William Cureton, Eusebius of Caesarea

History of the Martyrs in Palestine

Discovered in a very Ancient Syriac Manuscript

William Cureton, Eusebius of Caesarea

History of the Martyrs in Palestine
Discovered in a very Ancient Syriac Manuscript

ISBN/EAN: 9783337236496

Printed in Europe, USA, Canada, Australia, Japan

Cover: Foto ©Lupo / pixelio.de

More available books at **www.hansebooks.com**

HISTORY

OF THE

MARTYRS IN PALESTINE,

BY

EUSEBIUS, BISHOP OF CÆSAREA,

DISCOVERED IN A VERY ANTIENT SYRIAC MANUSCRIPT.

EDITED AND TRANSLATED INTO ENGLISH

BY

WILLIAM CURETON, D.D.,

MEMBER OF THE IMPERIAL INSTITUTE OF FRANCE.

WILLIAMS AND NORGATE:

14, HENRIETTA STREET, COVENT GARDEN, LONDON;

AND

20, SOUTH FREDERICK STREET, EDINBURGH.

PARIS: C. BORRANI.

MDCCCLXI.

THIS ACCOUNT OF

MARTYRS FOR THE TRUTH OF THE HOLY RELIGION OF OUR LORD JESUS CHRIST

IS

Dedicated to the Memory

OF

FRANCIS EGERTON EARL OF ELLESMERE

K. G.

IN PIOUS RECOGNITION OF MUCH AND LONG-CONTINUED KINDNESS AND IN GRATEFUL REMEMBRANCE OF THE PRIVILEGE OF ENJOYING THE FRIENDSHIP OF ONE WHO SO EMINENTLY ADORNED THE HIGH STATION TO WHICH HE WAS BORN BY HIS OWN PERSONAL VIRTUES AND ADDED REAL DIGNITY TO THE RANK WHICH HE INHERITED BY THE ACQUIREMENTS OF A SCHOLAR THE ACCOMPLISHMENTS OF A GENTLEMAN AND THE GRACES OF A CHRISTIAN.

PREFACE.

THE manuscript from which this work of Eusebius has been at length recovered, after the lapse of several centuries, is that wonderful volume of the Nitrian Collection[a] now in the British Museum, whose most curious and remarkable history I have already made known in the Preface to my edition of the Festal Letters of St. Athanasius.[b] It is not necessary, therefore, for me in this place to give any further account of it than to state that it was transcribed fourteen hundred and fifty years ago,—as early as the year of our Lord four hundred and eleven.

The several works contained in it are now all printed, and thereby rescued from the chance of being lost for all future time. The first—a Syriac translation of the Recognitions of St. Clement, which I once intended to publish, and had transcribed the greater part of it for that purpose—has been edited by Dr. P. de Lagarde,[c] to whom I

(a) British Museum, Additional MS. No. 12,150.

(b) P. xv. The Festal Letters of Athanasius, discovered in an antient Syriac version. 8vo. London, 1848.

(c) Clementis Romani Recognitiones Syriace. Paulus Antonius de Lagarde edidit. 8vo, Lipsiæ, 1861.

gave my copy. The transcript was completed by him, and compared with another manuscript of the same work, and afterward printed with that great care and accuracy which gives so much value to all the Syriac texts which he has edited. The second treatise in this manuscript is the book of Titus, Bishop of Bostra, or Bozra, in Arabia, against the Manicheans. We are also indebted for the publication of this important work to Dr. de Lagarde.[a] The third is the book of Eusebius on the Theophania, or Divine Manifestation of our Lord. The text of this was edited by the late Dr. Lee,[b] who also published an English translation of it,[c] with valuable notes and a preliminary dissertation. The last is this history of the Martyrs of Palestine, also written by the same Author.

In the eighth book of the Ecclesiastical History, upon the occasion of his giving a short account of certain Bishops and others, who sealed their testimony for their faith with their blood, Eusebius stated his intention of writing, in a distinct treatise, a narrative of the confession

(a) Titi Bostreni contra Manchæos libri quatuor Syriace. Paulus Antonius de Lagarde edidit. 8vo. Berolini, 1859.

(b) Eusebius, Bishop of Cæsarea, on the Theophania, or Divine Manifestation of our Lord and Saviour Jesus Christ. A Syriac Version, edited from an ancient Manuscript recently discovered. By Samuel Lee, D.D. 8vo. London, 1842.

(c) Eusebius, Bishop of Cæsarea, on the Theophania, or Divine Manifestation of our Lord and Saviour Jesus Christ. Translated into English with Notes, from an ancient Syriac Version of the Greek Original now lost. To which is prefixed a Vindication of the Orthodoxy and Prophetical Views of that distinguished writer By Samuel Lee, D.D. 8vo. Cambridge, 1843.

of those Martyrs with whom he had himself been acquainted.[a] Up to the time of the discovery of this Syriac copy, no such work was known to exist in a separate form, either in Latin or Greek. There is indeed a brief history of those contemporaries of Eusebius who suffered in the persecution of the Christians in Palestine, found in several antient Greek manuscripts, inserted as a part of it, and combined with the Ecclesiastical History: but it does not occupy the same place in all the copies of that work. In one it is placed after the middle of the thirteenth chapter of the eighth book;[b] in two[c] at the end of the tenth book; and in several,[d] at the end of the eighth; while from two

(a) *Οις γε μην αυτος παρεγενομην, τουτους και τοις μεθ' ημας γνωριμους δι' ετερας ποιησομαι γραφης.* "Moreover, there were many other eminent martyrs who have an honourable mention among the Churches, which are in those places and countries. But our design is not to commit to writing the conflicts of all those who suffered for the worship of God over the whole world, nor yet to give an accurate relation of every accident that befel them; but this rather belongs to those who, with their own eyes, beheld what was done. *Moreover, those ourselves were present at, we will commit to the knowledge of posterity in another work.*" See Ecc. Hist., B. viii. ch. 13, *Eng. Trans.* p. 148.

(b) Codex olim Regiæ Societatis, nunc vero Musei Britannici. This is G. of Dr. Burton's edition: Oxford, 1838. See the same, pp. 572 and 591.

(c) Duo Codices Florentini Bibliothecæ Mediceo-Laurentianæ. Plut. lxx. n. 7 et 20. I. and K. of Burton. See *Ibid.* p. 591.

(d) 1. Codex Regius Bibliothecæ Parisiensis n. 1436; 2. Codex Mediceus, *ibid.* n. 1434; 3. Codex Mazarinæus, *ibid.* n. 1430; 4. Codex Fuketianus, *ibid.* n. 1435; 5. Codex Savilianus, in Bibliotheca Bodleiana, n. 2278; being A. B. C. D. and F. respectively of Burton. *Ibid.*

others,[d] as well as from the Latin version made by Ruffinus, it is omitted altogether. There is no distinct title prefixed to it in any copy but one, the Codex Castellani,[a] where it bears the inscription:—*Ευσεβιου συγγραμμα περι των κατ' αυτον μαρτυρησαντων εν τῳ οκταετει Διοκλητιανου και εφεξης Γαλεριου του Μαξιμινου διωγμου;* but two copies, the Mazarine and Medicean, have at the end—*Ευσεβιου του Παμφιλου περι των εν Παλαιστινῃ μαρτυρησαντων τελος.*[b]

That this was the history of the martyrs who were known to Eusebius which he had promised, has never been doubted by any one; while, on the other hand, almost every one who has undertaken to write on the subject has judged it to be but an abridgment of the original work which formerly existed in a more extended form.[c] The

(d) Codex Bibliothecæ Regiæ Parisiensis n. 1431, and Codex Venetus n. 838; being E. and H. of Burton. *Ibid.*

(a) See N. of Burton. *Ibid.*

(b) See Valesius, note (a), p. 154, *Eng. Trans.*

( ) See Valesius and Ruinart, cited in the notes to this, pp. 50, 51, 55, 59, 60, 64, 69, 84. Also S. E. Assemani remarks:—"Græcam S. Procopii, Martyrum Palæstinorum in Diocletiani persecutione antesignani, historiam, quæ in laudato de martyribus Palæstinæ libro habetur; ab alia fusiori, atque explicatiori fuisse contractam atque truncatam, certum et exploratum est, nam quæ ad patriam atque institum pertinent omittere nunquam consuevit Eusebius."—*Acta SS. Mart.*

"Horum sanctorum martyrum historiam concisam pariter jejunamque exhibet nobis Græcus Eusebii Cæsariensis textus in libro de martyribus Palæstinæ; eandemque prorsus fortunam experta est, quam prior Procopii, ex latiori scilicet narratione in brevem summam. Atque priorem illam Latina, quæ superfuit, versio suppleverit, hæc autem suppleri aliter non potuissent, nisi, favente Deo, Chaldaicus

antient Latin copy of the Acts of Procopius,[a] the Acts of Pamphilus and his companions, as exhibited by Simeon Metaphrastes,[b] in much fuller detail than they are now found in the Greek text of Eusebius, and the additional facts respecting other martyrs who suffered in Palestine, supplied by the Greek Menæa and Menologia, were adduced as evidence of the existence at one time of a more copious work, and as a proof that the narrative inserted in the Ecclesiastical History was only an abridgment.

The correctness of this critical induction has been completely established by the discovery of this copy of the work of Eusebius of Cæsarea on the Martyrs of Palestine, in the vernacular language of the country where the events took place, and actually transcribed within about seventy years after the death of the author.[c]

S. E. Assemani goes so far as to express his conviction that this history of the sufferings of the martyrs in Palestine was originally composed in Syriac, a language with which Eusebius, Bishop of Cæsarea, was necessarily well acquainted,

Codex noster e tenebris Ægypti vindicatus emersisset in lucem."—*Ibid.* p. 173.

Baillet:—" Eusebe de Cesarée avait recueilli à part les Martyrs de Palestine: et quoique les Actes qu'il en avoit ramassez avec beaucoup de soin et de travail ne paroissent plus, il nous en reste un bon abbregé dans le livre qui se trouve joint à son histoire generale de l'Eglise." See *Les Vies des Saints*, vol. i. p. 55.

(a) See these printed p. 50 below and Valesius' note thereon.

(b) The Latin, by Surius, of this, will be found in the Notes, at p. 69.

(c) Eusebius died A.D. 339 or 340 (Fabricius, *Bibliotheca Græc.* lib. v. c. 4. p. 31), and this copy was transcribed A. D. 411.

as being the vernacular speech of his own country and diocese.[a] It is not at all improbable that Eusebius might made have use of the Syriac for ordinary purposes, or, indeed, as a safer deposit for any memoranda which he might wish to commit to writing than the Greek, during the time that the persecution continued. Could this inference of S. E. Assemani be established, it would give still additional interest and value to the work which I now publish. I must, however, own that I cannot admit the supposition that this work was originally written in the Syriac language. Indeed, it seems to me to be sufficiently disproved by the fact, that the Syriac copy of such of the Acts of Martyrs in Palestine as have been published by S. E. Assemani, while it agrees completely in substance with this, is evidently a translation by another hand; and that the variation and errors which occur in some of the proper names are of such a kind as could only have arisen from confounding two similar Greek letters of the writing at that period;[b] and further, there are some obscure passages in this Syriac, which obviously seem to be the result of a translator not fully apprehending the meaning of the Greek passage before him.[c]

How long the entire Greek text of the original work continued to be read, we have now no means of learning with any degree of certainty. It must have been in existence in the time of Simeon Metaphrastes, in the tenth century, for he has supplied many facts[e] from it

(a) See Note, p. 51, below.
(b) See Notes, pp. 57, 60 below.
(c) See p. 66, below.

which the abridged form of the Greek does not contain, and has also given entire the long passage relating to Pamphilus and his companions.[a] Neither can there be any doubt of its having been in use at the period when the Greek Menæa and Menologia were compiled.[b] The fact that many of the circumstances and events which it described had been inserted in the abovementioned books, and that an abridgment, which, I cannot doubt, was made by Eusebius himself, had also been incorporated into the Ecclesiastical History, seems to have led to the discontinuance of the transcription of the larger work, and to have been mainly the cause of its being no longer found in the Greek in a separate form. The preservation of this work in its complete state up to the present time, in the Syriac, is chiefly due to the circumstance of its having been transported, at a very early period, to the Syrian Monastery in the solitude of the Nitrian Desert, where the dryness of the climate kept the vellum from decay, and the idleness and ignorance of the monks saved the volume from being worn out and destroyed by frequent use.

Independently of the great interest of the subject of which it treats, this work of Eusebius has especial claims to consideration, on the ground of the author having been himself an eyewitness of most of the events which he de-

(a) A Latin version of this, as it is found in Simeon Metaphrastes, translated by Lipomannus, I have printed in the Notes, p. 69, below, for the sake of comparison with this text. It also still exists in Greek, and was first published by D. Papebrochius from a Medicean MS. in the *Acta Sanctorum*, June, vol. i. p. 64; and afterwards reprinted by J. Alb. Fabricius in *S. Hippoliti Opera*, 2 vols. fol. Hamb. 1716—19, vol. ii. p. 217.

(b) See notes pp. 53, 56, 59, 60, 64, 68.

scribes. There are some, indeed, at which he could not have have been present; for instance, the Confession of Romanus, who suffered at Antioch on the same day as Alphæus and Zacchæus did at Cæsarea, where he was then residing. He has, given a narrative of the sufferings of Romanus, in his history of the Martyrs of Palestine, because he was a native of Palestine, and had also been a deacon and exorcist in one of the villages of Cæsarea; and Eusebius was anxious to claim for his own country and diocese the honour of this man's confession. This may perhaps be the reason why there are found two distinct accounts of the Acts of Romanus in Syriac, as well as in Greek and Latin.

It is not my intention to enter into any discussion respecting the time of the composition of this treatise, or that of the great Church History by Eusebius: nor will I consider at any length the question of the abridgment of the account of the Martyrs of Palestine inserted in most of the copies of the Ecclesiastical History, or that of the different recensions of this latter work by the author himself.[a] These are certainly very interesting subjects of literary and historical inquiry; and doubtless this book will supply the critic with new data, to enable him to elucidate and determine them in a more complete and satisfactory manner than it has been hitherto possible for any one to do. These matters I would rather leave to other scholars. All now have the same materials as I have, and some may be possessed of other greater facilities and appliances, as well as better capacities for the task. I

(a) See Heinichen, *Notitia Codicum, Editionum et Translationum Historiæ Ecclesiasticæ Eusebianæ*, § vi.

believe it to be my duty to employ my own time and exertions in another way.

I will therefore content myself with briefly observing that this work of Eusebius on the Martyrs of Palestine bears evidently upon it the stamp of being a record of facts which were noted down at the time as they severally occurred, and were afterwards revised and arranged in due order at a subsequent period, when some events, which, in the earlier years of the Persecution, the author thought it probable might happen, had actually taken place; and when other occurrences of earlier date were no longer so fresh and vivid in the minds of men as they had been when all were still living who had witnessed them.

I would observe, also, that it seems to be evident that this work, in which Eusebius recounts the martyrdom of Pamphilus and his companions, was composed before he wrote the fuller history of that noble Martyr, to which he refers in the Abridgment; for no reference whatever is made to the existence of any such history in this original and more copious narrative of the Martyrs of Palestine. It must, therefore, have been composed before he wrote the Ecclesiastical History, in which he several times adverts to the life of Pamphilus as having been already completed.

The first edition of the Ecclesiastical History does not appear to have contained the history of the Martyrs of Palestine. This seems to be the copy used by Ruffinus, who neither gives any such history, nor has the passage in the thirteenth chapter of the eighth book which refers to it.

Indeed, it is evident from his own words that the abridgment must have been made by Eusebius himself.[a] When,

(a) See Note below, p. 79.

therefore, he condensed the narrative for the purpose of incorporating it into the subsequent editions of the Ecclesiastical History, he also took that opportunity of supplying several facts which, either from considerations of prudence, or from not having had knowledge of them at the time when the work was originally composed, he had previously omitted; and also ventured to speak more plainly of persons, because the altered condition of circumstances after the accession of Constantine enabled him to do this without any apprehension of danger. This, I think, will be obvious to those who will be at the pains to compare the general narrative of the events as they are recorded year by year, with the notes which I have added, even without having recourse to fuller and more minute researches.

The translation I have endeavoured to make as faithful as I could without following the Syriac idiom so closely as to render the English obscure. There are a very few passages in which I cannot feel quite sure that I have obtained the precise meaning of the Syriac; but the obscurity of these passages is certainly due to the Translator, who does not seem to have fully understood the Greek text which he had before him. My English translation of the long account of Pamphilus and his companions was printed before I read either the Greek text printed by Papebrochius, or the Latin translation made by Lipomannus from the same Greek, as it was preserved by Simeon Metaphrastes. The comparison of all of these together will be a good means of testing both the integrity of the transmission of the original Greek to the present day, and the fidelity of the Syriac translation.

In the notes, my chief object has been to collect such observations as may tend especially to throw light upon the time of the composition 'of this work and of the Ecclesiastical History by Eusebius, and serve to elucidate the text; but in order to keep them from extending to too great a length, I have omitted all those matters which it appeared to me an ordinarily well-informed scholar might be presumed to be acquainted with.

ON THE MARTYRS IN PALESTINE,

BY EUSEBIUS OF CÆSAREA.

THOSE Holy Martyrs of God, who loved our Saviour and Lord Jesus Christ, and God supreme and sovereign of all, more than themselves and their own lives, who were dragged forward to the conflict for the sake of religion, and rendered glorious by the martyrdom of confession, who preferred a horrible death to a temporary life, and were crowned with all the victories of virtue, and offered to the Most High and supreme God the glory of their wonderful victory, because they had their conversation in heaven, and walked with him who gave victory to their testimony, also offered up glory, and honour, and majesty to the Father, and to the Son, and to the Holy Ghost. Moreover, the souls of the martyrs being worthy of the kingdom of heaven are in honour together with the company of the prophets and apostles.

Let us therefore, likewise, who stand in need of the aid of their prayers, and have been also charged in the book of the Apostles, that we should be partakers in the remembrance of the Saints,—let us also be partakers with them, and begin to describe those conflicts of theirs against sin, which are at all times published abroad by the mouth of those believers who were acquainted with them Nor, indeed, have their praises been noted by monuments of stone, nor by statues variegated with painting and colours and resemblances of earthly things without life, but by the word of truth spoken before God: the deed also which is seen by our eyes bearing witness.

[P. 2.] Let us therefore, relate the manifest signs and glorious proofs of the divine doctrine, and commit to writing a commemoration not to be forgotten, setting also their marvellous virtues as a constant vision before our eyes. For I am struck with wonder at their all-enduring courage, at their confession under many forms, and at the wholesome alacrity of their souls, the elevation of their minds, the open profession of their faith, the clearness of their reason, the patience of their condition, and the truth of their religion: how they were not cast down in their minds, but their eyes looked upwards, and they neither trembled nor feared. The love of God also, and of His Christ, supplied them with an all-effective power, by which they overcame their enemies. For they loved God, the supreme sovereign of all, and they loved Him with all their might. He, too, requited their love to Him by the aid which He afforded them: and they also were loved by Him, and strengthened against their enemies, applying the words of that confessor who had already borne his testimony before them and exclaiming "Who shall separate us from Christ? shall tribulation, or affliction, or persecution, or hunger, or death, or the sword? as it is written, For thy sake we die daily: we are reckoned as lambs for the slaughter." And again, when this same martyr magnifies that patience which cannot be overcome by evil, he says—"that in all these things we conquer for Him who loved us." And he foretold that all evils are overcome by the love of God, and that all terrors and afflictions are trodden down, while he exclaimed and said: "Because I am persuaded that neither death, nor life, nor things present, nor things to come, nor powers, nor height, nor depth, nor any other creature, shall be able to separate us from the love of God which is in our Lord Jesus Christ."

At that time then, Paul, who exulted in the power of his Lord, was himself crowned with the victory of martyrdom in the midst of Rome, the Imperial City [p. 3.], because he had entered the contest there, as in a superior conflict. In that victory also which Christ granted to his triumphant martyrs, Simon, the chief and first of the disciples, likewise received the crown; and he suffered in a manner similar to our Lord's sufferings. Others of the Apostles too, in other places, closed their lives in martyrdom. Nor was this grace given only to those of former times, but it has also been bestowed abundantly upon this our own generation.

As for those conflicts, which were gloriously achieved in various other countries, it is meet that they who were then living should describe what took place in their own country; but for myself I pray that I may be enabled to write an account of those with whom I had the honour of being cotemporary, and that they may rank me also among them—I mean those of whom the whole people of Palestine is proud, for in the midst of this our land also the Saviour of all mankind himself arose like a thirst-refreshing fountain. The conflicts, therefore, of these victorious combatants I will proceed to relate, for the common instruction and benefit of all.

THE CONFESSION OF PROCOPIUS,

IN THE FIRST YEAR OF THE PERSECUTION IN OUR DAYS.

The first of all the martyrs who appeared in Palestine was named Procopius. In truth he was a godly man, for even before his confession he had given up his life to great endurance: and from the time that he was a little boy had been of pure habits, and of strict morals: and by the vigour of his mind he had so brought his body into subjection, that, even before his death, his soul seemed to dwell in a body completely mortified, and he had so strengthened his soul by the word of God that his body also was sustained by the power of God. His food was bread only, and his drink water; and he took nothing else besides these two. [P. 4.] Occasionally he took food every second day only, and sometimes every third day; oftentimes too he passed a whole week without food. But he never ceased day nor night from the study of the word of God: and at the same time he was careful as to his manners and modesty of conduct, so that he edified by his meekness and piety all those of his own standing. And while his chief application was devoted to divine subjects, he was acquainted also in no slight degree with natural science. His family was from Baishan; and he ministered in the orders of the Church in three things:—First, he had been a Reader; and in the second order he translated from Greek into Aramaic; and in the last, which is even more excellent than the preceding, he opposed the powers of the evil one, and the devils trembled before him. Now it happened that he was sent from Baishan to our city Cæsarea, together with his brother confessors. And at the very moment that he passed the gates of the city they brought him before the Governor: and immediately upon his first entrance the judge, whose name was Flavianus, said to him: It is necessary that thou shouldest sacrifice to the gods: but he replied with a loud voice, There is no God but one only, the Maker and Creator of all things. And when the judge felt himself smitten by the blow of the martyr's words, he furnished himself with arms of another kind against the doctrine of truth, and, abandoning his former order, commanded him to sacrifice to the emperors, who were four in number; but the holy martyr of God laughed still more at this saying, and repeated the words of the greatest of poets of the Greeks, which he said that "the rule of many is not good: let there be one ruler and one sovereign." And on account of his answer, which was insulting to the emperors, he, though alive in his conduct, was delivered over to death, and forthwith the head of this blessed man was struck off, and an easy transit afforded him along the way to heaven. [P. 5.] And this took place on the seventh day of the month Heziran, in the first year of the persecution in our days. This confessor was the first who was consummated in our city Cæsarea.

THE CONFESSION OF ALPHÆUS, AND ZACCHÆUS, AND ROMANUS,

IN THE FIRST YEAR OF THE PERSECUTION IN OUR DAYS.

It happened, at the same time, that the festival, which is celebrated on the twentieth year of the emperor's reign, was at hand, and a pardon was announced at that festival for the offences of those who were in prison. The governor, therefore, of the country came before the festival, and instituted an inquiry respecting the prisoners which were in confinement, and some of them were set at liberty through the clemency of the emperors; but the martyrs of God he insulted with tortures, as though they were worse malefactors than thieves and murderers.

Zacchæus, therefore, who had been a deacon of the Church in the city of Gadara, was led like an innocent lamb from the flock—for such indeed he was by nature, and those of his acquaintance had given him the appellation of Zacchæus as a mark of honour, calling him by the name of that first Zacchæus—for one reason, because of the smallness of his stature, and for another, on account of the strict life which he led; and he was even more desirous of seeing our Lord than the first Zacchæus. And when he was brought in before the judge, he rejoiced in his confession for the sake of Christ: and when he had spoken the words of God before the judge, he was delivered over to all the tortures of punishment, and after having been first scourged, he was made to endure dreadful lacerations, and then after this he was thrown into prison again, and there for a whole day and a whole night his feet were strained to four holes of the rack.

Alphæus, also, a most amiable man, endured afflictions and sufferings similar to these. His family was of the most illustrious of the city Eleutheropolis, and in the church of Cæsarea he had been honoured with the dignity of Reader and Exorcist. But before he became a confessor he had been a preacher and teacher of [p. 6.] the word of God; and had great confidence towards all men, and this of itself was a good reason for his being brought to his confession of the truth. And because he saw that there was fallen upon all men at that time laxity and great fear, and many were swept along as it were before the force of many waters, and carried away to the foul wórship of idols, he deliberated how he might withstand the violence of the evil by his own valour, and by his own courageous words repress the terrible storm. Of his own accord, therefore, he threw himself into the midst of the crowd of the oppressors, and with words of denunciation reproached those, who through their timidity had been dragged into error; and held them back from the worship of idols, by reminding them of the words which had been spoken by our Saviour, respecting confession. And when Alphæus, full of courage and bravery, had done these things openly with boldness, the officers seized him, and took him at once before the judge. But this is not the time for us to relate what words he uttered with all freedom of speech, nor what answers he gave in words of godly religion, like a man filled with the Spirit of God. In consequence of these things he was sent to prison. And after some days he was brought again before the judge, and his body was torn all over by severe scourgings without mercy, but the fortitude of his mind still continued erect before the judge, and by his words he withstood all error. Then he was tortured on his sides with the cruel combs, and, at last, having wearied out the judge himself, and those who were ministering to the judge's will, he was again committed to prison, together with another fellow-combatant, and stretched out a whole day and night upon the wooden rack. After three days they were both of them brought together before the judge, and he commanded them to offer sacrifice to the emperors: but they confessed, and said, We acknowledge one God only, the supreme sovereign of all; and when they had uttered these words in the presence of all the people (p. 7.) they were numbered among the company of Holy Martyrs, and were crowned as glorious and illustrious combatants in the conflict of God, for whose sake also their heads were cut off. And better than all the course of their lives did they love their departure, to be with Him in whom they made their confession. But the day that they suffered martyrdom was the seventh of Teshri the latter, on which day the confession of those of whom we have been speaking was consummated.

And on this selfsame day also Romanus suffered martyrdom in the city of Antioch. But this Romanus belonged to Palestine, and he was a Deacon, and an Exorcist likewise, in one of the villages of Cæsarea. And he, too, was stretched out upon the rack, and like as the martyr Alphæus had done in Cæsarea, so did the blessed Romanus by his words of denunciation restrain from sacrificing those who, from their timidity, were relapsed into the sin of the error of devils, recalling to the minds of them all the terrors of God. He had also the courage to go in together with the multitude who were dragged by force into error and to present himself there in Antioch before the judge: and when he heard the judge commanding them to sacrifice, and they, in trepidation from their fears, were driven with trembling to offer sacrifice, this zealous man was no longer able to endure this sad spectacle, but was moved with pity towards them as towards those who were feeling about in thick darkness, and on the point of falling over a precipice, and so he made the doctrine of the religion of God to rise up before them like the sun, crying aloud and saying: Whither are ye being carried, oh men? Are ye all stooping down to cast yourselves into the abyss? Lift up the eyes of your understanding on high, and above all the worlds ye shall recognise God and the Saviour of all the ends of the world; and do not abandon for error the commandment which has been committed to you: then shall the godless error of the worship of devils be apparent to you. Remember also the righteous judgment of God supreme. [p. 8.] And when he had spoken these things to them with a loud voice, and stood there without fear and without dread, at the command of him who was constituted judge there, the officers seized him, and he condemned him to be destroyed by fire, for the crafty judge perceived that many were confirmed by the words which the martyr spake, and that he turned many back from error. And because the servant of Jesus had done these things in the place where the emperors were, they at once brought out this blessed man into the midst of the city of Antioch. And he was arrived at the spot where he was to undergo his punishment, and the things which were required for the fire were got ready, and they were busying themselves to fulfil the command with haste, when the emperor Diocletian, having heard of what was done, gave orders that they should withdraw the martyr from the death by fire, because, said he, his insolence and folly were not suitable for punishment by fire; and so, like a merciful emperor, he gave order for a new kind of punishment for the martyr, that his tongue should be cut out. Nevertheless, when that member by which he spoke was taken away, still was his true love not severed from his God; neither was his intellectual tongue restrained from preaching, and immediately he received from God, the sovereign of all, a recompense for his struggle in the conflict, and was filled with power much greater than he had before. Then did great wonder seize upon all men; for he, whose tongue had been cut out, forthwith, by the gift of God spake out valiantly, and heartily exulted in the faith, as though he were standing by the side of Him in whom he made his confession; and with a countenance bright and cheerful he saluted his acquaintance, and scattered the seed of the word of God into the ears of all men, exhorting them all to worship God alone, and lifting up his prayers and thanksgiving to God, who worketh marvels [p. 9.]: and when he had done these things he mightily gave testimony to the word of Christ before all men, and in deed shewed forth the power of Him in whom he made his confession. And when he had done so for a long time he was again stretched upon the rack; and by the command of the governor and the judge they threw upon him the strangling instrument, and he was strangled. And on the same day as those blessed martyrs who appertained to Zacchæus he was consummated in his confession. And although this man actually passed through the conflict, and suffered martyrdom in Antioch, nevertheless, because his family was of Palestine, he is properly described among the company of martyrs in this our country.

THE CONFESSION OF TIMOTHEUS, IN THE CITY OF GAZA,

IN THE SECOND YEAR OF THE PERSECUTION IN OUR DAYS.

It was the second year of the persecution, and the hostility against us was more violent than the first; and Urbanus, who at that same time had superseded the governor Flavianus in his office, was governor over the people of Palestine. There came then again the second time edicts from the emperor, in addition to the former, threatening persecution to all persons. For, in the former, he had given orders respecting the rulers of the Church of God only, to compel them to sacrifice; but, in the second edicts there was a strict ordinance, which compelled all persons equally, that the entire population in every city, both men and women, should sacrifice to dead idols, and a law was imposed upon them to offer libations to devils; for such were the commands of the tyrants who, in their folly, desired to wage war against God, the king supreme. And when these commands of the emperor were put into effect, the blessed Timotheus, in the city of Gaza, was delivered up to Urbanus while he was there, and was unjustly bound in fetters, like a murderer [p. 10.], for indeed he was not bound in fetters on account of any thing deserving of blame, because he had been blameless in all his conduct, and during the whole of his life. When, therefore, he did not comply with the law as to the worship of idols, nor bow down to dead images without life, for he was a man perfect in every thing, and was in his soul acquainted with his God, and because of his piety and his conduct and his virtues, even before he was delivered up to the governor, he had already endured severe sufferings from the inhabitants of his own city, having lived there under insults and frequent blows and contumely, for the people of the city of Gaza were accursed in the heathenism; and when they were present in the judgment hall of the governor, this champion of righteousness came off victorious in all the excellence of his patience. And the judge cruelly employed against him severe tortures, and showered upon his body terrible scourgings without number, inflicting on his sides horrible lacerations, such as it is impossible to describe; but, under all these things this brave martyr of God sustained the conflict like a hero, and at last obtained the victory in the struggle, by enduring death by means of a slow fire: for it was a weak and slow fire by which he was burned, so that his soul could not easily make her escape from the body, and be at rest.

And there was he tried like pure gold in the furnace of a slow fire, manifesting the perfection and the sincerity of his religion towards his God, and obtaining the crown of victory which belongs to the glorious conquerors of righteousness. And because he loved God, he received, as the meet recompense of his will, that perfect life which he longed for in the presence of God the sovereign of all. And together with this brave confessor, at the same time of the trial of his confession, and in the same city, the martyr Agapius, and the admirable Theekla (she of our days) were condemned by the governor to suffer punishment and to be devoured by wild beasts. [p. 11.]

THE CONFESSION OF AGAPIUS, AND OF THE TWO ALEXANDERS, AND OF THE TWO DIONYSIUSES, AND OF TIMOTHEUS, AND OF ROMULUS, AND OF PAESIS,

IN THE SECOND YEAR OF THE PERSECUTION IN OUR DAYS, IN THE CITY OF CÆSAREA.

It was the festival at which all the people assembled themselves together in their cities. The same festival also was held in Cæsarea. And in the circus there was an exhibition of horse races, and a representation was performed in the theatre, and it was customary for impious and barbarous spectacles to take place in the Stadium: and there was a rumour and a report generally current, that Agapius, whose name we have mentioned above, and Theekla with him, together with the rest of the Phrygians, were to be sent into the theatre in the form of martyrs, in order that they might be devoured by the wild beasts; for the governor Urbanus would present this gift to the spectators. When the fame of these things was heard abroad, it happened further that other young men, perfect in stature, and brave in person (they were in number six) arrived. And as the governor was proceeding to the theatre, and passing through the city, these six men stood up courageously before him: and having bound their hands behind them, they drew near before the judge Urbanus, and, in fact, by binding themselves, shewed what was about to be done to them by others, and exhibited their excellent patience, and the readiness of their mind for martyrdom, for they confessed, crying aloud and saying, We are Christians; and beseeching the governor Urbanus that they also might be thrown to the wild beasts in the theatre in company with their brethren who appertained to Agapius. For all this confidence of Jesus our Saviour, in his own champions did He manifest to all men; extinguishing the menaces of the tyrants by his champion's valour, and manifestly and clearly shewing, that neither fire, nor steel, nor even fierce wild beasts, were able to subdue his victorious servants [p. 12.], for He had girded them with the armour of righteousness, and strengthening them with victorious and invincible armour, he made them despise death. And they struck at once the governor and the whole band with him with astonishment at this their courage: and the governor gave command that they should be delivered up to prison; and there they were detained many days. And while they were in prison, Agapius, a meek and good man, the brother of one of the prisoners, arrived from the city of Gaza, and went frequently to the prison to visit his brother, and having already striven in many contests of confession before, he went with confidence to the place of imprisonment: and so he was denounced to the governor as a man prepared for martyrdom, and consequently was delivered over to bonds, in order that he might endure the trial of a second conflict. And things similar to these did Dionysius also suffer. And this good recompense was given to him from the martyrs of God as the reward of his service to them. And when the governor was made aware of this recompense of the compassion of Dionysius towards the martyrs, he gave the sentence of death against him. And thus he became associated with those who preceded him. And all together they were eight in number; namely, Timotheus, whose origin was from Pontus; and Dionysius, who came from the city of Tripolis; and Romulus, a sub-deacon of the church of the city of Diospolis; and two were Ægyptians, Paesis and Alexander; and again another Alexander, and those two respecting whom we have said that they were at last cast into prison.

All these were delivered up together at one time, to be beheaded. And this matter took place on the twenty-fourth of Adar. But there was, at the same time, a sudden change of the emperors, both of him who was the chief and emperor, and of him who was honoured in the next place after him: and those [p. 13.] who had divested themselves of the power of empire and put on the ordinary dress, having given up the empire to their associates, were rent asunder from their love towards each other, and they raised against one another an implacable war; nor was any remedy given to this malady of their hostility, until the peace in our time, which was spread throughout the whole empire of the Romans; for it arose like light out of clouds of darkness, and forthwith the Church of the supreme God and the divine doctrine was extended throughout the whole world.

THE CONFESSION OF EPIPHANIUS (Gr. *Apphianus*),

IN THE THIRD YEAR OF THE PERSECUTION WHICH TOOK PLACE IN OUR DAYS IN THE CITY OF CÆSAREA.

THAT bitter viper, and wicked and cruel tyrant, which in our time held the dominion of the Romans, went forth, even from his very commencement, to fight as it were against God, and was filled with persecution and rage against us in a far greater degree than any of those who had preceded him—I mean Maximinus: and no little consternation fell upon all the inhabitants of the cities, and many were scattered abroad into every country, and dispersed themselves, in order that they might escape the danger which surrounded them.

What words then are adequate to describe, as it deserves, the divine love of the martyr Epiphanius, who had not yet attained the age of twenty years? He was sprung from one of the most illustrious families in Lycia, famous also for their extensive worldly wealth, and, by the care of his parents, he had been sent to be educated in the city of Beyrout, where he had also acquired a great stock of learning. But this incident is not in any way connected with the narrative which we are writing: if, however, it be befitting that we make any mention of the virtuous conduct of this all-holy soul, it is very right to admire, how in a city such as this he used to withdraw himself from the society and company [p. 14.] of young men, and practised the virtues and the habits of old men, adorning himself with pure conduct and becoming manners, nor suffered himself to be overcome by the vigour of his body, nor to be led away by the society of youth. But he laid the foundation of all virtues for himself in patience, cherishing perfect holiness and temperance, and applying himself with purity, as it is right, to the worship of God. And when he had finished his education and quitted Beyrout, and was returned to the house of his parents, he was no longer able to live with those who were of his own family, because their manners were dissimilar to his own. He therefore left them, without taking care to carry with him the means of providing sustenance even for a single day. He conducted himself, however, in his travels, with purity, and by the power of God which accompanied him, he came to this our city, in which the crown of martyrdom was prepared for him, and resided in the same house with us, confirming himself in godly doctrine, and being instructed in the Holy Scriptures by that perfect martyr, Pamphilus, and acquiring from him the excellence of virtuous habits and conduct.

And for this reason I have applied myself to the narrative of the martyrdom of Epiphanius, in order that I may declare, if I be able, what a consummation he also had. All the multitudes that beheld him were struck with admiration of him. And who is there, even now-a-days, that can hear of his fame without being filled with astonishment at his courage, and at his boldness of speech, and at his daring, and at his patience, at his words addressed to the governor, and his answers to the judge? And more than all to be wondered at is the resolution with which he dedicated as it were with incense the offering of his zeal for God. For when the persecution had been raised against us the second time, in the third year of this same persecution, the former edicts of Maximinus arrived—those by which he gave command that the governors of the cities should use great pains and diligence in order to compel all men to offer sacrifices [p. 15.] and libations to devils. The heralds, therefore, through all the cities made a diligent proclamation, that the men, together with their wives and children, should assemble in the temples of the idols, and before the Chiliarchs and Centurions, as they went round about to the houses and the streets making a list of the inhabitants of the city. Then they summoned them by name, and compelled them to offer sacrifice as they had been commanded. And while this boundless tempest was threatening all men from all sides, Epiphanius, a perfectly holy man, and a witness of the truth, performed an act which surpasses all words. While no one was aware of his purpose; he even concealed it from us who were in the same house with him, he went and drew near to the governor of the place, and stood boldly before him; having also escaped the observation of the whole band that was standing near the governor, for they had not given heed when he approached the governor: and while Urbanus was offering libations, he came up to him and laid hold of his right hand, and held him back from offering the foul libation to idols, endeavouring with an excellent and gentle address and godlike suavity to persuade him to turn from his error, saying to him: That it was not right for us to turn away from the one only God of truth, and offer sacrifice to lifeless idols and wicked devils. Thus did He, who is more mighty than all, reprove the wicked through the youth Epiphanius, whom, for the sake of his reproof, the power of Jesus had taken from the house of his fathers, in order that he might be a reprover of the works of pollution. He therefore despised threatenings and all deaths, and turned not aside from good to evil, but spake gladly with pure knowledge and a glorifying tongue, because he was desirous to carry speedily, if it were possible, persuasion even to his persecutors, and to teach them to turn away from their error, and become acquainted with our common deliverer, the Saviour and God of all. When then this holy martyr of God had done these things, the servants [p. 16.] of devils, together with the officers of the governor, were smitten in their hearts as if by a hot iron; and they struck him on the face, and when he had been thrown down on the ground they kicked him with their feet, and tore his mouth and lips with a bridle. And when he had endured all these things bravely, he was afterwards delivered up to be taken to a dark prison, where his legs were then stretched for a day and a night in the stocks. And after the next day they brought Epiphanius, who, although a youth in age, was a mighty man in valour, into the judgment hall, and there the governor Urbanus displayed a proof of his own wickedness and hatred against this lovely youth by punishment and every kind of torture inflicted upon this martyr of God. And he ordered them to lacerate his sides until his bones and entrails became visible: he was also smitten upon his face and his neck to such a degree, that his countenance was so disfigured by the severe blows which he had received, that not even his friends could recognise him. This martyr of Christ, however, was strengthened both in body and soul like adamant, and stood up even more firmly in his confidence upon his God. And when the governor asked him many questions, he gave him no further answer than this—that he was a Christian: and he questioned him again as to whose son he was, and whence he came and where he dwelt; but he made no other reply than that he was the servant of Christ. For this cause therefore the fury of the governor became more fierce, and he thundered forth the more in his rage, on account of the indomitable speech of the martyr, giving command that his feet should be wrapped up in cotton that had been dipped in oil, and then be set on fire. So the officers of the judge did what he commanded them. And the martyr was hung up at a great height, in order that, by this dreadful spectacle, he might strike terror into all those who were looking on, while at the same time they tore his sides and ribs with combs, till he became one mass of swelling all over, and the appearance of his countenance was completely changed. [p. 17.] And for a long time his feet were burning in a sharp fire, so that the flesh of his feet, as it was consumed, dropped like melted wax, and the fire burnt into his very bones like dry reeds. But at the same time, although he was in great suffering from what befel him, he became, by his patience, like one who had no pain, for he had within, for a helper, that God who dwelt within him; and he appeared evidently to all like the sun: and in consequence of the great courage of this martyr of Christ many Christians also were assembled together to behold him, and stood up with much open confidence*; and he, with a loud voice and distinct words, made his confession for the testimony of God, publishing by this his valour the hidden power of Jesus, that He is ever near to those who themselves draw near to Him.

And all this wonderful spectacle did the glorious Epiphanius exhibit, as it were in a theatre: for they who were the martyr's oppressors became like corrupt demons, and suffered within themselves great pain; being also themselves tortured in their own persons, as he was, on account of his endurance in the doctrine of his Lord. And while they stood in bitter pains, they gnashed upon him with their teeth, burning in their minds against him, and trying to force him to tell them whence he came, and who he was, and questioning him as to whose son he was, and where he lived, and commanding him to offer sacrifice and comply with the edict. But he looked upon them all as evil demons, and regarded them as corrupt devils: not returning an answer to any of them, but using only this word in confessing Christ, that He is God and the Son of God: [p. 18.] testifying also that he knew God his Father only. When therefore those who were contending against him were grown weary and overcome, and failed, they took him back to the prison, and on the next day they brought him forth again before that bitter and merciless judge, but he still continued in the same confession as before. And when the governor and his officers, and the whole band that ministered to his will, were foiled, he gave orders at last that he should be cast into the depths of the sea.

But that wonderful thing which happened after this act I know will not be believed by those who did not witness the wonder with their own eyes, as I myself did: for men are not wont to give the same credence to the hearing of the ear as to the seeing of eye. It is not, however, right for us also, like those who are in error and deficient in faith, to conceal that prodigy which took place at the death of this martyr of God; and we also call as witnesses to you of these things, which we have written, the whole of the inhabitants of the city of Cæsarea, for there was not even one of the inhabitants of this city absent from this terrific sight. For after this man of God had been cast into the depths of the terrible sea, with stones tied to his feet, forthwith a great storm and frequent commotions and mighty waves troubled the vast sea, and a severe earthquake made even the city itself tremble, and every one's hands were raised towards heaven in fear and trembling, for they supposed that the whole place, together with its inhabitants, was about to be destroyed on that day. And at the same time, the sea, even as if it were unable to endure it, vomited back the holy body of the martyr of God, and carried it with the waves and laid it before the gate of the city. And there was at that time vast affliction and commotion, for it seemed like a messenger sent from God to threaten all men with great anger [p. 19]. And this which took place was proclaimed to all the inhabitants of the city, and they all ran at once and pushed against each other in order that they might obtain a sight, both boys and men and old men together, and all grades of women, so that even the modest virgins, who kept to their own apartments, went out to see this sight. And the whole city together, even the very children as well, gave glory to the God of the Christians alone, confessing with a loud voice the name of Christ, who had given strength to the martyr in his lifetime to endure such afflictions, and at his death had shewed prodigies to all who beheld.

Such was the termination of the history of Epiphanius, on the second of the month Nisan, and his memory is observed on this day.

THE CONFESSION OF ALOSIS (Gr. *Ædesius*).

LIKE what had befallen the martyr Epiphanius, so after a short time the brother of Epiphanius, both on the father's and the mother's side, became a confessor, whose name was Alosis. He too, as he contended against them with the words of God, made use of his faith in the truth as armour; they also fought against him with smiting and scourging, and they stood up against each other as it were in battle array, and strove which side should get the victory. But even before his brother had given himself up to God, this admirable Alosis had applied his mind to philosophy, and meditated upon all the learned investigations of the greatest minds. Nor was he a proficient in the learning of the Greeks only, but he was also well acquainted with the philosophy of the Romans, and he had passed a long time in the society of the martyr Pamphilus, and by him had been embued with the godly doctrine as with purple suited for royalty. This same Alosis, after his admirable confession, which was accomplished before our eyes, and his sufferings of the evils (p. 20) of imprisonment for a long period, was first of all delivered over to the copper mines which are in our country, Palestine; and after that he had passed through many afflictions there, and then been released, he went thence to the city Alexandria, and fell in with Hierocles, who held the government of the province in all the land of Egypt. Him also he beheld judging the Christians severely, and contrary to just laws, making mock of the confessors of God, and delivering up the holy virgins of God to fornication, and to lust, and to bodily shame. When therefore these things were perpetrated before the eyes of this brave combatant, he devoted himself to an act akin to that of his brother; and the zeal of God was kindled within him like fire, and its heat burned within his members as in dry stubble, and he drew near to Hierocles, the wicked governor, with indignation, and put him to shame by his words of wisdom and his deeds of righteousness, and, having struck him on the face with both his hands, he threw him on his back upon the ground; and as his attendants laid hold upon him to help him, he gave him some severe blows, saying to him, Beware how thou darest to commit acts of pollution contrary to nature against the servants of God. And, being well instructed, he convicted him from the laws themselves of acting contrary to the laws.

And after Alosis had so courageously done all these things, he endured with great patience the torments which were inflicted upon his body; and as he resembled his brother in his appearance, and conduct, and in his zeal and confession, so also did they resemble each other in their punishment, and at the last, after their death the terrible sea received them from the hand of the judge.

Now this servant of Jesus exhibited his contest for the truth in [p. 21] the city of Alexandria, and was there adorned with the crown of victory; but the next confessor after Epiphanius who was called to the conflict of martyrdom in Palestine was Agapius.

THE CONFESSION OF AGAPIUS,

IN THE FOURTH YEAR OF THE PERSECUTION IN OUR DAYS.

It was in the fourth year of the persecution in our days, and on Friday the twentieth of the latter Teshri: it was on this same day that the chief of tyrants, Maximinus, came to the city of Cæsarea. And he made a boast that he would exhibit some novel sight to all the spectators that were assembled together on his account; for that was the same day on which he celebrated the anniversary of his birthday. And it was requisite upon the arrival of the tyrant that he should exhibit something more than what had ordinarily been done. What then was this new spectacle, but that a martyr of God should be cast to wild beasts to be devoured by them? while of old it had been the practice upon the arrival of the emperor that he should set before the spectators competitive exhibitions of various forms and different kinds, such as recitation of speeches, and listening to new and strange songs and music, and also spectacles of all sorts of wild beasts, and likewise that the spectators might have much delight and amusement in a show of gladiators.

It was therefore requisite that the emperor at this festival of his birthday should also do something great and extraordinary, for at all the previous exhibitions which he had furnished for them he had not done any thing new. So that—what was at once a thing desired by himself, and acceptable to the wicked tyrant—a martyr of God was brought forth into the midst, adorned with all righteousness, and remarkable for the meekness of his life; and he was cast into the theatre in order that he might be devoured by the wild beasts. His name was Agapius, respecting whom, together with Theckla, an order had been given that they should be devoured by wild beasts. The fair name of Theckla has been already mentioned in another chapter [p. 22]. They therefore dragged the blessed Agapius forward, and took him round about in mockery in the midst of the Stadium. And a tablet, with an inscription upon it, was carried about before him, on which no other accusation was exhibited against him, but this only—That he was a Christian. And the same time also a slave, a murderer, that had killed his master, was brought forward, together with the martyr of God, and they both received equally one and the same sentence. And very closely did this passion resemble that of our Saviour; for while the one was to suffer martyrdom for the sake of the God of all, the other also was to be put to death for the murder of his master; and one and the same sentence of evil went forth against both of them without any distinction. And the judge in this case was the governor Urbanus, for he was still governor in Palestine: but when Maximinus came to be present at this spectacle which has been described above, as if on account of the promptitude of Urbanus, he increased his power of evil, and liberated from death that murderer which had slain his master, and put him beyond all torture; but as for the martyr of God, he took delight in looking on with his own eyes while he was being devoured by the savage beasts. When therefore they had led the martyr Agapius round about in the Stadium, they asked him in the first place if he would deny his God, but he cried out with a loud voice and said to all those who were assembled together—Oh ye that are looking on at this trial in which I am now placed, know that it is not for any evil crime which I have committed that I am brought to this trial, for I am a witness of the true doctrine of God, and I bear testimony to you all, in order that ye may have knowledge of the one only God, and of that Light which he has caused to arise, that ye may know and adore Him who is the creator of the heavens and of the earth. And all this which is come upon me for his name's sake, I receive with joy in my mind; for they have not brought me to this place against my will, but I desire this of my own free choice, by which I stand even unto death. Moreover, I am contending for the sake of my faith, that I may afford encouragment to those who are younger than myself, that they too may despise death while [p. 23] they follow after their true life, and may disregard the grave in order to obtain a kingdom; that they should make light of that which is mortal, and keep in their recollection the life of the Giver of life, nor have any dread of punishment which is momentary, but be in fear of those flames of fire which are never quenched.

When therefore this martyr of God had cried with a loud voice and said these things, and stood erect in the midst of the Stadium, like one who felt confident that there was no danger, the wicked tyrant was filled with rage and fury, and gave orders for the wild beasts to be let loose upon him: but he, being full of courage and despising death, turned not aside to the right hand or to the left, but with lightness of feet and courage of heart advanced to meet the savage beasts. And a fierce bear rushed upon him and tore him with her teeth: he was then remanded to prison, while life was still left in him, and there he lived one day. After this, stones were tied about him, and his body was thrown into the sea; but the soul of the blessed Agapius winged her flight through the air to the kingdom of heaven, whither she was previously hastening, and was received together with the angels and the holy company of martyrs. So far then was the contest and the valour of Agapius victorious.

THE CONFESSION OF THEODOSIA, A VIRGIN OF GOD,

IN THE FIFTH YEAR OF THE PERSECUTION WHICH TOOK PLACE IN OUR DAYS.

The persecution in our days had been prolonged to the fifth year. And it was the month Nisan, and the second day of the same month, when a godly virgin, and holy in all things, one of the virgins of the Son of God in the city of Tyre, who was not yet eighteen years old, out of pure love for those, who on account of their confession of God were set before the tribunal of the governor, [p. 24] drew near and saluted them, and entreated them to remember her in their prayers: and because of these words which she had spoken to them, the wicked men were filled with anger, as if she had been doing something unjust and improper; and the officers seized her forthwith, and took her before the governor Urbanus, for he still held the power in Palestine. And I know not what happened to him, but immediately, like one much excited by this young woman, he was filled with rage and fury against her, and commanded the girl to offer sacrifice: and because he found, that although she was but a girl, she withstood the imperial orders like a heroine, then did this savage governor the more inflict tortures on her sides and on her breast with the cruel combs; and she was torn on the ribs until her bowels were seen. And because this girl had endured this severe punishment and the combs without a word, and still survived, he again commanded her to offer sacrifice. She then raised her lips and opened her eyes, and looking around with a joyful countenance in that time of her suffering, (for she was charming in beauty and in the appearance of her figure), with a loud voice she addressed the governor: Why, oh man, dost thou deceive thyself, and not perceive that I have found the thing which I prayed to obtain at thy hands? for I rejoice greatly in having been deemed worthy to be admitted to the participation of the sufferings of God's martyrs: for indeed, for this very cause, I stood up and spake with them, in order that by some means or other they might make me a sharer in their sufferings, so that I also might obtain a portion in the kingdom of heaven together with them, because so long as I had no share in their sufferings, I could not be a partaker with them in their salvation. Behold therefore now, how, on account of the future recompense, I stand at present before thee with great exultation, because I have obtained the means of drawing near to my God, even before those just men, whom but a little while ago I entreated to intercede for me. Then that wicked judge [p. 25], seeing that he became a laughing-stock, and that his haughty threats were manifestly humbled before all those who were standing in his presence, did not venture to assail the girl again with great tortures like the former, but condemned her by the sentence which he passed to be thrown into the depths of the sea.

And when he passed on from the condemnation of this pure girl, he proceeded to the rest of those confessors, on whose account this blessed maiden had been called to this grace, and they were all delivered over to the copper mines in Palestine, without his saying a word to them, or inflicting upon them any sufferings or torture; for this holy girl prevented all those confessors by her courageous conduct against error, and received in her own body, as it were on a shield, all the inflictions and tortures which were intended for them, having rebuked in her own person the enemy that opposed them; and subdued by her valour and patience the furious and cruel judge, and rendered that fierce governor like a coward with respect to the other confessors. It was on the first day of the week that these confessors were condemned in Cæsarea; and in the month above written and in the year noted by us was this act accomplished.

THE CONFESSION OF DOMNINUS,

IN THE FIFTH YEAR OF THE PERSECUTION IN OUR DAYS, IN THE CITY OF CÆSAREA.

URBANUS was governor in Palestine; and it was the first day of the latter Teshri; and so, from day to day, he renewed himself in his wickedness, and every year prepared some devices against us. I will therefore relate how many evils he inflicted on this one day which I have mentioned. On the day then which we have spoken of, a certain man, admirable in all his conduct, and excellently skilled in the science of medicine, [p. 26] and he was a young man of tall stature and handsome, and celebrated for the holiness of his life, and the purity of his soul, and his modesty, and his name was Domninus; he was also well known to all those in our time who had been confessors. Moreover, this same man, previously to his receiving consummation by martyrdom, had endured torture in the copper mines; and on account of his patience under his confession he was condemned to the punishment by fire.

When that same judge, cunning in his wickedness (for it is not meet that those should be called wise who boast themselves in the bitterness of their wickedness), had passed on from this martyr, he lighted upon three young men of fine stature, and handsome in their person, and praiseworthy as to their souls, on account of their courage in worshipping God; and in order that he might afford amusement thereby, he sent them to the Ludus. Then he passed on from these, and delivered up an excellent and godly old man to be devoured by the wild beasts. Then the mad man passed on from this old man, and came to others, and commanded them to be castrated and turned into eunuchs. Then he left them also, and proceeded to those who appertained to Sylvanus, whose own lot also it was some time afterwards to become a martyr of God, and these he condemned to the mines of Phæno. Afterwards he passed on from these and came to others whom he insulted with tortures. Nor was the fury of his malice content with males, but he also threatened to torment the females, and delivered over these virgins to fornicators for the violation of their persons. Others again he sent to prison. Now all these things which we have described did this arrogant judge perpetrate in one hour.

And after all these things which I have described had been accomplished, that heavenly martyr of God, Pamphilus, a name very dear to me (p. 27), who was holy in all things, and adorned with every virtue, was tried in the conflict of martyrdom. He was indeed the most famous of all the martyrs in our time, on account of his accomplishments in philosophy, and his acquirements both in sacred and profane literature. Of this same man, admirable in all things, Urbanus first made a trial of his wisdom by questions and answers; and at last endeavoured to compel him by threats to offer sacrifice to dead idols; and when he had ascertained by trial that he was not to be persuaded by words, and also perceived that his threats were not heeded by him, he applied cruel torture, and lacerated him grievously on his sides. But he was not able to subdue him by this means, as he had expected. The wicked judge then considered that if he bound him in prison together with those confessors of whom mention has been already made, he might by this means subdue this holy martyr.

Now as to this cruel judge, who employed all these wicked devices against the confessors of God, what recompense and punishment must await him? For this is easy for us to know from what we are writing. For forthwith, and immediately, and without any long delay, the righteous judgment of God overtook him on account of those things which he had dared to do, and took severe and bitter vengeance upon him; and he that sat on the judgment-seat on high in his pride, and boasted himself in his soldiers that stood before him, and considered himself above all the people in Palestine, was in one night stripped of all his splendour and all his honours, and reduced to the condition of a private individual. And here, in our city of Cæsarea, where he had perpetrated all those crimes which have been written above, he was by the sentence of Maximinus, a wicked tyrant like himself, delivered up to a miserable death; and insult and humiliation, which is worse than all deaths, was heaped upon him, so that reproachful words from women, with dreadful imprecations from the mouths of all, were poured into his ears before he died [p. 28]. Wherefore, by these things we may perceive that this was a foretaste of that vengeance of God which is reserved for him at the last, on account of all his maliciousness and unmercifulness towards the servants of God.

These things we have related in a cursory manner for those believers, of whom some still remain unto this present time, omitting to relate many afflictions which passed over him, in order that we may arrange these things briefly, and in a few words, as a record for those who are to come after us; but there may come a time when we may recount in our narrative the end and fall of those wicked men who exerted themselves against our people.

THE CONFESSION OF PAULUS, AND VALENTINA, AND HATHA,

IN THE SIXTH YEAR OF THE PERSECUTION IN OUR DAYS IN CÆSAREA.

Up to the sixth year of the persecution which was in our days, the storm which had been raised against us was still raging; and great multitudes of confessors were in the mines which are called Porphyrites, in the country of Thebais, which is on one side of Egypt; and on account of the purple marble which is in that land, the name of Porphyrites has also been given to those who were employed in cutting it. This name, therefore, was also extended to those great multitudes of confessors who were under sentence of condemnation in the whole of the land of Egypt: for there were a hundred martyrs there all but three. And these confessors were sent, the men together with the women and children, to the governor in Palestine, whose name was Firmillianus. For he had superseded the governor Urbanus in his office, and he was a man by no means of a peaceful turn; indeed he even surpassed his predecessor in ferocity, having been a soldier that had been engaged in war, and had had much experience in blood and fighting. [p 29.]

There is a large city in the land of Palestine, teeming with population, of which all the inhabitants were Jews. It is called in the Aramaic tongue Lud, and in the Greek it is called Diocæsarea. To this city the governor Firmillianus went, and took thither the whole assembly of those hundred confessors. And this was a great sight which well deserves to be recorded in writing. And the Jews were spectators of this marvellous contest, having surrounded the place of judgment on all sides; and as if it were for a rebuke to themselves, they looked on with their own eyes at what took place, while the whole company of the confessors, with much confidence and immense courage, made their confession of belief in God's Christ. And they being Jews, to whom the coming of that Christ had been foretold by their prophets, whose coming their fathers looked for, had not received him when he was come; but these Egyptians, who had been of old the enemies of God, confessed, even in the midst of persecutions, their faith in God, the Lord of all, and in the Manifestation from him. And these Egyptians, who had been taught by their fathers to worship idols only, were at that time, from the conviction of their reason, undergoing this conflict, in order that they might avoid the worship of idols; while those Jews, who had always been accused by their prophets on account of their worship of idols, were surrounding them, standing and looking on, and listening as the Egyptians repudiated the gods of their own fathers, and confessed their faith in the same God as they also did; and bare witness for Him whom they had many times denied. And they were still more cut to the heart and rent, when they heard the criers of the governor shouting and calling Egyptians by Hebrew names, and addressing them with the names of the prophets. For the crier, shouting aloud, called to them and said: Elias, Isaiah, Jeremiah, Daniel, and other appellations similar to these, which their fathers had chosen from among the Hebrews, [p. 30.] in order that they might call their sons after the names of the prophets. Moreover, it also came to pass that their deeds corresponded with their names; and the Jews greatly wondered both at them and at their names, as well as at their words and their deeds, being rendered despicable themselves both by their own vice and infidelity. And I myself am convinced that these things were not done without the will of God. However, after this trial they were deprived of the use of their left leg, by having the muscles of the knee cauterized with fire, and then again they had their right eyes blinded with the sword, and then destroyed by fire. And not only were they men who endured these things, but really children and many women. And after this they were delivered over to the copper mines to see afflictions there.

And after a short time, the three men from Palestine, whom I mentioned a little while ago as having been for the moment handed over to the Ludus, were called to undergo similar sufferings, because they would not take the food from the royal provision, nor would give themselves up to that exercise and instruction which were requisite for pugilism; and they suffered many evils which we are not competent to describe: and at the end of all their afflictions they underwent this severe sentence. And others in the city of Gaza, being in the habit of assembling themselves for prayer, and being constant in reading the Holy Scriptures, were seized, and had to endure the same sufferings as their companions, being tortured on their legs and eyes. Others also had to contend in conflicts even greater than these, and after having been tortured both in their legs and eyes, were severely torn on their sides with combs. And others again more than these attained to this great excellence, and at the end of all contended with death itself.

And when he had turned himself away from these, he came to judge one who, although a woman in body, was a hero in the bravery of mind, which she possessed [p. 31]: she was also a virgin in her mode of life, and could not bear the threat of pollution which she heard, but at once gave utterance to harsh words against the tyrannical emperor, for having given authority to a vile and wicked judge. On this account, therefore, he in the first place bruised her body all over with stripes; then she was hung up and her sides were lacerated; and this not once only, but two and three times in one hour, and for a great while and also repeatedly, until those who inflicted the punishment became wearied and tired; then others succeeded them against her, and, at the commands of the furious governor, tortured her most severely. For these judges were barbarous in their manners, and enemies in their hearts. Moreover, it happened that while this furious judge was insulting this girl with his tortures, another young woman, small indeed in person, but courageous in soul—for she was possessed of a large mind, which supplied strength to the smallness of her person—being no longer able to tolerate the wickedness and cruelty of those things which were inflicted upon her sister, called out from the midst of the crowd of persons who were standing before the governor, and cried out complaining, and said: How long dost thou intend to tear my sister to pieces in so cruel and merciless a manner? And when the wicked Firmillianus heard this saying, he was bitterly incensed, and gave orders for the young woman who had complained to be brought before him. Her name was Valentina. Having therefore caught her up they brought her into the midst of the place of judgment. But she placed her trust in the holy name of Jesus. Then the murderous governor in his fury commanded her to offer sacrifice. But the maiden Valentina despised the word even of the threatener. Then he gave orders for those who were ministering to his will to lay hold upon the girl by force, and to take her up to the side of the altar, so that she might be polluted by the sacrifices. Then at that time of terror [p. 32.] the noble maiden shewed the courage of her mind, and gave the altar a kick with her foot, and it was overturned, and the fire that had been kindled upon it was scattered about; and because she did all these things without shewing any fear, the rage of the governor was roused like a wild beast, and he gave command for her to be tortured with the combs, without any mercy, so that no one man was ever torn to such a degree; and I think that, had it been possible, he would even have devoured the girl's flesh. And when at length his fury was satisfied with the sight of her blood, and he had learned, both by deeds and words, how divine is that invincible power which arms and strengthens even little girls with courage and valour, he caused both the young women, Hatha and Valentina, to be bound together, and gave sentence against them of death by fire. The name of the first was Hatha, and her father's house was in the land of Gaza; and the other was from Cæsarea, our own city, and she was well known to many, and her name was Valentina.

And after these things, Paul the confessor was called to the conflict. And he also endured it bravely, and in the same hour was condemned to be put to death, and his sentence was to be beheaded by the sword. When, then, this blessed man came to the place of execution where he was to be put to death, he besought the officer who was to behead him to have patience with him for a little while; and when the officer had granted him this desire, in the first place, with a mild and cheerful voice, he offered up thanksgiving, and worship, and glory, and supplication to God for having accounted him worthy of this victory. Then he prayed for tranquillity and peace for our people, and entreated God speedily to grant them deliverance. After this he offered up prayer for our enemies, the Jews, many of whom at that time were standing around him: then he went on in his supplication, and prayed for the Samaritans, and for those among the Gentiles [p. 33] who were without knowledge; he prayed that they might be converted to the knowledge of the truth. Nor was he unmindful of those who were standing around him, but prayed also for them. And oh, the perfection—which cannot be described—that he prayed even for that judge who had condemned him to death, and for all rulers in every place; and not only for them, but also for that officer who was then going to cut off his head. And as he was offering his supplications to God, the officers heard him with their own ears praying for them, and beseeching God not to lay to their charge that which they did to him. And as he prayed for all with a suppliant voice, he turned the whole multitude that was standing by and looking on to sorrow and tears; and then, of his own accord, he bent down his body, and put out his neck to be cut off by the sword. The conflict of this victorious martyr was consummated on the twenty-fifth of the month Thamuz.

THE CONFESSION OF ANTONINUS, AND ZEBINAS, AND GERMANUS, AND MANNATHUS (Gr. *Ennathas*),

IN THE SIXTH YEAR OF THE PERSECUTION IN OUR DAYS IN CÆSAREA.

And when some time had elapsed after these things which I have related, another company of God's martyrs, amounting in number to one hundred and thirty, was sent from the land of Egypt into our country. And all of these had also undergone the same tortures in their eyes and legs as the former martyrs; and some of them were sent to the mines of Palestine, and some of them were delivered over to the judges in Cilicia to be chastised with injurious and insulting tortures. But from us the flame of the persecution ceased a little, the sword having been satiated with the blood of the holy martyrs; and a little rest and cessation threw some check upon the persecution which took place in our days. And continuously the scourge of God was sent upon Maximinus, the wicked tyrant, of all these evils, of which the governors of the countries were the instructors and cunning ministers, [p. 34], and that duke who was the general of the army of the Romans. And because of those things which took place, they urged the Logistæ of the cities, and the military commander, and the Tabularii to rebuild with diligence what was fallen of the temples of idols, and to compel all the men, together with their wives and children and slaves, and even the infants at the breast, to sacrifice and offer libations to devils, and also to force them to eat of the sacrifices. And a command was given that every thing that was sold in the market should be polluted with the libations and the sprinkling of the blood of the sacrifices. When these things, therefore, were done in this manner, these actions which were performed were abominated, even by the heathen who were without faith.

Great tumult, therefore, and consternation, such as there had never been the like before, overwhelmed all those who belonged to us in every place; and the souls of every one were set in affliction and trouble. But the Divine Power, on account of those things which had taken place, gave encouragement to such as belonged to Him, so that they were able to tread under foot the threats of the judges, and to depise their tortures.

But some servants of Christ's people, who in the stature of their bodies were only youths, but their soul was armed with the worship of God, both came of themselves, and when the governor was offering libations to idols in the midst of the city, suddenly rushed upon him, and called upon him to abandon his error, For there is no other God but one, the Maker and Creator of all things; and when they were asked who they were, they confessed they were Christians. No sooner, then, were these words uttered than they received sentence of death, and so passed on easily and without delay to Him in whom they made their confession. The name of the first of them was Antoninus, and the second was called Zebinas, and the third's name was Germanus; and these things were done on the thirteenth of Teshri the latter.

And they had at the same time a companion, a sister, one of the Lord's virgins, [p. 35] a chaste and courageous maiden, who came from the city of Baishan. She, however, had not acted in the same manner as those had done with whom she became confessor; for she had been brought by force from Baishan, and suffered insults and cruel tortures from the judge before she was condemned. But one of those who was set over the streets of the city was the originator of these evils. His name was Maxys, and he proved to all men that he was worse even than his name. This same blessed woman he stripped naked, and she was only left covered from the groin downwards, in order that he might indulge his lustful eyes in looking at the rest of her limbs; and he carried her about through the whole city, being tortured with straps; and afterwards took her before the tribunal of the governor, where with great boldness of speech she made the confession of her faith—that she was a Christian; and there also displayed her courage and patience under every kind of torture; and was afterwards delivered over by the governor to be burnt with fire. Moreover, the same judge became day by day more ferocious, displaying both his merciless disposition and cruelty, and he was carried away even beyond the laws of nature, so that he wreaked his vengeance and hatred even upon the lifeless corpses of the Christians, and forbade their burial. And of this same maiden of whom it has been just spoken, and of those who on the same day were consummated by confession, orders were issued that their bodies should be devoured by animals, and be carefully guarded night and day till they should be consumed by birds. Persons were therefore appointed to watch over this barbarous order from a distance, and to keep guard to prevent the bodies of the confessors from being carried away by us by stealth. So the beasts of the field, and the dogs, and the fowls of the heaven, were here and there tearing to pieces the flesh of men, so that men's bones and entrails were found even in the middle of the city; and all men were clad in sorrow on account of these things, because never before had such atrocities been done. [p. 35.] And great sorrow and grief came even upon those who were aliens from us in the faith, because of these things which their own eyes beheld; for even before the gates of the city was exhibited the dreadful spectacle of men's bodies devoured by wild beasts. When, therefore, things had continued in this manner for many days, there happened in the midst of the city a prodigy which will scarcely be believed. The atmosphere was perfectly calm and clear, when, all on a sudden, many of the columns of the porticos in the city emitted spots as it were of blood, while the market-places and the streets became sprinked and wet as with water, although not a single drop had fallen from the heavens. And it was declared by the mouth of every one, that the stones shed tears and the ground wept; for even the senseless stones and the ground without feeling could not endure this foul and barbarous deed; and that the blood which flowed from the stones, and the earth which without any rain emitted as it were tears from its body, rebuked all these godless folk. And perhaps it may seem to such as did not see with their own eyes the things which I have described, that what I have related must be attributed to a fable devoid of truth. Far from it, for these things which we have described were actually seen by those who were living at that time, some of whom are alive unto this very day.

Such then was the consummation of those holy martyrs of God, whose struggles and conflicts against error were exhibited before our eyes.

THE CONFESSION OF ARES, AND PRIMUS (Gr. *Promus*), AND ELIAS,

IN THE SIXTH YEAR OF THE PERSECUTION IN OUR DAYS AT ASHKELON.

In the month Canun the former, on the fourteenth of the same—on this day some Egyptian martyrs of God were seized before the gates of Ashkelon; and because, when they were questioned as to who they were, they acknowledged that they were Christians, [p. 38] and confessed that they had undertaken the journey, and were come from their own country for the purpose of taking sustenance to the confessors who were in Cilicia, they also were brought as malefactors before the judge. For the keepers of the gates of the city were cruel men, and laid hold upon these martyrs, and took them before Firmillianus the governor, because he was also, up to that time, still over the people of Palestine; and he decreed a cruel sentence against them: and some of them he ordered to have their eyes and their feet injured by fire and steel, and some of them to be delivered over to death by the sword; but one of them, whose name was Ares, was consummated in his confession by a fierce fire, and Primus and Elias were beheaded by the sword.

THE CONFESSION OF PETER, WHO WAS SURNAMED ABSALOM,

IN THE SEVENTH YEAR OF THE PERSECUTION IN OUR DAYS IN THE CITY OF CÆSAREA.

On the tenth day of the month Canun the latter, Peter, who was called Absalom, appeared, a famous confessor of the kingdom of God; and so manfully did he behave in his struggle for the worship of God, and so victorious was he in the conflict of his martyrdom, that he even excited admiration in the judge himself, and made those who were standing by him wonder greatly. Much, therefore, did they strive to induce him to have pity upon himself, to spare his own person, and save himself from the evils which were hanging over him; but he disregarded in his mind all that they said. And those who surrounded him—not those only who knew him, but those also who were not acquainted with him—urged him, and intreated him one after another, and besought the blessed man as if it were for their own lives. But some of them confirmed his good resolution; others, again, by what they said, suggested irresolution [p. 39], bidding him to regard with pity his own youth and person. Those of the same mind as himself called to his remembrance that hell fire which is to come, while others tried to make him afraid of the fire which was visible before him. Some endeavoured to terrify him by the mortal judge, while others reminded him of the Judge of all judges. Some called upon him to regard this transitory life, while others persuaded him to look to the kingdom of heaven. Those who belonged to the right hand invited him to turn towards them, while they who belonged to the left hand tried to persuade him to mind earthly things. But he was a young man, handsome in person, brave in mind, and active and able in body; and being such he proved his purity like gold in the furnace and the fire, and loved his confession in our Saviour better than the life of this time, which so soon passes away. And there was burned together with him in the same fire one who belonged to the heresy of Marcion, and called himself a bishop; and he gave himself up to this as in the zeal for righteousness, although he was not in true knowledge, and endured martyrdom by fire in company with this God's martyr. And this holy martyr of whom we have spoken came from Aia (Gr. *Anea*), a village which is on the confines of Beth Gobrin; and he contended in the consummation which we have described, and obtained in the conflict the crown of the glorious victory of the martyrs of Christ.

THE CONFESSION OF PAMPHILUS, AND VALES, AND SELEUCUS, AND PAULUS, AND PORPHYRIUS, AND THEOPHILUS (*Theodulus*), AND JULIANUS, AND ONE EGYPTIAN,

BEING IN NUMBER EIGHT, IN THE SEVENTH YEAR OF THE PERSECUTION IN OUR DAYS.

The time now calls upon us to describe that grand spectacle which was displayed of the all-holy martyr Pamphilus, and of those [p. 39] who together with him were consummated by martyrdom; men admirable and brave, who exhibited, under many forms, contests for the sake of the worship of God. For indeed there are many whom we know to have been victorious in this persecution; but in none altogether like these whom we have just mentioned did we behold so completely all kinds of bodily stature, and of moral qualities of soul and education, and of deaths by different tortures, receiving the glory of the consummation of martyrdom by various triumphs. For all of the Egyptians who were with them appeared to be youths and boys; others were young men in the prime of life, among whom was Porphyrius; others again were in the full vigour both of mind and body, namely, those who were of the house of Pamphilus, that name dearly beloved by me; and Paulus, who came from Iamna; and Seleucus and Julianus, both of whom came from the country of Cappadocia. There were also among them some venerable seniors who were bent down with deep old age, as Vales, a deacon of the church of Jerusalem, and that other, whose conduct was conformable to his name, Theodulus. There was, likewise, a variety of bodily stature: and they differed too in their mental acquirements, for some of them were very simple-minded and ordinary like children, while others were possessed of profound understandings and courageous habits. There were also some among them who were also instructed in theology, and in all of them was their praiseworthy courage remarkable. But like the sun which giveth light to the day among the stars, so in the midst of them all shone forth the excellency of My Lord Pamphilus—for it is not meet that I should mention the name of that holy and blessed Pamphilus without styling him My Lord, for he indeed had no slight acquaintance with that learning which those among the Greeks admire; while there was no one in our time who was [p. 40] so well instructed in those scriptures which proceed from the Spirit of God, and also in the whole range of theology. And what is even greater than these acquirements, he was possessed of natural wisdom and discernment, that is, he received them by the gift of God. Moreover, Pamphilus was by birth of an illustrious family, and his mode of living in his own country was as that of the noble. Seleucus also had held a place of authority in the army. Some of them again were of the middle rank of life, and one also, who was called to this honour together with the rest, was a slave of the governor. Porphyrius too was reckoned the slave of Pamphilus, but in his love towards God and in his admirable confession he was his brother; and by Pamphilus himself he was considered rather as a beloved son; and, indeed, in every thing he closely resembled him who had brought him up. And were any one to say of this company of them all that they were a perfect representation of a congregation of the church, I should say that he did not go beyond the truth. For among them Pamphilus had been honoured with the presbytery, and Vales was in the orders of the diaconate, and others among them had the rank of readers; and Seleucus, even before the consummation of his confession, had been honoured as a confessor by the suffering of cruel scourgings, and had endured with patience his dismissal from his command in the army. And the remainder of the others who came after these were hearers and receivers (catechumens). And thus, under a small form, they completed the representation of a perfect church of many persons. And so this admirable selection of all these martyrs and such as these, while we looked upon them, although they were not many in number, lo! they still bore the semblance of a many-stringed harp, which consists of chords that do not resemble each other—the tenor and base, and flat, and sharp, and medial, all of which are well arranged together by the art of music. Like this resemblance, also, there were among them young men and old men together, and slaves and free, [p. 41] and clever and simple, and noble and common, and believers together with hearers (catechumens), and deacons with presbyters: all of which were variously harmonized together by one all-skilful—the Word—the only (begotten) of God. And they displayed each individually the excellency of the power within them by the endurance of tortures, and at the place of judgment produced the melody of a glorious confession.

It is also worthy of our admiration, when we look to their number, how they were twelve like the prophets and the apostles. Nor is it fit that we should omit the all-patient readiness of every one of them, each in his own part; the combs on their sides, and their incurable scourgings, and their tortures of every kind, and how they forced by violence these martyrs to do that which was abominated by them. And what necessity is there for our telling of the divine sayings which they uttered, as though stripes were reckoned by them as nothing, while with a cheerful and joyous countenance they answered the interrogatories of the judge, and jested with readiness under the very tortures themselves. And when he asked them over again whence they came, they avoided speaking of the city to which they belonged on earth, and spake of the city which in truth is theirs, and said that they were from Jerusalem which is above in heaven, confessing that they were hastening to go thither. And because of these things the judge became the more enraged at them, and prepared himself against them with cruel scourgings, in order that he might accomplish his will upon them; but when hefa iled in his expectations, he gave command that one of them should receive the crown of victory.

Moreover, the modes of their deaths also were of all kinds; for two of them were hearers (catechumens), and they were baptized at their deaths with the baptism of fire only, while others of them were delivered up to be crucified like our Saviour.

But Pamphilus, that name so especially dear to me—one who was a lover of God in truth, and a peacemaker among all men—[p. 42] received a triumph different from these. He was the ornament of the church of Cæsarea, because he also sat in the chair of the presbytery, both adorning it and being himself adorned thereby during his ministry in that place. In all his conduct too he was truly godly, being at all times in communion with the Spirit of God; for he was eminently virtuous in his mode of life, shunning wealth and honours, despising and rejecting them, and devoting himself entirely to the word of God. For every thing that he possessed from his parents he sold and distributed to the naked, and the sick, and the poor, and continued in private life without any possessions, and passed his time in the patient study of divine philosophy. He therefore quitted Beyrout, the city in which he had grown up in stature and learning together; and for the sake of his knowledge and understanding he attached himself to men seeking perfection. Human wisdom he abandoned, and loved the word of God. He also adopted the heavenly habit of the prophets, and was crowned with martyrdom.

The next after him that was brought to the conflict was Vales, a man venerable for his comely grey hairs, being in appearance a pure and respectable old man. Nor was he worthy of honour on this account only, but also for his great knowledge of the holy scriptures; for his memory was completely stored with the scriptures, so that he could repeat God's scriptures by rote like one in whose memory the whole scriptures were deposited. Moreover, he was a deacon of God's church.

And he that was reckoned third among them was named Paul, a man who was fervent in the Spirit of God; and he came from the city Iamna. And he also had previously to this his confession contended with the suffering [p. 43] of the cautery of confession.

And when they had endured affliction in prison for about two years, the immediate cause of their martyrdom was the arrival of those Egyptians who were also consummated in martyrdom at the same time together with them. For having accompanied those men who had been sent to suffer affliction in the mines of Cilicia, and being then on their way back to return to their own country, as they entered in at the gate of Cæsarea, they were questioned as to who they were and whence they came; and when they made no concealment of the truth, but said, We are Christians, they were at once seized, just as if they had been malefactors. And they were in number five. So when they were carried before the judge, and spake in his presence with openness of speech, they were forthwith committed to prison; and on the next day—the sixteenth of the month Shebat—they, together with those who appertained to Pamphilus, were brought before Firmillianus. First of all, then, the governor tried the Egyptians, and proved them by every kind of torture; and he brought forward the first of them into the midst, and asked him what was his name; but instead of his real name he heard from them the name of a prophet. Also the rest of the Egyptians who were with him, instead of those names which their fathers had given them after the name of some idol, had taken for themselves the names of the prophets, such as these—Elias, Jeremiah, Isaiah, Samuel, Daniel. And when the judge heard from the same martyrs some such name as these, he did not perceive the force of what they said, and asked them again what was the city to which they belonged. He then gave a reply similar to the former, and said, Jerusalem is my city; for he was acquainted with that city of which St. Paul spake, Jerusalem which is above is free, and our mother in whom we confess is the holy church. And the governor inquired diligently about this. Then he brought against them the combs and cauteries of fire. But he, when his hands had been bound behind him, and his feet were twisted in the stocks, sealed what he had said before, [p. 44.] and spake the truth. And again, when he questioned him many times as to what city and in what country was that Jerusalem which was said to belong to the Christians only, he replied, It is in the east, and on the side of the light of the sun, again making use of this artifice as it were in his own mind, while those who surrounded him continued to torture him with combs. Nor was he at all changed, but seemed as one who had no body. Then the judge grew furious in his mind, and imagined that perchance the Christians had built in some place a city for themselves; and so he became much more instant with tortures against them, making inquiries respecting this city, and the country in the east. When, therefore, he had punished this young man with scourging, and perceived that he varied not at all from what he had said to him at the first, he gave sentence of death against him that he should be beheaded. The rest then of the Egyptians he tried with tortures similar to his, and they likewise agreed in their confession with him who had preceded them.

And then, after these things he turned to those of the house of Pamphilus; and when he learned that they had been previously tried by many tortures, he thought that it would be folly in him to apply to them the same tortures again, and so labour in vain. He therefore only put to them the question whether they would now comply; and when he heard from them one after another the words of confession, he condemned them in the same manner as those who had preceded them, and gave sentence against them that they should be beheaded. And before the whole of the sentence was uttered, a youth from among the men, who was a slave of Pamphilus, cried out from the midst of the crowd which was standing round about the place of judgment; and then came forward into the midst, and cried out again with a loud voice to persuade the governor to grant permission for the bodies of the confessors to be buried. And he was no other than the blessed Porphyrius, the beloved disciple of Pamphilus, the mighty man of valour. [p. 45.] But Porphyrius himself was not yet eighteen years old; and he had been instructed in literature and writing, and for his modesty and manners was deserving of all praise. This youth then, who had been brought up by such a man, when he was informed of the sentence which had been issued against his master, cried out from the middle of the crowd, and begged the bodies of the confessors. Then that wretch, who is not worthy to be called a man, but rather a savage brute, not only refused to grant this becoming request, but also neither spared nor had pity upon one who in years was but a youth; and having learnt this one thing only, that he was a Christian, gave orders to those who applied the tortures to tear him with all their might: and after this, having commanded the blessed youth to sacrifice, and experiencing a refusal, he now applied the torture upon him, not as if it were upon a human body, but rather as if it were upon lifeless wood or stone, and commanded him to be torn even till they came to his bones and entrails. And when he had done this for a long while, he perceived that he was labouring to no purpose; and thus having exhibited his own cruelty and brutality upon this youth, he condemned him to be given up to a slow and lingering fire. Now, he was brought to the conflict before Pamphilus was consummated, and so departed from the body before his master who had brought him up. And thus Porphyrius exhibited himself as a warrior who was crowned with victory in all his conflicts; and although he was weak in body, he was of a cheerful countenance and courageous mind, and trod along the path of death without fear, and in truth he was full of the Holy Ghost. And when he arrived at the place where he was put to death, having put on his cloak like a philosopher, with his shoulder uncovered, he looked with his eyes up towards heaven, and in his mind looked down upon all the life of man, and approached the fire with a soul unmoved, like one who had no harm near him, and with a watchful mind, and undisturbed, he gave charge to his friends respecting his human affairs, and then was anxious to go speedily [p. 46] to the presence of God. When, therefore, the fire had been kindled at a distance around him, he caught at the flames here and there with his mouth, and his soul hastened to the journey which lay before him. Such was the conflict of Porphyrius.

Then Seleucus carried to Pamphilus a report of all these things which had been done to Porphyrius, and as the reward for this intelligence it was granted of God to Seleucus that he should become a martyr with Pamphilus. For immediately after he had given information to Pamphilus respecting the struggle and conflict of Porphyrius, as he saluted one of the martyrs with a kiss, the soldiers laid hold upon him and took him before the governor; and as Seleucus himself was anxious to go in company with the confessors, commandment was given for him to be beheaded. And this Seleucus came from the country of Cappadocia, and had acquired a glorious reputation by his military service, having held an important command in the ranks of the army. And not only this, but he also surpassed most men in stature by the size of his person and his prowess. His appearance, too, was very handsome. Moreover, at the commencement of the persecution he had been famous for his endurance of scourgings in confession; and after he had been dismissed from his military service on account of his religion, his zeal suffered not him to abstain from doing good, and so he was anxious to serve in the beloved ranks of Christ. As a visitor, therefore, of lonely orphans, and of destitute widows, and of those who were afflicted with poverty and sickness, he became a visitor and supporter of these, and, like a tender father, endeavoured to heal their afflictions. And after all these things, in which God delighteth more than sacrifices, and burnt-offerings, and incense, he was counted worthy of being consummated by confession. And this was the tenth combatant of those who have been mentioned above as having received all together on the same day their consummation and crown. And it seemed as if a great door of the kingdom of heaven had been opened by the confession of Pamphilus [p. 47], and an abundant entrance been effected for others as well as himself into the paradise of God.

The next that was brought forward after Seleucus was the pure and pious Theodulus; and he was one of the slaves of the governor, and the oldest of them all, and was much respected by them all, both on account of his manners and his years; and although he was the father of three generations, and had served his master with fidelity, still he had no mercy on him when he heard that he had saluted the martyrs in the same way as Seleucus. For after this had been told to his master, he was excited with fury against him much more than against the rest; and gave command that he should be put to death by the same mode of suffering as our Saviour, and suffer martyrdom on the cross.

But there was still one wanted after these to complete the number twelve; and so Julianus arrived from a journey, and, as if it were on purpose to make up the number of martyrs twelve, the moment he arrived, before he was yet entered into the city, immediately on the way he was told by some one respecting the matter of the confessors, and ran to have a sight of the confessors; and when he beheld the bodies of the saints lying upon the ground, he was filled with joy, and embraced them one after another with heavenly love, and saluted them all with a kiss. And while he was still visiting them, and lamenting that he himself had not suffered martyrdom with them, the officers seized him, and took him before the judge; and that judge commanded what his evil heart conceived, and delivered him also to a slow fire. So this Julianus, also, with joy and gladness praised God with a loud voice for having counted him worthy of this; and his soul ascended to his Lord with the company of the confessors. And this man was by family of Cappadocia, and in his soul he was filled with the fear of God, being a quiet and religious man, and diligent in the practice of every virtue. There was also in him a glorious savour of the Holy Spirit; and he was counted worthy to be associated with the company of these who received the consummation of confession together with the blessed Pamphilus. [p. 48.]

Four days and nights then were the bodies of the all-holy martyrs of God exposed to be devoured by wild beasts, by the command of the governor Firmillianus. When, therefore, nothing had touched them, not even the wild beasts, they were taken up whole without the permission of the governor, and with due reverence committed to an honourable burial; and were laid in the interior of the churches, and so consigned to a never-to-be-forgotten memorial in the temples of the house of prayer, that they might be honoured of their brethren who are with God.

THE CONFESSION OF HADRIANUS AND EUBULUS,

IN THE SEVENTH YEAR OF THE PERSECUTION IN OUR DAYS.

WHEN the consummation of Pamphilus and of those martyrs who were with him was published abroad by the mouths of all men, both Hadrianus and Eubulus, from a place which is called part of Batanea, had hastened to the rest of the martyrs at Cæsarea: and when they drew near to the gate of the city, they were interrogated as to the cause for which they were come, and having stated the truth, they were taken before Firmillianus; and he at once, without any delay, ordered them, in the first place, to have their sides torn with combs, and punished them in a peculiar manner, as if they had been enemies and were hated by him; and not being satisfied with this, he condemned them to be devoured by wild beasts. And after an interval of two days, the confessor Hadrianus was cast before a lion on the fifth of Adar, and bravely accomplished his conflict, and after having been torn by the beast, he was at last put to death by the sword. Eubulus, also, on the second day following, the seventh of Adar, when the judge had made many attempts with him, and said to him, If thou wilt sacrifice to devils thou shalt be set at liberty in peace, both despised the whole existence of this passing time, and chose for himself everlasting life rather than this fleeting and transitory life. He was then cast to a lion, and after [p. 49] he had been torn by the teeth of the lion, he suffered in the same manner as those who were gone before him. He was the last of all that suffered martyrdom and finished his conflict in Cæsarea.

THE CONFESSION OF PAULUS (Gr. *Peleus*) AND NILUS, AND PATRIMYTHEAS (Gr. *Patermutheus*) AND ELIAS,

IN THE SEVENTH YEAR OF THE PERSECUTION IN OUR DAYS.

It was the nineteenth day of Ilul, and during the same wonderful conflict of the martyrs of God, that a great spectacle was assembled in Phæno, in this same Palestine; and all the combatants were perfect, and in number they were about a hundred and fifty. Many of them, also, were Egyptians, amounting to more than a hundred. And the same in the first place had their right eyes and their left legs in their sinews destroyed by cautery of fire and by the sword. And then after these things they were delivered over to dig copper in the mines. Those, also, who belonged to Palestine had to endure afflictions in the same manner as the Egyptians; and they were all assembled together in a place called Zauara, as a congregation consisting of many persons. There was also much people with them, who came from other places to see them, and many others who ministered to them in their necessities, and visited them in love, and filled up their lack. And all the day they were occupied in the ministry of prayer, and in the service of God, and in teaching and reading; and all the afflictions which passed over them were esteemed by them as pleasures, and they spent all that time as if it had been in a festive assembly. But the enemy of God and wicked envier was not able to bear these things, so there was immediately sent out against them one of those generals of the Romans that is styled Dux; and first of all he separated them one by one from each other, and some of them were sent to that wretched place Zauara, and some not; and some of them to Phæno, the place where the copper is dug; [p. 50.] and the others went to different places. Afterwards he selected from among those in Phæno four of them who were of great excellence, in order that by them he might terrify the rest. Having, therefore, brought them to the trial, and not one of them having shewn any signs of dismay, this merciless judge, thinking that no punishment was so severe as that by fire, delivered up God's holy martyrs to this kind of death. When, therefore, they were brought to the fire, they cast themselves into the flames without fear, and dedicated themselves as an offering more acceptable than all incense and oblations; and presented their own bodies to God as a holocaust more excellent than all sacrifices. And two of these were Bishops Paulus and Nilus; and the other two were selected of the laity, Patermytheus and Elias; and by race they were all of them Egyptians. They were pure lovers of that exalted philosophy which is of God, and offered themselves like gold to the fire to be purified. But He who giveth strength to the weak, and multiplieth comfort to the afflicted, deemed them worthy of that life which is in heaven, and associated them with the company of angels.

THE CONFESSION OF SILVANUS, AND OF THOSE WITH HIM,

IN THE EIGHTH YEAR OF THE PERSECUTION IN OUR DAYS.

This blessed Silvanus came from Gaza, and he was one of the veteran soldiers; and when his freedom from service proved to be contrary to his habits, he enlisted himself as a good soldier of Christ. For he was a perfectly meek man, and of bright turn of mind, and used his faith with simplicity and purity. And he was a presbyter of the church in the city of Gaza, and conducted himself there with great propriety. And because the conflict for life was proclaimed against the soldiers of Christ [p. 51], he, an old man, of a noble person, went down to the Stadium, and there, in his first confession before the people of Cæsarea, he acquitted himself valiantly, being tried with scourgings. And when he had endured these bravely, he fought in a second conflict, in which the old man endured the combs on his sides like a young man. And at the third conflict he was sent to the copper mines; and during a life of much length he exhibited great probation. He was also deemed worthy of the office of the episcopate, and also rendered himself illustrious in this office of his ministry. But on the fourth day of Iyar the great gate of heaven was fully opened to him, and this blessed man went up with a company of martyrs, not being left alone, for a great assembly of brave men followed him. And suddenly a mandate of wickedness was issued, and command was given that all those in the mines who were become enfeebled through old age or sickness, and those who were not able to work, should be put to death by the sword; and God's martyrs, being all together forty in number, were beheaded all in one day. And many of them were Egyptians, but their leader and guide was this same martyr and bishop of martyrs, Silvanus, a man truly blessed and beloved of God.

Being now arrived at this place in our narrative, we will inform you how God in a short time took vengeance upon those wicked rulers, and they speedily experienced the punishment of their crimes. For he that was excited against these martyrs of God in a barbarous manner, like some fierce wild beast, suffered a wretched punishment; and by the command of him who possessed the power of the time, perished after the manner of a cruel wild beast. And all the rest perished by various kinds of deaths, and received that punishment which they deserved for their crimes.

So, then, we have described and made known the things which were done during the whole time of the persecution among the people in Palestine. And all these were blessed martyrs [p. 52] of God, who triumphed in our time; who made light of this temporary life, and prized the worship of God far above every other thing, and have received the hidden hope of those good things which are invisible to the bodily eyes.

Oh! the blessed confessors of the kingdom of Christ, who were tried like gold in the excellence of their righteousness, and obtained through the conflict in which they were set the heavenly life of angels, and laid hold upon the promises of the hidden good things of the victory of the high calling—For eye hath not seen nor ear heard, neither hath it entered into the heart of man, what God has prepared for them that love him.

Here end the chapters of the narrative of the victories of the holy confessors in Palestine.

NOTES.

P. ii. l. 18.—"Who shall separate us ..... slaughter." Rom. viii. v. 35. This passage varies slightly both from the Greek and the Peshito. There is nothing here to correspond with *της αγαπης* and *η γυμνοτης*; and also ܡܘܬܐ, "death," for *κινδυνος*.

l. 23.—"For him who loved us," v. 37: as if the Syriac translator had read *δια τον αγαπησαντα ημας*, or had mistaken the meaning of *δια* with a genitive.

l. 27.—v. 38. *ουτε αγγελοι, ουτε αρχαι* omitted.

l. 31.—Eusebius gives the account of the martyrdom of Peter and Paul at Rome in his Eccl. Hist. book ii. ch. 25.

P. iii. l. 6.—"As for those conflicts." Eusebius makes a similar statement, book viii. ch. 13, on which passage Valesius has the following note:—([d]) "He means doubtless his book *concerning the Martyrs of Palestine.* For no other book but that can be found, wherein Eusebius relates the conflicts of the Martyrs which he himself had seen. The opinion of Christophorson is from this passage further disproved, who supposed the book *concerning the Martyrs of Palestine* was a part of this eighth book." In speaking here of Christophorson, Valesius alludes to a note immediately preceding, which runs thus—" ([c]) To wit, in the book *concerning the Martyrs of Palestine,* which is placed after this eighth book. For in that Eusebius at large declares the martyrdom of Pamphilus, as may there be seen. Moreover, from this place it appears that that book *concerning the Martyrs of Palestine* was written by Eusebius after his *Ecclesiastical History,* and after his books *concerning the life of Pamphilus the Martyr.* Christophorson, who had inserted the whole Appendix before this chapter, was forced to omit these words of Eusebius here, lest Eusebius should seem to have forgot himself." See English Translation of Eusebius's Ecclesiastical History in "*The History of the Church*: fol., London, 1709, p. 148. I shall cite this in the following notes as *Eng. Trans.*

l. 18.—"Procopius." There is an antient Latin copy of these Acts, as they stand here, published by Valesius in his notes upon the first chapter of the Martyrs of Palestine as they exist in the Greek at the end of the eighth book of the Eccl. Hist. of Eusebius. Respecting these, he writes thus:—"The same relation is in the *Acts of the Passion of Procopius the Martyr*, which begins thus: '*The first of the Martyrs that appeared in Palestine was Procopius*,' &c. From whence it is evident that those acts were translated out of the Greek copy of Eusebius into Latin. To make this more apparent, it will in no wise be unuseful to insert here the entire acts. For many things worth our knowledge are contained in these which neither Baronius nor Molanus happened to have a sight of."

Passio Sancti Procopii Martyris, qui passus est sub Fabiano judice 4 Nonas Augusti.

Primus martyrum qui sunt in Palæstina, apparuit Procopius, vir cœlestis gratiæ, qui et ante martyrium sic suam vitam disposuit, ut etiam a parva ætate castitati semper et morum virtutibus studeret. Corpus quidem suum sic confecit, ut pæne mortuum putaretur, animam vero ejus sic verbis confortabat divinis, ut etiam corpori virtutem ex hujus refectione ministraret. Cibus et potus ei panis et aqua fuit. Solis his utebatur, cum post biduum triduumque, diem interdum etiam post septimam ad cibum rediret. Sacrorum quoque meditatio sermonum ita mentem ejus obstrinxerat, ut nocte ac die in hoc infatigabilis permaneret. Clementiæ autem et mansuetudinis tanquam ceteris inferior documentum sui præbebat copiam. In verbis divinis ei tantum studium erat. Illa vero quæ extrinsecus sunt, mediocriter attigerat. Igitur genere quidem Æliensis, conversatione autem vel habitatione Scythopolitanus erat. Ibi ecclesiæ tria ministeria præbebat, unum in legendi officio, alterum in Syri interpretatione sermonis, et tertium adversus dæmones manus impositione consummans. Cumque ab Scythopoli una cum sociis in Cæsaream transmissus fuisset, ab ipsis portis ad præsidem ducitur, et priusquam carceris vel vinculorum experiretur angustias, in ipso ingressu suo a judice Flaviano ut diis sacrificaret impellitur. At ille magna voce non esse deos multos sed unum factorem omnium opificemque testatus est. Judex autem plaga sermonis ictus et conscientia saucius, consensit ejus sermoni. Atque ad alia se rursum argumenta constituit, ut vel regibus sacrificaret. Sanctus autem Dei martyr sermonem ejus despiciens, Homeri, inquit, versum dicens: non est bonum multos dominos esse. Unus dominus est, unus rex. Itaque hoc verbo ejus audito, quasi qui infausta in regibus deprompsisset, jussu judicis ducitur ad mortem, et capite amputato ingressum vitæ cœlestis, vel compendium beatus invenit: Desii septima Julii mensis, quæ Nonas Julias dicitur apud Latinos, primo anno quo adversus nos fuit persecutio. Hoc primum in Cæsarea martyrium consummatum est, regnante Domino nostro Jesu Christo, cui honor et gloria in sæcula sæculorum. Amen.

And in a note following this Latin copy he writes ([r])—“ Many things are omitted in the Greek text of Eusebius, which must be made perfect by these Acts in Latin. For when Eusebius had here said expressly, that Procopius upon his first arrival was brought before the judge, he adds nothing concerning the place from whence he came, where he was apprehended, or to what place he was brought: nothing of which ought to have been omitted. Besides, Eusebius does accurately relate the descent and country of other Martyrs mentioned in this book; and if any of these had attained to any Ecclesiastical honour, he does usually take notice of that also. But of this person, who was the chief and leader of all the Palestine Martyrs, we see no such relation made. This, it is probable, was not the fault of Eusebius, but of his exscribers; for in the Latin Acts, which, as we before evinced, were translated out of Eusebius, all these circumstances are manifestly declared.” See Ecc. Hist. *Eng. Trans.*, p. 154. This Latin version is also printed by Th. Ruinart, p. 353, *Acta primorum*

Martyrum Sincera et Selecta, fol. Amstel. 1713. There is also another Syriac version of these Acts taken from Cod. Nit. Vat. 1. (See Assemani, *Bibl. Orient.* vol. 1. p. 56); and published with a Latin translation and notes, by S. E. Assemani, in *Acta SS. Martt. Orient. et Occident.*, 2 vol. fol. Romæ, 1748, part ii. p. 169. I have collated it with this version. It is not of importance to note the variants, which seem to be chiefly due to separate translations.

l. 20.—"The first year of the persecution in our days." The preface to the account of the *Martyrs of Palestine*, in the eighth book of *Ecc. Hist.*, says this was the 19th year of Diocletian, or A. D. 303. See Ruinart *Acta primorum Martt.* p. 316.

P. iv. l. 2.—"His family was from Baishan." The Latin has—"Igitur genere quidem Æliensis, conversatione autem vel habitatione Scythopolitanus erat," with which the other Syriac agrees in reading, ܫܪܒܬܗ ܕܝܢ ܡܢ ܐܘܪܫܠܡ ܐܝܬܘܗܝ، ܗܘܐ ܘܡܥܡܪ ܒܡܕܝܢܬܐ ܒܝܫܢ ܗܘܐ—"But his family was from Jerusalem, and he dwelt in the city Baishan." Scythopolis was the Greek name of Baishan, and Ælia occupied the scite of Jerusalem. See, respecting Baishan, S. E. Assemani, *Ibid*, not. p. 171.

l. 4.—"In the second order he translated from Greek into Aramaic." He was an interpreter; on which passage S. E. Assemani observes—"Ad munus interpretis recte adnotat Valesius, apud Syros olim Divinas Scripturas Græce fuisse lectitatas, quas deinde Interpres Syriacus redderet," *Ibid.* p. ii. p. 171. I should feel much disposed to question this assertion without greater proof. Doubtless before this time the Scriptures were translated into Syriac. The meaning of the passage may also imply that Procopius was engaged in translating other ecclesiastical works into Syriac from the Greek. This very copy of Eusebius was transcribed only 108 years after the Martyrdom of Procopius. *Ibid.* p. 166. S. E. Assemani gives his opinion in these words:—"Imo vero quum S. Procopius Sanctorum librorum a Græco in Syriacum sermonem in ecclesia Scythopolitana Interpres dicatur, plane inde colligitur, Syriacum seu Chaldaicum idioma Palæstinis tunc vernaculum fuisse, atque adeo ejusdem Procopii, quemadmodum et aliorum martyrum in Palæstina coronatorum, Acta Syriace seu Chaldaice ab Eusebio fuisse primum exarata, eademque ipsa esse, quæ præ manibus habemus, omnino tenendum est. Neque enim verisimile est, Eusebium, quam in usum popularium suorum, et in ovium sibi concreditarum solatium scribebat, martyrum historiam iis literis consignasse, quas omnes non callerent." *Ibid.* p. 166.

l. 12.—"Flavianus." The other Syriac has ܦܘܠܝܢܘܣ, Paulinus, evidently a mistake of the scribe.

l. 21.—"Greatest of the poets of the Greeks." The Latin has "Homeri inquit versum, dicens;" and the other Syriac, ܗܘܡܪܘܣ ܡܫܒܚܐ ܕܦܘܐܛܣ ܕܝܘܢܝܐ, "Homer, the celebrated of the poets of the Greeks." Those words of Homer, *Iliad* ii. 24, were often cited by the early Christians, and do not therefore prove that Procopius was acquainted with his poems. See *Heinichen's note.*

l. 19.—"The Emperors, who were four in number." These were Diocletianus, Maximianus, Constantius, and Galerius. See Eusebius *Ecc. Hist.* b. viii. c. 13; and supplement to same book; and Valesius's notes, *Eng. Trans.* pp. 148. 153.

l. 27.—"On the seventh day of the month Heziran." See Valesius's note on this passage in the Greek; *Eng. Trans.* p. 157.

l. 31.—"The confession of Alphæus, Zacchæus, and Romanus." Their festival is celebrated on the 18th of November. See Baillet, *Vies des Saints.* There is also a Syriac version of these Acts published by S. E. Assemani in *Acta SS. Martt.* part ii. p. 177.

l. 35.—"Festival—on the twentieth year." That is, Diocletian's Vicennalia. See Valesius's note on this place, *Eng. Trans.* p. 158; and also on Life of Constantine, *ibid.* p. 529.

P. v. l. 9.—"Of Gadara." So in the other Syriac. This is not in the Greek, but Valesius has supplied the fact in the following note ([g]):—"He was of Gadara, concerning whom we have this passage in the Menology at 18th of November—*The comme-*

moration of the holy Martyrs, Michæus, Zacchæus, deacon of Gadara, and Alphæus, ibid. p. 158. See also Ruinart, n. 4. p. 317, *Acta prim. Martt.*

l. 22.—"Four holes of the rack." Valesius has the following note on Eusebius, *Ecc. Hist.* b. v. c. i.—"The fashion of this engine for punishment, and the manner how persons were punished in it, seems to have been this. It was a piece of timber wherein five pairs of holes were made at a certain distance one from the other. Into these holes, as it were into boots, they put the feet of the offenders, and fastened them therein with cords and fetters. The meaning of *their feet being strained to the fifth hole* is, they forced them to straddle so wide as to put their feet into the last pair of holes, which posture (those holes being at the greatest distance one from the other) was the sharpest degree of torture in this engine."—*Eng. Trans.* p. 71. See also *Gallonius De SS. Martt. cruciatibus*, Parisiis, 1659.

l. 25.—"Exorcist." Valesius has this note on Exorcists (°):—"There was in former times a twofold use of the *Exorcists* in the Church; for their business was to cleanse both those possessed with devils, and also the *catechumens*, who were exorcised more than once; for after every examination in their catechism they were brought to the Exorcist ungirt and with their shoes off, that they might be purged by him. See Cyril Hierosol. in *Procatechesi ad Illuminandos*, and Chrysostom in his first Homily *ad Illuminandos*." *Eng. Trans.* p. 158. See also Bingham, *Antiquities of the Christian Church*, book iii. ch. 4. Respecting Readers or Lectors, see *ibid.* ch. v.

P. vi. l. 16.—"Combs." See Gallonius de *SS. Martt. Cruciat.* ch. v.

l. 33.—"Romanus." There are other Acts of Romanus, in Syriac, giving a much longer and fuller account than this. *British Museum Cod. Add.* 12,174, fol. 300 b. In these the day of his martyrdom is given the 19th of Teshri the latter. See L. Surius, *de Probatis Sanctorum vitis*, at the 18th of November, and Baillet, *Vies des Saints*, at the same day. See a further account of him from Eusebius *de Resurrectione*; Prudentius περι σεφανων, &c., collected and published by Ruinart. *Acta prim. Martt.* p. 357 seq.

P. vii. l. 7.—"The judge." His name was Asclepiades. See Prudentius *Hymn* περι στεφανων, l. 687, in Ruinart, *Acta prim. Martt.* p. 361. S. E. Assemanni also observes:—"Hunc Asclepiadem vocant *Acta* apud Mombritium et Prudentius in *Hymno.*" See *Acta SS. Martt.* ii. p. 182, and the other Syriac Acts, *Mus. Brit. Cod. Add.* 12,174.

l. 24.—"The officers," ܩܣܛܘܢܪ̈ܐ, "Quæstionarii." They were the persons who inflicted the punishment, as appears from the following passage of the acts of Trypho:—"Præfectus autem admirans tantam eorum perseverantiam, jussit eos manibus post tergum ligatis nudos cædi: et cum acerrime cæderentur, quæstionarii deficiebant, Præfectus ira repletus jussit ungulas et lampades eorum lateribus applicari. Quæstionarii accedentes jussa complebant." See Ruinart, *Act. prim. Martt.* p. 163. He also has this note, *ibid.* p. 172.—"Quæstionis nomine designat tormenta, quæ ad confessionem eliciendam adhibentur: vox etiam nunc ad eandem rem significandam usurpata est. Ab ea *Confessores quæstionati et torti* dicuntur apud Cyprian, *Epist. ad Florentium*, 66.

l. 34.—"The emperor Diocletian." The name is not given in the Greek. It appears from this that Valesius was mistaken when he wrote,—"I suppose he means Galerius Cæsar, for Diocletian made his abode then at Nicomedia." See *Eng. Trans.* p. 158. The other Syriac Acts, however, give the name ܡܟܣܝܡܝܢܘܣ ܚܬܢܗ ܕܕܝܘܩܠܛܝܢܘܣ. "Maximinus, the son-in-law of Diocletianus." *Mus. Brit. Cod. Add.* fol. 304.

P. viii. l. 8.—"Then did great wonder." The miraculous part of this narrative, which savors so strongly of the superstitious, is omitted from the Greek; and that passage added which, in the Syriac, commences the account of Zacchæus, but is not found at that place in the Greek. The story of Romanus having spoken after his tongue was cut out is, however, repeated in the other Syriac Acts, and is also told in the Greek *Menæum.* See Valesius, note (ᵃ) *Eng. Trans.* p. 158. Ruinart has the following note:—"Omittit miraculum Romani, etiam abscissâ linguâ loquentis, quod alias adeo exaggerat. Hinc patet non omnia isto libello contineri." p. 318. Eusebius himself also, in his book *de Resurrectione,* affirms the miracle. See Ruinart, *Acta prim. Martt.* p. 359; and Chrysostom, *Orat.* 43 et 48. *Ibid.* See also S. E. Assemani's note, *Act. SS. Martt.* p. ii. p. 182.

l. 20.—"Upon the rack." The other Syriac version adds here, "to five holes," ܒܚܡܫܐ ܢܘܩ̈ܒܝܢ. *Ibid.* p. 181.

l. 22.—"Strangling instrument." ܒܡܚܢܩܬܐ. Greek, *τῷ ξυλῳ βροχῳ.* The other Acts have, "He was strangled in Prison," fol. 304.

l. 30.—"Confession of Timotheus." These Acts are also given in the other Syriac Translation by S. E. Assemani, *Act. SS. Martt.* p. ii. p. 184. See Surius, at the 19th of August, and Baillet, at the same day.

P. ix. l. 2.—"Edicts from the Emperors." Respecting these Edicts Valesius has the following note on the Ecc. Hist. b. viii. c. vi. (ᶠ)—"By the first Edict of the Emperors against the Christians it was ordered that the churches should be ruined and the scriptures burnt, and that those who were honoured with any preferment (if they refused to sacrifice) should be deprived of their dignity. The meaner sort were to lose their liberty. See chap. 2. Another Edict soon followed this, that Bishops, Priests, and Deacons should be imprisoned, and by all ways compelled to sacrifice. The third Edict comprehended all sorts of Christians, as well those of the laity as the clergy; which Edict was proposed (says Eusebius in the chap. 3 of his book *concerning the Martyrs of Palestine*) in the second year of the Persecution. But this seems rather to have been the fourth Edict: for the second and third concerned the Presbyters only. By the second it was ordered they should be imprisoned, and by the third it was enjoined that they should by tortures be compelled to sacrifice." *Eng. Trans.* p. 143.

l. 25.—"The people of the city of Gaza were accursed in their heathenism." See the account given by Theodoretus, book iii.

c. 6 and 7; and S. E. Assemani, *Acta SS. Martt.* p. ii. p. 186, note (4).

P. x. l. 9.—"Theckla (she of our days)." There were several martyrs of this name. S. E. Assemani has published the Acts of two others. See *Acta SS. Martt.* vol. i. pp. 101, 123; but Eusebius seems especially to draw the distinction with reference to Theckla, the companion of St. Paul, so celebrated in the early ages of Christianity. See Grabe, *Spicilegium*, vol. i. p. 95 Jer. Jones, *New and Full Method,* vol. ii. p. 353; Tischendorf, *Acta Apost. Apocr. Lips.* 1851, p. 40. There are also antient copies in Syriac of the Acts of Theckla, brought from the Nitrian Convent, now in the British Museum. The account of Theckla is in one or two instances found in a volume containing also the Books of Ruth, Esther, and Judith, and called in Syriac "The Book of Women." See *Cod. Add.* 12,174; 14,641; 14,652.

l. 15.—"Timotheus." The Greek has *Τιμολαος*. See Surius, at March 24th, and Baillet, at the same day.

l. 16.—"Paesis." The Syriac is ܦܠܣܝܣ, "Plasis," which I have corrected here from the reading below, where it is ܦܝܣܝܣ. Paesis, or Pausis, for some Greek MSS. read *Παησις* and others *Παυσις*. Valesius notes (c)—"In the *Maz.* and *Med.* MSS. his name is ***Paesis.*** In the ***Greek Menology*** (which ***Canisius*** published) at the 5th of March, instead of ***Paesis*** he is called ***Publius.***" ***Eng. Trans.*** p. 159. The variation in the Syriac doubtless arose from confounding *Α* with *Λ* in the word *ΠΑΗCΙC* or *ΠΛΗCΙC.*

l. 27.—"The Phrygians." There is no mention of Phrygians in the Greek; but in *Ecc. Hist.* book viii. ch. 11, Eusebius speaks of the destruction of a whole city of Christians in Phrygia. These, perhaps, were some of them who had been reserved for a spectacle in the theatre.

P. xi. l. 35.—"A subdeacon." Syriac ܦܪܝܩܐ, evidently a blunder for ܦܕܝܩܐ. Greek *υποδιακονος*.

P. xii. l. 5.—"A sudden change." See respecting this, Eusebius, *Life of Constantine,* book i. ch. 18, *Eng. Trans.* p. 537, where Valesius has the following note(a):—"This place is highly remarkable, for from it this conclusion may be made, that the persecution began in Dioclesian's eighth, and Maximian's seventh consulate, and not on the foregoing year, as Baronius will have it. Concerning which matter I have spent many words in my notes on Eusebius, *Ecc. Hist.* book viii. c. 2, note (c). For whereas Eusebius affirms that the Emperors Dioclesian and Maximian divested themselves of their purple in the year after the persecution was begun; and whereas it is manifest that they did that on the year of Christ 304; what I have said does necessarily follow, that Dioclesian's persecution was begun in the year of Christ 303." Ruinart has this note:—"Diocletianus scilicet prope Nicomediam, Herculius Mediolani, cogente Galerio Maximinano, non autem sponte, uti hactenus putabatur. Totam hunc historiam egregie describit Lactantius in lib. de *Mortibus Persecut.* cap. 18 seq. *Acta Prim. Martt.* p. 319.

l. 16.—The Greek adds a passage, "But we will give an exact account of these matters at a more opportune place and time," referring perhaps to the Life of Constantine.

l. 18.—"Epiphanius." Syriac, ܐܦܝܦܢܘܣ; but the Greek reads *Απφιανος*; the other Syriac version published by S. E. Assemani, *Acta SS. Mart.* P. ii. p. 189, ܐܦܝܢܘܣ; and an Arabic account cited by him, امفيانوس, "Amphianus." In Latin he is called *Apianus*, *Apphianus*, and *Amphianus*. *Ibid.* See Surius and Baillet, at the 2d of April.

l. 33.—"He was sprung from one of the most illustrious families in Syria." For which the Greek is, *ει τις αρα Παγας επισταται της Λυκιας, ουκ ασημον πολιν, εντευθεν ορμωμενος*. On this Valesius has the following note (c):—"In the *Med.* MS. this city is called *Arpagas*; in the *Maz.* MS. *Arapagas*, in the *Fuk* MS. *Harpagas*; but in the margin a notice is given that it should be *ἁραγας* with an aspirate. I never met with any thing concerning *Aragas*, a city of Lycia.—In the *Menæum* of the Greeks, Amphianus is said to have been born in Lydia."—*Eng. Trans.* p. 160. There seems, therefore, to have been some mistake in the copies in this place at an early period.

l. 36.—"Educated at Beyrout." (c) "At Berytus there was a

school of civil law, as many have taken notice from Gregory Thaumaturgus, Eunapius, Nonnus, and others. Gregorius Nazianzenus calls Berytus *Φοινικης κλυτον αστυ, νομων εδος Αυσονιηων, a famous city of Phœnicia, the seat of Ausonian laws.*" See Valesius, *ibid.*

P. xiii. l. 20.—"This our city." The Greek has *την Καισαρεων πολιν.*

l. 23.—"Pamphilus." His name is not mentioned in the Greek, and Valesius has this note on the passage (f):—"Simeon Metaphrastes, who professes that he transcribed the Martyrdom of *Apphianus* (or, as he calls him, Amphianus), out of Eusebius, has altered this passage thus:—*And having been conversant with us in divine studies, and instructed in the sacred scriptures by the great Martyr Pamphilus, he obtained no mean habit of virtue; by which he opened a passage for himself, whereby he procured the crown of Martyrdom.*" See *Eng. Trans.* p. 160. And in note (c), on the same page, Valesius writes:—"In the Menologies of the Greeks at the 2d of April, Amphianus, with his brother Ædesius, is mentioned to have been instructed in the Christian religion by Pamphilus the Martyr, at Berytus;" but not having the knowledge of the fact that Pamphilus himself had been educated at the same place—supplied in the Syriac, but omitted in the Greek—Valesius supposed the Menologies to be mistaken. See note (f), *Ibid.* It is evident from this that Simeon Metaphrastes, and the compilers of the Menologies, read these Acts as in the Syriac.

P. xv. l. 12.—"His bones and entrails became visible." The same thing is said of the Martyr Alexander, whose Acts were published by Ruinart:—"Ita enim laniatum fuerat corpus crudelitate verberantium, ut carne soluta costarum, patefactisque visceribus, secreta animæ panderentur." *Acta Prim. Martt.* p. 77.

l. 28.—"Was hung up at a great height." See, respecting the various modes of suspension in torture, Gallonius *de SS. Martt. cruciatibus*, p. 6.

P. xvii. l. 30.—After the Martyrdom of Apphianus the Greek adds the following account of Ulpianus:—"At the same time, and almost on the same day, a young man in the city of Tyre, by name Ulpianus, after he had been cruelly scourged, and endured most grievous stripes, was sewn up in the raw hide of an ox, together with a dog and a venomous serpent, and cast into the sea. Wherefore we thought it agreeable to make mention of this person at [this place wherein we have related] the Martyrdom of Apphianus."—*Eng. Trans.* p. 161. On this Valesius has the following note (a):—"*Διο μοι δοκει κ.τ.λ.*: that is, *Although Ulpianus suffered not in Palestine, but in Phœnicia, yet because he suffered martyrdom at the same time, and died by the same sort of punishment that Apphianus had inflicted on him, we judged it not unfit to make mention of him here.* It is therefore apparent from these words that Eusebius in this book designed to give an account of the Martyrs of the Province of Palestine only."—*Ibid.*

l. 33.—"Alosis." In the Greek Ædesius, *Αιδεσιος*, the variation has doubtless arisen from the similarity of the names *ΑΛΟCΙΟC* and *ΑΔЄCΙΟC* in a MS. partly effaced. The other Syriac published by S. E. Assemani has [illegible]. See *Acta SS. Martt.* P. ii. p. 195. The account of this martyrdom is given by Baillet, at the 2d of April.

l. 36.—"Both on the father's and the mother's side." And so also in the other Syriac.—*Ibid.* p. 195. The Greek has here *ομοπατριος αδελφος* only. Valesius has this note (b):—"In the *Greek Menæum*, at the second day of April, Ædesius is styled Apphianus's brother by the mother's side."—*Eng. Trans.* p. 161. Hence it appears they both followed a text like this, each omitting one part of it.

P. xviii. l. 12.—"In the society of the martyr Pamphilus." There is no mention of this or of Pamphilus in the Greek; but in the *Menæa* and in the *Menology* Apphianus, with his brother Ædesius, is said to have been instructed by Pamphilus. See Valesius, note (f), *Eng. Trans.* p. 160.

l. 20.—"Hierocles." His name is also omitted in the Greek, but it is given in the Menæum of the Greeks, which Valesius quotes in explanation of the passage, otherwise obscure, as it is found in the Greek, but plain enough from the facts supplied in the Syriac. "The explanation of this place is to be had from the Menæum of the Greeks, where Ædesius is said to have struck Hierocles, Prefect of Egypt, with his fist. The words there are these:—*But Ædesius, who was condemned to work in the mines of brass, having seen (at Alexandria in Egypt) Hierocles, the president, punishing the Christians, he accounted him a despicable person, and struck the president with his own hand.*—Epiphanius and Lactantius mention this Hierocles, Prefect of Egypt, who was famous for the great slaughter he made amongst the Christians. This was the Hierocles against which our Eusebius wrote a book." See *Note* (d) p. 161, *Eng. Trans.* See also *Acta SS. Martt.* S. E. Assemani, p. 1, p. 197. The last and best edition of Eusebius *Against Hierocles* was published by the late most excellent and learned Dr. Gaisford, Dean of Christ Church: *Eusebii Pamphili contra Hieroclem et Marcellum* libri, 8vo., Oxonii, 1852.

P. xix. l. 15.—"Agapius." The Syriac is ܐܓܦܘܣ, which would be more correctly transcribed "Agapus;" but the other Syriac, published by S. E. Assemani, *Acta SS. Martt.* P. ii. p. 198, has ܐܓܦܝܘܣ. The omission of the vowels causes frequently great discrepancy in the transcription of Greek proper names in the Syriac character. The Acts of Agapius are given by Baillet, at the 19th of August.

P. xx. l. 10.—"In another chapter." See above, p. 10. Valesius was mistaken in supposing that this was a different Agapius from the one there mentioned. For it is distinctly stated here, that although he had been condemned by the Judge Urbanus to be devoured by wild beasts two years before, the sentence had not yet been put into execution, but was kept back till now, when Maximinus was present See note (b) p. 162. *Eng. Trans.* He is called in the Greek the *second Agapius*—*Αγαπιος ουτος ο δευτερος*—because, although he had been condemned before, he was not put to death till after the other Agapius mentioned above, p. 11, who was beheaded.

l. 12.—Concerning the leading about in the Stadium Valesius has this note on the *Ecc. Hist.* b. v. c. 1 (*):—"The Gladiators and the Bestiarii, before they began the encounter, were wont to be led about in the presence of the spectators. See Lucian, in *Toxari*. This was usually done, not only with those who let themselves out to play prizes, but also with those offenders, which were condemned to the sword and to the wild beasts. So Martial, "Traducta est gyris, nec cepit arena nocentes." *Eng. Trans.* p. 72.

l. 25.—"Maximinus." The Emperor's name is not mentioned in the Greek; but the following passage, not found in the Syriac, is added:—"The Emperor himself being then present, being reserved as it were on set purpose for that opportunity, that that saying of our Saviour's which, by his divine knowledge, he foretold his disciples might be accomplished in him, *that they should be brought before kings for their testimony of him.* See *Eng. Trans.* p. 162.

P. xxi. l. 3.—"That Light which he had caused to arise." Syriac, ܠܕܢܚܐ ܕܐܕܢܚܗ; and again below, P. xxvii. l. 20.—"The manifestation from him." Eusebius's work, *Περι Θεοφανειας*, which having been long lost, was discovered in this same MS., and has been published both in Syriac and English by the late lamented Dr. Lee, bears the Syriac title, ܕܥܠ ܕܢܚܐ ܐܠܗܝܐ, On the "Divine Manifestation," or, more literally, on "The Divine Sunrise," the *Ανατολη;* which is the Septuagint version of צמח of Zech. vi. 12. *ιδου ο ανθρωπος ῳ ονομα Ανατολη.* In our English translation, "Behold the man whose name is the BRANCH." So in Luke i. 78, *ανατολη εξ υψους;* and Matt. iv. 16, *φως ανετειλεν;* Epist. to Heb. vii. 14, *εξ Ιουδα ανατεταλκεν ο Κυριος ημων:* all referring to the coming of Christ.

P. xxii. l. 1.—"Theodosia." There is another Syriac version of these Acts, published by Assemani in *Acta SS. Martt.* P. ii. p. 203. Ruinart notes:—"Celebris est ejus memoria apud Latinos et Græcos die 2 Aprilis. Alii tamen aliis diebus ejus festum peragunt. Ejusdem Martyris Acta prolixiora vidimus in multis codd. MSS. sed aliquatenus amplificata. Ipsius vero sacrum corpus in Monasterium Dervense allatum ab ipso S. Berchario fuisse dicitur. Vide Mabillon, sæc. 2; Bened. p. 848; et

Bolland, ad diem 2 April." See *Acta Prim. Martt.* p. 323. Her martyrdom is given by Baillet, at the 2d of April.

l. 10.—" One of the virgins of the Son of God." The other Syriac has " *Christian* virgins," ܡܫܝܚܝܬܐ; the Greek, *παρθενος, πιστον και σεμνοτατον κορασιον.*

l. 18.—" Urbanus." The name of the Governor is omitted in the Greek.

P. xxiii. l. 19.—" Copper mines in Palestine." The Greek adds the name of the place Phæno, which occurs also in the Syriac below. See P. xxiv. l. 35; P. xlvi. l. 9, and note thereon.

l. 28.—" The first day of the week." The Greek has *εν αυτῃ κυριακῃ ημερᾳ της του Σωτηρος ημων αναστασεως*, upon which Valesius has a note ([a]):—" In the MS. Acts of the passion of Theodosia, she is said to have suffered, not on Easter-day, but only on a Sunday.—*Eng. Trans.* p. 162.

P. xxiv. l. 1.—" Confession of Domninus." In the Greek mention is made of Sylvanus before him, and the account of both much abridged. See Surius and Baillet, at the 4th of October.

l. 28.—" Ludus." " Munera seu ludi, pugnæ cum bestiis appellabantur, quod in populorum vel militum delectationem darentur. Dicebantur autem ludi castrenses, si in castris fierent. Sermonem in *die Munerum* habuit Augustinus in *Basilica Restituta*, qui est in nova edit. 19, tomi v. vide notas ibi appositas." See Ruinart, *Acta Prim. Martt.* p. 96, in not.; also p. 111. The Greek, however, has in this place, *και τρεις μεν εις το μονομαχειν επι πυγμῃ καταδικαζει*, on which Valesius has this note ([c]):—" See the following chapter; from whence we are informed that those who were condemned to such combats were delivered to the procurators of Cæsar, who caused them to practise exercise daily, so that at last they might be fit to engage in combat." *Eng. Trans.* p. 163.

l. 29.—" An excellent and godly old man." The Greek gives his name " Auxentius." See Baillet, at the 13th of December.

l. 33.—" Silvanus." A further account is given of him below, p. 47. The Greek adds here—" who was then a Presbyter and a Confessor, but some time after was honoured with a Bishopric."—*Eng. Trans.* p. 162.

P. xxv. l. 26.—"Without any long delay." For this the Greek has, *και ουκ εις μακρον τοις κατα Παμφιλου τετολμημενοις*.

l. 31.—"Considered himself above all the people of Palestine." The Greek adds here—"Who also was companion of the tyrant himself, for he was his chief favourite, and did usually eat at the same table with him." *Ibid.* p. 163.

P. xxvi. l. 8.—"The servants of God." The Greek more boldly, "against us," *καθ' ημων*; and so at line 15 below. Instead of "There may come a time ..... against our people," the Greek has, "There may happen a seasonable opportunity, wherein we shall be more at leisure to relate the exits and calamitous deaths, by which those impious wretches (especially Maximinus and those about him who were his advisers) that were the greatest sticklers in the persecution against us, finished their lives." See *Eng. Trans.* p. 163. This account is given in the Appendix to the Eighth Book of the *Ecc. Hist. Ibid.* p. 153. See also *Ecc. Hist.* b. viii. c. 16; and Valesius, note (b) *Eng. Trans.* p. 151, and b. ix. c. 9, *Ibid.* p. 177.

l. 19.—"Hatha." The Greek gives no name, but only *η αδελφη*, "The Sister." The word *Hatha* means "Sister." *Hathai* ܚܬܝ, was not an uncommon woman's name.—See S. E. Assemani, *Acta SS. Martt.* P. i. p. 101, &c. In the Greek Menology she is called *Thea.* Valesius gives this note (c):—"This virgin's name is wanting here, but we will supply this defect from the *Grecian Menology;* where this passage occurs at the 15th of July. *On the same day the holy Martyrs* Valentina *and* Thea, which were Egyptians, *being brought to the city* Dio Cæsarea, *before* Firmillianus *the judge, made confession of Christ's name, who is our God; after which, their left feet being burnt and their right eyes pulled out, they were killed with a sword, and their bodies burnt.* But this account disagrees with Eusebius's relation here. For he says the one was born at Gaza and the other at Cæsarea; and he makes no mention of the burning of their feet or the pulling out of their eyes." See *Eng. Trans.* p. 164. The mistake in the Menologium perhaps arose from the compiler having read that the Egyptians, who are spoken of in the beginning of this same chapter, had their eyes put out and their feet burnt, and therefore concluding that these two virgins, mentioned immediately afterwards, were Egyptians, and had suffered like the rest. See Surius and Baillet, at the 25th of July.

P. xxvii. l. 6.—"Lud:" and in the Greek it is called *Dio Cæsarea*." Lydda is the same as Diospolis. It seems, therefore, that Dio Cæsarea, which is the same as Sepphoris, is a mistake for Diospolis. See Van de Velde, *Memoir to accompany the Map of the Holy Land*, p. 331 and 347. If, however, it be a mistake, it has been copied into the Greek Menology. See the preceding note.

l. 31.—"Calling Egyptians by Hebrew names." Eusebius refers to this in his Commentary on Isaiah as a fulfilment of the prophecy contained in ch. 44, v. 5:—"One shall say, I am the Lord's, and another shall call himself by the name of Jacob, and another shall subscribe with his hand unto the Lord, and surname himself by the name of Israel." Eusebius's words are—*Θαυμασαι δε εστι, και καταπλαγηναι αληθως την των προφητικων λογων δυναμιν, ως αυτοις εργοις τα αποτελεσματα παρειληφαμεν· εν γουν τοις καθ' ημας αυτους γενομενοις διωγμοις, πολλους των αλλοφυλων εθνων εθεασαμεθα, προσαρπαζοντας εαυτοις τας των αγιων ανδρων προσηγοριας. ων ο μεν εαυτον Ιακωβ εκαλει, και ετερος Ισραηλ, αλλος δε Ιερεμιαν, και Ησαιαν ετερος, και Δανιηλ παλιν αλλος. τοιαυτα γουν επιγραφομενοι ονοματα επι το μαρτυριον του Θεου συν πολλῳ θαρσει και παρρησιᾳ παρηεσαν· α δη σημαινουσα η προφητεια φησιν, Ουτος ερει, του Θεου ειμι.* Hoc est: Mirari plane subit prophetiæ vim et efficaciam, et quam vere rei eventum oculis perceperimus. Nam in persecutionibus nostro tempore concitatis, multos ex alienigenis gentibus vidimus, qui sanctorum virorum nomina usurpabant; alius quippe sese Jacobum appellabat, alius Israelem, alius Jeremiam, hic Hesaiam, iste Danielem. Etenim his sibi adscriptis nominibus, ad martyrium pro Deo subeundum cum fiducia et constantia accedebant. Quæ prophetia indicat dum ait, Hic dicet, Dei Sum, &c. See

Eusebius's *Comm. in Hesaiam*, in *Collectio Nova Patt.*, edited by Montfaucon, vol. ii. pp. 353 et 527.

P. xxviii. l. 17.—"Food from the Royal provision —— pugilism." The Greek is *επει μητε τας εκ του βασιλικου ταμειου τροφας, μητε μην τας επιτηδειους τῃ πυγμῃ μελετας υπεμενον*; and also adds, which is not in the Syriac, *ηδη δε ουκ επιτροποις αυτο μονον οι δηλουμενοι, αλλα και αυτῳ Μαξιμινῳ τουτου γε ενεκεν παραστ αντες*: on which Valesius observes (d):—"He means, as I judge, the Procurators of the company of gladiators and of the morning exercises; of whom there is frequent mention in the inscriptions. For the gladiators that were maintained by stipends paid out of the imperial exchequer, were committed to their care, and they gave them their allowances out of the treasury." *Eng. Trans.* p. 163, note.

P. xxx. l. 8.—"Our own city." Omitted in the Greek; and so probably for the same purpose below, *υπερ των ομοεθνων* instead of "for our people." l. 20.

P. xxxi. l. 8.—"Mannathus." The Greek has *Ενναθας* below, on which Valesius remarks (f)—"In the Greek Menology she is called Manatho." *Eng. Trans.* p. 165. Ruinart observes—"Hoc ipso die memorantur (*i.e.* Antoninus, Zebinas, et Germanus) cum Ennatha virgine in Martyrol. Romano, ac Menologio Basilii Imp., sed in magnis Menæis et Menologio Canisii die præcedenti. Porro hæc omnia Menologia *Nicephorum* tribus his martyribus adjiciunt, et pro Ennatha habent *Manatho*." *Acta Prim. Martt.* p. 327. See Baillet, *Vies des Saints*, at the 13th of November.

l. 23.—"And continuously —— Romans." This passage is evidently corrupt, and it is difficult to understand it. I subjoin the corresponding Greek:—*αθροως δ' ουν αυθις Μαξιμινου διαφοιτᾳ καθ' ημων πανταχου γραμματα κατ' επαρχιαν. ηγεμονες τε και προσετι ο των στρατοπεδων αρχειν επιτεταγμενος, κ. τ. λ.*

l. 28.—"They urged the Logistæ of the cities, and the military commander, and the Tabularii." On this Valesius notes (e)—"I judge he means the Prefect of the Prætorium. For at that time they took care of the military matters. Indeed, Eusebius's following words are a sufficient evidence that the Prefect of the Prætorium is meant here. For he speaks of the injunctions and public orders given to the Curators, Magistrates, and Tabularii of every city: which orders were issued out by the Prefect of the Prætorium only; as might be made to appear from several places. See Book 9, ch. 1 & 9, where Eusebius speaks of Sabinus, Prefect of the Prætorium to Maximin." *Eng. Trans.* p. 165. Concerning the Logistæ or Curators he writes ([b])—"The *Curator* of the city was he, who looked after the Treasure and whatever else belonged to the revenue of the city: this is manifest from the *Pandects of the Law.* He is also called *Logista* (from the Greek word λογιστης, which is the term here in the original) in Lege 3, *Cod. de modo mulctandi.* Hence λογιστευειν was used to signify *the performance of the Curator's office.*" See *Ecc. Hist.* b. viii. c. 9; *Eng. Trans.* p. 146. Respecting the Tabularii he writes ([c])—"These officers had in their custody the public tables or rolls of the cities, and looked after the accounts of the tribute. They were first called *Numerarii.* Afterwards Valens made a law that they should be called Tabularii." He then refers for further information to his observations on Ammianus Marcellinus, *ibid.* p. 165, which Heinichen has incorporated into his notes at this place.

P. xxxii. l. 18.—"They received sentence of death." The Greek says this was passed upon them by Firmillianus. It also adds that Zebinas was from Eleutheropolis.

l. 20.—"Antoninus." Valesius ([e]):—"In the Greeks' Menology this man is called Antonius, where, besides Zebinas and Germanus, there is a fourth companion of their's named, to wit, Nicephorus. For the 12th day of November this passage occurs:—*The birthday of the holy Martyrs Antonius and his fellows, who were in the times of Maximinus. Antonius was an old man, Nicephorus, Zebinas, and Germanus were in the flower of their age. They were taken at Cæsarea, and after they had boldly confessed Christ, were slain.* Here you see the author of the Menology has rendered πρεσβυτερος an *old man,* and *not a Presbyter.*" *Ibid.* p. 165.

l. 23.—"A sister, one of the Lord's virgins, a chaste and courageous maiden." For this the Greek has *τις γυνη παρθενιας στεμματι και αυτη κεκοσμημενη*; and also adds the name *Ενναθας*, omitted here in the Syriac.

l. 30.—"Maxys." Greek *Μαξυς*. Ruinart, *Acta Martt.* p. 327, has this note:—"Hæc vox Græca non est. An a Syris repetenda, apud quos *mochos* est pulicanus a *casas* increpare?" That is ܡܟܣܣ from ܟܣܣ; but the form here is ܡܟܣܣܘܣ, which seems rather to follow the Greek.

P. xxxiii. l. 33.—"The stones shed tears," &c. This, which doubtless was produced by natural causes, seemed miraculous to Eusebius, more especially if he looked upon it as fulfilling a prophecy of our Lord—Luke xix. 40: "I tell you, that if these should hold their peace, the stones would immediately cry out." See also Habak. ii. 11. Compare note p. 55 above.

P. xxxiv. l. 12.—"Primus." The Greek is *Προμος*, on which Valesius observes ([a])—"In the Greek this man's name is Promus; but I suppose it should be Probus, for I have never met with such a proper name as Promus. This mistake rose from hence: in antient MSS. *Beta* is usually written like *My*. In the *Fuk.* and *Sav.* MSS. it is *Probus.*" *Eng. Trans.* p. 166.

P. xxxv. l. 1.—"Peter, who was surnamed Absalom." In the Greek he is called *Πετρος ασκητης, ο και Αψελαμος*. Valesius has this note: ([b])—"Mention is made of this person in the *Greek Menæa* at the 14th of October, although Eusebius says he suffered on the 3d of the Ides of January. In the Menæum he is called *Auselamus,* but in the Menology *Anselamus* is, by a mistake, put for *Auselamus* or *Abselamus*. The import of the passage there is this:—'On the same day is the commemoration of the holy Martyr Petrus Anselamus of Eleutheropolis, who, being in the flower of his age and of a vigorous mind, behaved himself most admirably in the conflicts he underwent for religion; and having despised earthly things, was by fire offered up as a victim well pleasing to God in the sixth year of Dioclesian's and Maximian's empire. In which passage this is observable, that the sixth year of Dioclesian's empire is put for the sixth year of the Persecution." See *Eng. Trans.* p. 166. Ruinart has published *Passio Sancti Petri Balsami,* who, although some have doubted the fact, can hardly be a different person from the one here described as "as Peter, who was surnamed Absalom." See *Acta Prim. Martt.* p. 501. The account is given by Baillet in the *Vies des Saints* at the 3d of January.

P. xxxvi. l. 1.—"One who belonged to the heresy of Marcion." The Greek gives the name *Asclepius,* omitted here.

l. 6.—"Aia, a village which is on the confines of Beth Gobrin."—The Greek has *Ανεας, κωμης των ορων Ελευθεροπολεως.* The other Syriac version published by S. E. Assemani has ܐܢܐ, which he renders—"Ex agro Eleutheropolitano in vico Anea." *Acta SS. Martt.* P. ii. p. 207. See Van de Velde—*Eleutheropolis: Betogabra* (Ptolemy xvi. 4), *Betogabri, Bethgebrim;* also *Geberin* of the Crusaders, identified with great care by Robinson and Smith (*Bib. Res.* 404—420, 642, seq.), with the Modern Beit-Jibrin. *Memoir to accompany the Map of the Holy Land,* p. 309.

l. 11.—"The Confession of Pamphilus," &c. This account is considerably abridged in the Greek. Valesius has the following note (a):—"Symeon Metaphrastes has transcribed this whole relation of the Martyrdom of Pamphilus and his companions, out of our Eusebius, adding some things and altering others, as he usually does. But he seems to have been furnished with more perfect copies of Eusebius, than those we now have; which will manifestly appear to the reader, who may meet with Metaphrastes' account hereof in the Latin version of him, which Lipomannus and Surius put forth, Tome the third, at the 1st of June, p. 139, Edit. Ven. at 1581." *Eng. Trans.* p. 166. This account of Pamphilus and his companions still exists entire in Greek. It was first printed from a Medicean MS. by D. Papebrochius in the *Acta Sanctorum,* June, vol. i. p. 64. J. A. Fabricius reprinted it in his edition of Hippolytus' works, vol. ii. p. 217. Both of these learned men supposed it to have been an extract of Eusebius' *Life of Pamphilus,* to which he frequently refers in his Ecclesiastical History, and of which Jerome speaks. See note, p. 78 below. It is quite evident that Metaphrastes had before him the same copy of the Martyrs of Palestine as this Syriac, with some very slight variations. I have thought that it would be useful, for the sake of comparison, to copy here the whole of Lipomannus' Latin version after Metaphrastes in Surius, *De Probatis Sanctorum Vitis*, at the 1st of June :—

Certamen SS. Martyrum Pamphili et Sociorum ex Symeone Metaphraste.

I. "Tempus invitat ad omnibus enarrandum magnum et gloriosum spectaculum Pamphili et sociorum, virorum admirabilium, cum eo consummatorum, et qui ostenderunt multiplicia certamina pietatis. Atque cum plurimi in nobis cognita persecutione se fortiter gesserint, eorum de quibus agimus rarissimun certamen quod nos cognovimus, conscripsimus, quod in se simul omne genus ætatis et corporis et animi vitæque diversorum studiorum est complexum, variis tormentorum generibus, et diversis in perfecto martyrio coronis exornatum. Licebat enim videre quosdam adolescentes et pueros, atque adeo plane infantes, ex illis qui erant ex ipsis, alios autem pubescentes, cum quibus erat Porphyrius, corpore simul vigentes et prudentia, nempe mihi carissimum Jamnitem Paulum, Seleucumque et Julianum, qui ambo orti erant ex terra Cappadocum. Erant autem inter eos sacris quoque canis et profunda ornati senectute, Valens quidam diaconus ecclesiæ Hierosolymitanæ, et cui verum nomen obtigerat, Theodulus.

II. Atque hæc quidem fuit in eis ætatum varietas. Animis autem inter se differebant. Nam alii quidem erant rudiores, utpote pueri, et quibus erat ingenium adhuc tenerius et simplicius, alii vero severi et morum gravitate præditi. Erant autem inter eos quoque nonnulli disciplinarum sacrarum non ignari. Aderat vero omnibus congenita, insignis et admirabilis animi fortitudo. Veluti autem quoddam in die resplendens luminare in astris fulgentibus, in medio eorum eminebat meus Dominus, non est enim fas mihi aliter appellare divinum et plane beatissimum Pamphilum. Is enim et eruditionem, quæ habetur apud Græcos in admiratione, non modice attigerat, et in divinorum dogmatum et divinitus inspiratarum scripturarum eruditione, si quid audacius, sed verum dicendum est, ita erat exercitatus, ut nullus æque ex iis qui erant suo tempore. Quod autem erat his longe majus et præstantius, habebat donum, nempe domi natam, vel potius ei a Deo datam, intelligentiam et sapientiam.

III. Et quod ad animum quidem attinet, omnes ita se habebant. Vitæ autem conditionis et conversationis erat inter eos plurima differentia, cum Pamphilus quidem duceret genus secundum carnem ex iis qui erant honesto loco nati, fuisset autem insignis in republica gerenda in patria sua; Seleucus vero fuisset insigniter ornatus militiæ dignitatibus; alii autem nati essent ex mediocri et communi loco. Non erat eorum chorus nec extra servilem conditionem. Nam et ex præsidis domo in eorum numerum relatus erat Theodulus, et Porphyrius, qui specie quidem erat Pamphili famulus; is autem ipsum affectione habebat loco fratris, vel germani potius filii, ut qui nihil omitteret, quo minus imitaretur dominum. Quid aliud? Si quis dixerit in summa, eos ecclesiastici cœtus typum esse complexos, is non procul abfuerit a veritate, cum inter eos presbyterio quidem dignatus esset Pamphilus; Valens vero diaconatu, et alii sortiti essent locum eorum, qui e multitudine consueverunt legere, et confessionibus per fortissimam flagrorum tolerantiam diu ante in martyrio præclarissime se gessisset Seleucus, et militaris dignitatis amissionem fortiter excepisset, et reliqui deinde per catechumenos et fideles reliquam implerent similitudinem innumerabilis ecclesiæ, ut in parva imagine.

IV. Sic adspexi admirabilem tam multorum et talium martyrum electionem, qui etsi non essent multi numero, nullus tamen aberat ex iis ordinibus, qui inveniuntur inter homines. Quomodo autem lyra, quæ multas habet chordas, et ex chordis constat dissimilibus, acutis et gravibus, remissisque et intensis, et mediis, arte musica concinne adaptatis omnibus, eodem modo in his adolescentes simul et senes, servi simul et liberi, eruditi et rudes, obscuri generis homines, ut multis videbatur, et gloria insignes, fideles simul cum catechumenis, et diaconi simul cum presbyteris. Qui omnes tanquam a sapientissimo musico, nempe Dei verbo unigenito, varie pulsati, et quæ erat in ipsis potentiæ unusquisque per tormentorum tolerantiam, hoc est confessionem, ostendentes virtutem, et clarissimos numerososque, et concinnos sonos edentes in judiiciis, uno et eodem fine in primis piam et longe sapientissimam, per Martyrii consummationem, Deo universorum impleverunt melodiam.

V. Opera pretium autem est admirari virorum quoque numerum, qui significat propheticam quamdam et apostolicam gratiam. Contigit enim omnes esse duodecim, quo numero patriarchas et prophetas et apostolos fuisse accepimus. Non est autem prætermittenda uniuscujusque singulatim laboriosa fortitudo, laterum lacerationes, et cum pilis caprinis laceratarum corporis partium attritiones, et flagella immedicabilia, multipliciaque et varia tormenta, gravesque et toleratu difficiles cruciatus, quos, jubente judice, manibus et pedibus infligentes satellites, vi cogebant martyres aliquid facere eorum quæ prohibita.

VI. Quid opus est dicere memoriæ perpetuo mandandas voces virorum divinorum, quibus labores nihil curantes, læto et alacri vultu respondebant judicis interrogationibus, in ipsis tormentis ridentes viriliter, et bonis moribus ludificantes ejus percontationes? Cum enim rogasset undenam essent, mittentes dicere, quam in terris habebant civitatem, ostendebant eam, quæ vere est eorum patria, dicentes se esse ex Hierusalem. Indicabant vero eadem sententia Dei quoque cœlestem, ad quam tendebant, civitatem, et alia quæ sunt ejusmodi, ignota quidem et quæ non possunt perspici ab iis, qui sacras literas non gustarunt, eis autem solis qui a fide divina sunt incitati, aperta adducebant. Propter quæ judex indignatus, et valde animo cruciatus, et plane quid ageret dubius, varia, ne vinceretur, in eos operabatur. Deinde cum a spe cecidisset, concessit unicuique auferre præmia victoriæ. Erat autem varius modus eorum mortis, cum duo quidem inter eos catechumeni, consummati sint baptismo ignis, alius vero fuerit traditus figuræ salutaris passionis, qui autem erat mihi carus, fuerit diversis braviis redimitus.

VII. Atque hæc quidem dixerit quispiam, horum magis faciens universam mentionem, singulatim autem unumquemque persequens, merito beatum pronuntiarit eum, qui in choro primum locum obtinet. Is autem erat Pamphilus, vir revera pius, et omnium, ut semel dicam, amicus et familiaris, re ipsa nomen sibi impositum verum esse ostendens, Cæsariensium ecclesiæ ornamentum. Nam presbyterorum quoque cathedram, cum esset presbyter, honestabat, ut qui simul ornaret ministerium et ex eo ornaretur. Quinetiam aliis quoque erat divinus et divinæ particeps inspirationis, quoniam tota sua vita fuit maxime insignis virtute, multum quidem jubens valere delicias et copiam divitiarum, cum se totum dedicasset Dei verbo, renuntians quidem iis quæ ad ipsum redibant a majoribus, nudis, mancis, et pauperibus omnia distribuit. Ipse autem degit in vita, quæ nihil possidebat, per valentissimam exercitationem, divinam persequens philosophiam. Atque ortus quidem erat ex Berytensium civitate, ubi in prima ætate educatus fuerat in illis, quæ illic erant, studiis litterariis. Postquam autem ejus providentia ad virilem pervenisset ætatem, transiit ab iis ad sacrarum litterarum scientiam. Assumpsit vero mores divinæ et propheticæ vitæ, et ipse se verum Dei martyrem exhibuit etiam ante ultimum vitæ finem. Sed talis quidem erat Pamphilus.

VIII. Secundus autem post ipsum accessit Valens ad certamen, qui senili, et quæ decet sacerdotem, erat ornatus canitie, ipsoque aspectu venerandus et sacro-sanctus senex; qui etiam divinarum scripturarum sciens, ut si quis alius, eas quidem certe ita erat complexus memoria, ut a lectione nihil discreparent, quæ memoriæ mandatæ ab eo conservabantur, sacrosanctorum discipulorum promissiones. Erat autem diaconus, etsi esset hujusmodi, ecclesiæ Eliensium.

Tertius in eorum numerum relatus erat Paulus, qui, vir acerrimus et spiritu fervens, agnoscebatur ex civitate Iamnitarum: qui etiam in martyrio per cauterii tolerantiam susceperat certamen confessionis.

IX. His in carcere duobus annis contritis, martyrii occasio fuit Ægyptiorum adventus, qui etiam cum eis fuêre consummati. Ii autem cum vel sic valde afflicti, in metallis usque ad loca pervenissent, domum revertebantur. Qui, cum in ingressu portæ Cæsariensium interrogati essent a custodibus, quinam essent et unde venirent, et nihil veri celassent, dixissent autem se esse Christianos; perinde ac malefici in ipso furto deprehensi, vincti sunt et comprehensi: erant vero quinque numero. Ad Præsidem autem adducti, et coram eo libere locuti, in vincula quidem statim conjiciuntur: die autem sequente, qui erat sextus decimus mensis Peritii, more vero Romano quartus decimus Calend. Martii, hos ipsos cum Pamphilo et sociis adducunt ad Firmillianum. Ille autem Ægyptiorum solum periculum fecit ante tormenta, omni ratione eos exercens. Atque eorum quidem principem, quum adduxisset in medium, rogavit quisnam esset, et unde? Qui cum pro proprio nomine quoddam propheticum audisset (hoc autem fiebat ante alia, ut qui pro patriis eis impositis idolicis nominibus sibi prophetica nomina impossuissent, ut qui Eliam, et Hieremiam, Esaiam, Samuelem et Danielem ipsi seipsos nominarent, et qui est in occulto, Judæum et germanum Israelitem, non solum factis, sed etiam vocibus proprie enunciatis judicarent).

X. Cum tale ergo Judex audivisset a martyre, vim autem nominis non attendisset, secundo rogavit, quænam esset ejus patria? Ille vero cœlestem Hierusalem dixit esse suam patriam, illam intelligens de qua dictum est Paulo. 'Quæ sursum est Jerusalem est libera, quæ est mater nostra.' Et 'accessistis ad montem Sion et civitatem Dei viventis, Hierusalem cœlestem.' Et hic quidem hanc cogitabat: ille autem humi suam abjiciens cogitationem, quænam hæc esset, et ubi terrarum sita esset, accurate perscrutabatur, atque adeo ei etiam inferabat tormenta, ut verum fateretur. Hic vero dum torqueretur, se verum dixisse affirmabat. Deinde eo hæc rursus et sæpe sciscitante quænam esset, et ubi sita esset dicta civitas Hierusalem? solum dicebat eam esse patriam Christianorum; nullos enim alios præter eos esse ejus participes, sitam autem esse ad orientem et ad ipsam lucem et solem. Atque hic quidem rursus per hæc mente sua philosophabatur, nihil sentiens eos, qui circumcirca ipsum tormentis afficiebant. Tanquam autem carnis expers et incorporeus, nihil videbatur pati molestum. Judex vero animi dubius, odio cruciabatur, et existimans Christianos hanc sibi civitatem, quæ esset infesta Romanis, constituisse, valde urgebat tormentis, et curiose scrutabatur eam, quæ dicta fuerat, civitatem, et quæ est in Oriente, inquirebat regionem. Cum autem adolescentem, diu cæsum flagellis, videret non posse dimoveri ab iis, quæ prius dixerat, statuit in eum ferre sententiam capitis.

XI. Et in eum quidem res hoc modo processit: reliquos autem Ægyptios cum simili palæstra exercicuisset, similem quoque in eos fert sententiam. Deinde cum ab his transisset ad Pamphilum, accepit quod ii jam prius essent plurima experti tormenta. Absurdum autem esse arbitratus, eosdem iisdem rursus afficere tormentis, et frustra laborare, hoc solum est percontatus, an nunc saltem obedirent? Cum vero ab unoquoque eorum audiisset ultimam vocem martyrii, in eos similiter fert sententiam capitis.

XII. Nondum autem dictum universum absolverat, et alicunde exclamat quidam adolescens ex familia Pamphili, et ex media turba accedens in medium eorum, qui circumsidebant judicium, alta voce corpora eorum petiit sepulturæ. Is autem erat beatus Porphyrius, Pamphili germanum pecus, nondum totos octodecim annos natus, recte scribendi scientiæ peritus, modestia vero morum has laudes celans, ut qui a tali viro fuisset institutus. Is, postquam adversus dominum latam cognovit sententiam, exclamavit ex media multitudine, Corpora rogo, ut humi mandentur. Ille autem non homo, sed fera, et quavis fera agrestior, neque honestam et rationi consentaneam admittens petitionem, neque juvenili ætati dans veniam, cum hoc solum intellexisset, cum fateri se esse Christianum, jubet tortoribus ut totis viribus in eum uterentur. Cum vero, eo jubente, sacrificare recusasset vir admirandus, non utique tanquam carnem hominis, sed tanquam lapides et lignum, aut aliquid aliud inanimum usque ad ipsa ossa et ima viscera jubet eum torquere et corpus ejus cædere. Cum autem hoc diu fieret, agnovit se hoc frustra aggredi, cum propemodum mutum et inanimum effectum esset corpus generoso Martyri. Perseverans vero Judex in sævitia et inhumanitate, iubet latera tormentis exagitata, pilorum textis amplius atteri. Deinde cum sic eum cepisset satietas et furore esset exsatiatus, pronunciat sententiam ut tradatur lento et molli igni. Atque hic quidem, cum ante Pamphili consummationem postremus accessisset, prior e corpore excessit ad Dominum.

XIII. Licebat autem videre Porphyrium, non secus affectum quam victorem in sacris certaminibus, qui in omnibus pugnis evaserat superior, corpore pulverulentum, vultu lætum, audenter et exultando ad mortem progredientem, re vera plenum divino spiritu. Philosophico autem habitu suo indumento amictus instar superhumeralis, rursum aspiciens et omnia humana despiciens, sicut vitam mortalem, quieto animo accedit ad rogum. Cum jam flamma ei appropinquaret, et tanquam nihil ei adesset molestum, sana mente et nulla affecta perturbatione de rebus suis mandavit suis necessariis, adhuc vultum et universum corpus lætum conservans et immutatum. Postquam autem notos suos satis allocutus, eos valere jussit, jam de cætero contendebat ad Dominum. Cum vero rogus, satis longo spatio disjunctus, circa eum esset accensus, hinc et illinc ore flammam arripiebat, se ipsum incitans ad iter propositum. Hoc autem faciebat nihil aliud quam Jesum invocans. Tale est certamen Porphyrii.

XIV. Cum ejus autem consummationis Pamphilo nuncius fuisset Seleucus, dignus habetur, cui sors eadem cum eis obtingeret. Cum primum itaque renuntiasset Pamphilo exitum Porphyrii, et uno osculo salutasset Martyres, comprehendunt eum milites et ducunt ad Præsidem. Ille autem perinde ac urgens, ut ipse abiret simul cum prioribus, jubet eum affici supplicio capitis. Is erat ex regione Cappadocum, cum autem militia se præclare gessisset, ad non parvos gradus dignitatum pervenerat in Romano exercitu. Quin etiam statura, viribusque et magnitudine corporis, reliquos omnes longe superabat: ipso quoque aspectu erat omnibus suspiciendus, et tota forma corporis plane admirabilis, tam propter magnitudinem quam propter pulchritudinem. Atque in principio quidem persecutionis, per flagellorum perpessionem clarus extitit in certaminibus confessionis. Postquam autem fuerat liberatus a militia, seipsum constituens æmulatorem eorum, qui se exercent in pietate, efficitur Christi germanus miles, orphanorum desertorum et viduarum, quæ carebant præsidio, eorumque qui paupertate opprimebantur et imbecillitate, tanquam episcopus quispiam et procurator, curam gerens et instar diligentis et soliciti patris, omnium, qui abjecti erant, labores recreans et affectiones. Quamobrem merito Deo his magis lætante quam quæ per fumum et sanguinem fiunt, sacrificiis, dignus fuit habitus consummatione, quæ fit per martyrium. Hic decimus athleta cum iis, qui dicti sunt, consummatus fuit uno eodemque die: in quo, ut est consentaneum, maxima Pamphili martyrio porta cœlorum aperta, facilis et expeditus ei fuit aditus regni cœlorum.

XV. Seleuci institit vestigiis Theodulus quidam, venerandus et pius senex, qui primum honoris locum obtinuerat inter servos præsidis, et morum et ætatis gratia, et quod trium filiorum esset pater, et maxime propter benevolentiam quam conservabat in suos. Is autem, cum similiter fecisset atque Seleucus, et quendam ex martyribus salutasset osculo, adducitur ad dominum. Quem cum magis ad iram irritasset quam alii, salutaris passionis cruci traditus, subiit martyrium.

XVI. Cum post hos unus adhuc restaret, qui inter eos, qui dicti sunt, numerum impleret duodecimum, eum impleturus aderat Julianus. Is, cum ea ipsa hora rediisset ex peregrinatione, ne ingressus quidem civitatem, ita ut erat ex itinere, hoc audito profectus ad videndos martyres, postquam adspexit sanctorum corpora humi jacentia, gaudio repletus, unumquemque amplectitur, omnes salutans osculo. Eo autem adhuc agente, eum comprehendunt lictores et adducunt ad præsidem. Impius vero suo instituto faciens consentanea, eum quoque tradit lento igni. Sic itaque Julianus lætans et exultans, et magna voce Deo, qui tantis bonis eum erat dignatus, agens gratias, assumptus fuit in choros martyrum. Erat autem is quoque genere quidem Cappadox, moribus plenus quidem pietate, plenus et fide, vir mitis et mansuetus, et alioqui vir bonus, et spirans bonum odorem Sancti Spiritus. Tanta turba comitatus, dignatus fuit consummatione martyrii cum beatissimo Pamphilo.

Et quatuor quidem dies et totidem noctes jussu Firmilliani sanctissima martyrum corpora exposita fuerunt bestiis carnivoris.

Cum autem Dei providentia nihil ad eos accessisset, non fera, non avis, non aliquid aliud, sed sana permansissent et integra, justum et convenientem honorem consecuta, consuetæ mandata sunt sepulturæ, reposita in pulchris templorum ædibus, et sacris traditæ oratoriis ad perpetuam memoriam, ut honorarentur a populo, ad gloriam Christi, veri Dei nostri."

P. xxxvi. l. 13.—"Theophilus." An error of the scribe for Theodulus. It is given correctly in the narrative below.

l. 15.—"Being in number eight." And so the names enumerated above are eight; but there were really twelve. See pp. 38 and 44. The Greek, which is here a good deal abridged, has at the beginning, *δωδεκα δ' ησαν οι παντες.*

l. 28.—"Youths and boys." Papebrochius corrects here the error of Lipomannus—"*Adolescentes et pueros atque adeo plane infantes.*" See *Hippolyti Opera*, curante J. A. Fabricio, vol. ii. p. 217. I have not the *Acta Martyrum* at hand, and therefore cite the reprint of the Acts of Pamphilus and his companions by Fabricius. When I use the term *the other Greek*, I mean these Acts, in contradistinction to *the Greek*, which I have used in these notes to signify the abridgement found in the Ecclesiastical History of Eusebius.

l. 29.—"Porphyrius." The Syriac has by mistake here ܦܘܪܦܘܢ, "Porphon."

l. 32.—"Iamna." "Jamnia sive Jamna urbs maritima Palæstinæ, haud procul a Joppe, sed totis 20 leucis horariis dissita a Cæsarea, cujus Archiepiscopo subest: etiam urbs maritima in confiniis Phœniciæ." Papebrochius. *Ibid.* p. 218.

l. 36.—"Conformable to his name, Theodulus." That is, *Servant of God.*

P. xxxvii. l. 7.—"But like the sun ..... My Lord Pamphilus." Eusebius speaks of him several times in his Ecc. Hist. Book vi. chap. 32, he says:—"But what necessity is there at present to write an exact catalogue of this man's works, which requires a work itself, which we have also written in our *History of Pamphilus's life*, the blessed martyr of our times.

In which, endeavouring to prove how great Pamphilus's care and love towards sacred learning was, we have published the catalogue of Origen's works, and of several other ecclesiastical writers which he collected." *Eng. Trans.* p. 107. And in the next chapter:—"But what things concerning him are necessary to be known, may be read at large in that *Apology* for him which was written by me and Pamphilus, the holy martyr of our times, which we conjointly composed." *Ibid.* In book vii. ch. 33. "In this man's (Agapius) times we knew Pamphilus, a most eloquent man and a true philosopher in the practices of his life, honoured with a presbytership of that church (Cæsarea). To declare what a person this man was, and whence descended, would be a copious subject. But all things relating to his life, the school he founded, the conflicts which, during the time of persecution, he underwent in several confessions, and lastly, the crown of martyrdom with which he was encircled, we have fully declared in a peculiar work. Indeed, this Pamphilus was the most admirable person of all that lived here." Valesius's note ([r]). Christophorson takes these words to signify one book only. But Eusebius wrote three books of the life of *Pamphilus*, which Hieromynus attesteth in his book, *De Scriptoribus Ecclesiasticis*, and in his *Apology against Ruffinus*. *Ibid.* p. 138. Book viii. c. 13—"Amongst which number we must in no wise omit the mention of *Pamphilus* the Presbyter, the most admirable person in our age, and the greatest ornament of the Church of Cæsarea, whose fortitude and courageous exploits we will declare at a fit and convenient opportunity." Valesius remarks ([b])—"I must indeed confess that in the *Maz.*, *Med.*, *Fuk.*, and *Savil* MSS, the reading is (*ανεγαψαμεν, we have declared*); but if that reading be true, Eusebius must mean his Books *concerning the life of Pamphilus the Martyr*, which, as we before observed, he wrote before his *Ecclesiastical History*, *Ibid.* p. 148. See the former part of this note which I have quoted above, p. 49. See also what Eusebius says in the *Confession of Domninus*, p. 25, above. The Greek, in the account of Pamphilus, here adds:—"This person's other virtues and egregious performances, which require a larger relation, we have already comprised in *three Books*, being a particular work which we wrote concerning his life. On this Valesius remarks ([d]):—"Moreover, hence we make this manifest conclusion, that the *Book concerning the Martyrs of Palestine* was Eusebius's own work, written by him after his Books concerning Pamphilus's life, and after his Ecclesiastical History." *Eng. Trans.* p. 166. We must bear in mind that this observation of Valesius applies to the *abridged* form of the Martyrs of Palestine, and not to the original copy; for the passage upon which he founds his conclusions does not exist, either in the Syriac or the other Greek. It therefore affirms that the *abridgment* was made by Eusebius himself. The Confession of Pamphilus is given by Baillet, *Vie des Saints*, at the 1st of June.

l. 10.—"Without styling him My Lord." Upon referring to the Syriac here it is seen that Simeon Metaphrastes, whom Lipomannus followed in translating "*non est mihi fas aliter appellare*," had ετερον correctly; and that the reading εταιρον of the *other Greek* is wrong. See Papebrochius' note in *Hipp. Oper.* vol. ii. p. 218.

l. 23.—"Porphyrius." His martyrdom and that of those who suffered with him is given by Baillet, *Vie des Saints*, Feb. 17.

l. 36.—"His dismissal from his command in the army." Lactantius speaks of the order of Diocletian respecting the dismissal of soldiers who professed Christianity thus:—"Tunc ira furens, sacrificare non eos tantum qui sacris ministrabant, sed universos qui erant in palatio, jussit, et in eos, si detractassent, verberibus animadverti; datisque ad Præpositos litteris, etiam milites cogi ad nefanda sacrificia præcepit, ut qui non paruissent, militia solverentur." See *De Mortibus Persecutorum*, ch. x.

P. xxxviii. l. 6.—"They bore the semblance of a many-stringed harp." Eusebius uses the same comparison in his Theophania, bk. i. ch. 28:—ܗܘ ܗܟܝܠ ܟܠܗ ܡܬܦܪܢܣܢܐ ܒܕܡܘܬ ܟܢܪܐ ܗܘ
ܘܥܠ ܩܠܐ ܕܡܬܩܢܝܢ ܡܢ ܩܢܝܐ ܕܠܐ ܕܡܢܐ ܡܢ ܡܦܠܓܘܬܐ
ܘܚܢܘܬܐ ܘܡܢ ܥܘܠܝܬܐ ܘܡܬܚܫܚܢܘܬܐ ܘܡܬܢܓܪܢܘܬܐ ܕܥܡܢܐ

ܡܪ̈ܟܒܝܢ ܚܠܝܡܝܢ ܒܐܘܡܢܘܬܐ ܕܡܘܣܩܘܣܘܬܐ ܐܟܘܬܗ
ܕܝܢ ܕܗܢܐ ܐܦ ܗܢܐ ܕܐܝܬܘܗܝ، ܟܢܝܫ ܠܪ̈ܟܒܐ ܚܕ ܘܟܠ
ܪ̈ܘܒܒܐ ܘܡܪ̈ܟܒܘܬܐ ܐܟܚܕܐ ܘܫܚܝܢܘܬܐ ܕܠܘܩܒܠܗ
ܘܪܛܝܒܘܬܐ ܘܝܒܝܫܘܬܐ ܕܐܘܣܝܐ ܠܝܫ. ܪ̈ܘܒܒܐ ܐܬܒܢܝ
ܘܡܐܢܐ ܐܝܬܘܗܝ، ܪܒܐ ܘܥܒܕܐ ܕܐܠܗܐ ܕܟܠ

which Dr. Lee translates as follows:—

"This sensible world is therefore, not unlike the lyre of many strings, consisting of many dissimilar portions: of acute and grave, lax and intense; and of others between these, all well combined together by the art of the musician. Such, then, is also this (universe), collected (as it is) into one compound, consisting of many parts, and many compositions; of cold at once, and warm its opposite; and of matter, wet and dry. It is, moreover, a mighty vessel, and is the work of the God of all." See *Eusebius, Bishop of Cæsarea, on the Theophania*, translated by S. Lee. 8vo. *Cambridge*, 1843, p. 18.

l. 19.—"Like the prophets." He means the Twelve Minor Prophets.

l. 20.—"Nor is it fit that we should omit." So also the Latin version of Lipomannus. The other Greek is corrupt here, reading *ου περυ ετερων*.

P. xxxix. l. 6.—"The baptism of fire." Martyrdom for the sake of Christ was held in antient times to supply the place of baptism to those who had not yet received that sacrament. It was generally called the "Baptism of Blood." Thus Cyprian, *letter* 57, to Cornelius:—"Qui martyrium tollit, sanguine suo batizatur." Edit. *Dodwell*, Amst. 1691, p. 118. And 73, to Jubaianus:—"Sanguine autem suo baptizatos et passione sanctificatos consummari, et divinæ pollicitationis gratiam consequi; declarat in Evangelio idem Dominus." *Ibid.* p. 208. *Exhort. ad Mart.*:—"Nos tantum, qui, Domino permittente, primum baptisma credentibus dedimus, ad aliud quoque singulos præparemus, insinuantes et docentes hoc esse baptisma in gratia majus, in postestate sublimius, in honore pretiosius: baptisma in quo angeli baptizant, baptisma in quo Deus et Christus ejus exultant, baptisma post quod nemo jam peccat, baptisma quod fidei nostræ incrementa consummat, baptisma quod nos de mundo recedentes statim Deo copulat. In aquæ baptismo accipitur peccatorum remissa, in sanguinis corona virtutum. *Ibid.* p. 168. See also *Bingham Antiquit.* Book 10, ch. 2, s. 20, and other passages cited by him. St. Cyril of Jerusalem, Cat. 3, ch. 10:—*ει μη τις λαβοι το βαπτισμα, σωτηριαν ουκ εχει, πλην μονων μαρτυρων, οι και χωρις του υδατος λαμβανουσι την βασιλειαν.* Eusebius speaks also of Herais, a catechumen, receiving *baptism by fire*, Book 6, ch. 4:—*και γυναικων δ' Ηραϊς ετι κατηχουμενη το βαπτισμα, ως φησιν που αυτος, το δια πυρος λαβουσα τον βιον εξεληλυθεν.*

l. 8.—"But Pamphilus, that name ..... different from these." The other Greek varies here from the Syriac. See Lipomannus's Translation above, vii.

l. 14.—"In communion with the Spirit of God." The other Greek, *Θειας μετεχων εμπνευσεως.*

l. 24.—"Men seeking perfection." Other Greek, *τελειους ανδρας.*

l. 26.—"Martyrdom." The other Greek adds here, *αλλ' ο μεν Παμφιλος τοιουτος ην.*

l. 27.—"Vales." There is added here in the Greek, "a deacon of Ælia." This had been stated of him before in the part omitted from the Greek, "a deacon of the Church of Jerusalem." See p. 37, l. 35, above.

P. xl. l. 4.—"In prison." The other Greek has *επι της κρητης*, which Papebrochius has corrected after Metaphrastes from Lipomannus's translation *in carcere*, to *της ειρκτης.*

l. 33.—"Our Mother in whom we confess is the Holy Church." The Greek here, as in Gal. iv. 26, *ητις εστιν μητηρ ημων*; and adds, Heb. xii. 12, *προσεληλυθατε Σιων ορει, και πολει Θεου ζωντος, Ιερουσαλημ επουρανιῳ*, and so the other Greek and Lipomannus' version. See p. 74 above.

P. xli. l. 3.—"In what country was that Jerusalem." At the time when these events took place, there was no city known to the Romans by the name of Jerusalem; otherwise, as Valesius observes, Firmillianus, president of Palestine, would never have been so earnest in his inquiries of the martyrs where Jerusalem was situated. Eusebius writes, Book 4, ch. 6:—"From that time the whole nation was altogether interdicted to enter into the country about Jerusalem, the law, edict, and sanctions of Adrian having commanded them that they should not so much as from afar off behold their paternal soil. Ariston of Pella relates this. Thus the city being destitute of the Jewish nation, and wholly cleared of its old inhabitants, was possessed by foreigners, who dwelt there, and afterwards made a Roman city; and changing its name, was, in honour of the Emperor *Ælius Adrianus*, called *Ælia*." Valesius, in his note on this place, says ([e]):—"Eusebius is here doubly mistaken; both in that he says Jerusalem was wholly destroyed in Adrian's time; and also because he thought Ælia Capitolina was built by the same Adrian after the siege of Betthera.—*Ælia Capitolina* was built long before; to wit, in the second year of Adrian: from whose times to those of Constantine the Great it was always called *Ælia*. But from the time of Constantine the Great it recovered again the name of Jerusalem, both upon account of the honour of that name, and also because of its prerogative, being the first episcopal seat." See *Eng. Trans.* p. 52.

P. xlii. l. 7.—"Wretch —— savage brute." Such epithets as this, and others—"that bitter viper," p. 12, "fierce wild beast,' p. 49, when applied to the persecutors of the Christians, are not peculiar to Eusebius. Cyprian calls Nero, *execrabilis ac nocens tyrannus, bestia mala;* and Decius, *execrabile animal:* also he calls Diocletianus, Maximinianus Herculius, and Galerius Maximinianus, *tres acerbissimæ bestiæ.* See *De mortt. Pers.* ch. 4, 9, 16, &c.

l. 24.—"Weak in body." Syriac, ܒܦܓܪܗ ܡܚܝܠ. The other Greek, κεκονιμενον το σωμα, and Lipomannus, *corpore pulverulentum.* Perhaps originally the translation was ܡܚܝܠ, afterwards altered by a transcriber.

l. 28.—"Having put on his cloak like a philosopher, with his shoulder uncovered." Valesius has this Note on Book 6, ch. 19 of Ecc. Hist. ([r]):—"The philosophic habit was the pallium or cloak, which was the usual badge of the Greek philosophers, different from that which was worn by the ordinary Greeks, which those Christians still kept to, who, before their conversion, were philosophers."—See *Eng. Trans.* p. 101. And on this place (*):—"This garment is in the Greek termed *εξωμις*: see its description, A. Gellius, Book 7, ch. 12." *ibid.* p. 168.

P. xliv. l. 2.—"The father of three generations." The Greek, *τῳ τριγονειας πατερα καθεσταναι,* and the other Greek, *διο τριγονειας αυτον πατερα καθεσταναι.* On which Papebrochius observes:—"Trium filiorum patribus præmia apud Romanos fuisse proposita notius est quam ut hic moneri debeat, atque id hic dici credo *τριγονειας πατερα.* Valesius, tamen aliter vertit *quod tertiæ jam stirpis nepotes haberet.*" See *Hippol. Opera*, vol. ii. p. 224.

l. 19.—"Officers," here "Quæstionarii," as above, p. 55. The Greek is, in this place, *οι των φονων διακονοι.*

l. 27.—"There was also in him a glorious savour of the Holy Spirit." Greek, *πνεων αυτου αγιου πνευματος*; and the other Greek, *πνεων ευωδιας αγιου πνευματος.*

l. 36.—"Without the permission of the Governor." Omitted in the Greek.

P. xlv. l. 1.—"And were laid in the interior of the Churches ..... with God." This passage is not found in the abridged Greek, but it is in the *other Greek.* Upon which Papebrochius has the following note: "Deest hæc clausula in historia: quam tamen Eusebio abjudicare nihil nos cogit, qui vitam Pamphili æque ac Historiam Ecclesiasticam scripsit, cum jam Constantinus lege lata permisisset Christianis sacras ædes condere et Martyrum corpora eis inferre." See *Hippol. Opera.* vol. ii. p. 224.

l. 13.—"Of Batanea." ܕܒܬܢܝܐ. Greek, *απο Μαγγανειας.*

l. 32.—"He was the last ..... in Cæsarea." The Greek here adds the account of Firmillianus having been put to death by the sword; and then a chapter concerning what happened to the prelates of the Church.

P. xlvi. l. 1.—"The confession of Paulus," &c. The name in the Greek is *Πηλευς*, both in this place and in Ecc. Hist., Book 8, ch. 13.

l. 9.—"Phæno." Eusebius has described this place thus in his book, *De locis Hebraicis*:—*Φινων, ην κατῳκησεν Ισραηλ επι του ερημου· ην δε και πολις Εδωμ. αυτη εστι Φαινων, ενθα τα μεταλλα του χαλκου, μεταξυ κειμενη Πετρης πολεως και Ζουρων.* And Athanasius:—*μεταλλον ουχ απλως, αλλα εις το του Φαινω, ενθα και φονευς καταδικαζομενος ολιγας ημερας μογις δυναται ζησαι.* See Reading's Note on Eusebius at this place.

l. 18.—"Zauara." This is *Ζουρα*, mentioned by Eusebius in the preceding note, now Zara, Zora, or Zoara. See Van de Velde, *Memoir to Map of the Holy Land*, p. 354.

P. xlvii. l. 8.—"Patermytheus." Above, *Patrimytheas*, with the usual inconsistency in writing proper names in Syriac.

l. 10.—"Lovers of that exalted philosophy which is of God." That is, the Christian religion. See Ecc. Hist. passim.

l. 25.—"Presbyter of the Church in the city of Gaza." The Greek has, *ων ηγειτο εκ της Γαζαιων επισκοπος ορμωμενος Σιλβανος.* And in the Ecc. Hist. Book 8, ch. 13:—*επισκοπος των αμφι την Γαζαν εκκλησιων.* And in the Greek of the Mart. Palest., ch. 7, he gives the same account of him as in this place, that he was at that time presbyter of Gaza, and afterwards was promoted to the episcopate:—*Σιλβανον ετι δη τοτε οντα πρεσβυτερον, ομολογησαντα, ον ουκ εις μακρον επισκοπη τιμηθηναι συνεβη.*

P. xlviii. l. 5.—"And suddenly a mandate of wickedness was issued." The Greek states that this order was given by Maximinus.

l. 9.—"Forty in number." The Greek says "thirty-nine."

l. 10.—"Many of them were Egyptians." The Greek adds in this place the account of one John, who had learned the Scriptures so thoroughly by heart, that Eusebius states, that when he saw him standing up and repeating portions of the Scripture to the congregation, he supposed that he had been reading, till he drew near, and discovered that he was quite blind.

l. 16.—"For he that was excited against us ..... perished after the manner of a cruel wild beast." It does not appear to whom this applies. Probably he means Firmillianus, of whose savage disposition and extreme cruelty he had spoken above in such strong terms, see p. 27, 29; some account of whose death he gives in the Greek, although omitted here. See note above, on P. xlv. l. 32, p. 84. Or he may mean the Maximinus whose death he describes in the Ecclesiastical History, b. xi. ch. 10.

W. M. WATTS, CROWN COURT, TEMPLE BAR.

ERRORS IN THE SYRIAC TEXT.

P. ܗ. l. 8. for ܡܬܒܪܝܢ read ܡܬܒܪܝܢ

P. ܝܚ. l. 20. „ ܬܗܕܐ „ ܬܗܪܐ

P. ܟܒ. l. 6. „ ܠܚܘܪ̈ܐ „ ܠܚܘܪܐ

P. ܟܘ. l. 24. „ ܒܘܠܦܠܐ „ ܒܘܠܦܢܐ

P. ܠܕ. l. 20. „ ܡܫܘܢܐ „ ܡܢܘܫܐ

P. ܠܗ. l. 18. „ ܕܗܘܢ „ ܘܕܗܘܢ

ܢܒ ܕܥܠ ܡܕܝܢܬܐ ܕܦܠܘܦܘܢܝܐ ܕܐܡܝܪ ܠܐܘܓܘܣܛܘܣ ܩܣܪܐ.

ܠܦܘܬܢܝܐ ܕܐܠܗܐ ܕܒܪܘܟ ܐܬܦܪܫܘ. ܗܢܘܢ ܕܡܢ ܫܢܐ ܕܐܘܒܠܐ
ܡܬܬܐܠܡ ܗܘܘ ܘܠܡܨܪܬܐ ܕܐܠܗܐ ܠܘܬ ܡܢ ܟܠ ܡܕܡ ܡܩܕܡܝܢ
ܗܘܘ. ܘܡܫܪܐ ܒܗܘܢ ܕܠܦܘܬܐ ܕܠܐ ܡܬܚܫܚ ܒܒܢܝ ܦܓܪܐ ܡܢ
ܐܠܗܐ ܡܠܘ. ܀

ܐܘ ܡܕܝܢܬܐ ܠܦܘܬܢܝܐ ܕܡܠܟܘܬܗ ܕܡܫܝܚܐ. ܗܢܘܢ ܕܒܗܡܘܬ
ܕܗܒܐ ܒܡܬܪܘܬܐ ܕܕܝܡܘܬܗܘܢ ܐܬܒܣܪܘ. ܘܫܢܐ ܥܬܝܩܐ
ܕܬܠܐܒܐ ܒܐܪܥܘܬܐ ܕܒܡܘ ܒܗ ܡܢܗ. ܘܒܬܘܠܬܐ ܕܠܦܘܬܐ
ܒܡܬܐ ܕܕܒܘܬܐ ܕܡܪܝܐ ܕܠܥܠ ܢܦܫܗ. ܒܝܬ ܚܝܐ ܠܐ ܝܕܥܬ
ܘܐܕܝܐ ܠܐ ܥܒܕܬ. ܘܥܠ ܠܒܐ ܕܒܪ ܐܢܫܐ ܠܐ ܣܠܩ. ܡܕܡ
ܕܠܒܢ ܐܠܗܐ ܠܗܢܘܢ ܕܪܚܡܝܢ ܠܗ. ܀

ܫܠܡܬ ܬܪܥܐ ܕܬܫܥܝܬܐ ܕܐܝܫܘܥ ܕܡܕܝܢܬܐ
ܩܕܝܫܐ ܕܦܠܘܦܘܢܝܐ. ܀

ܗܘܐ. ܗܟܢܐ ܗܕܝܢ ܒܡܘܡܬܗ ܠܐܘܦܛܪܝܣ ܢܨܚ. ܘܗܘ ܕܝܢ
ܒܡܘܕܝܢܘܬܗ ܡܕܡܫܬܐ ܡܢ ܒܢܝܢܐ ܕܗܘܝܢܐ ܐܬܚܙܝ
ܘܒܡܫܘܚܬܐ ܐܬܓܡܪ. ܘܟܕ ܗܟܢ ܗܠܝܢ ܒܒܢܝܢܗ ܒܐܝܠܘܢܐ
ܕܬܪܝܢ ܐܬܒܢܝ. ܘܗܪܘܢܐ ܒܝܘܡܘܗܝ ܗܘ ܗܟܢܐ ܐܝܟ ܒܠܒܘܫܐ
ܗܟܢ ܗܘܐ. ܘܟܐܝܠܘܢܐ ܕܐܬܬܐ ܠܟܠܗܘܢ ܥܒܕܘܗܝ ܕܢܫܐ.
ܘܩܝܣܐ ܕܒܝܬܐ ܗܠܝܢܐ ܒܡܘܬܐ ܪܒܐ ܣܘ. ܘܠܬܫܒܘܚܬܐ
ܕܐܦܘܣܩܘܦܬܐ ܥܒܕ. ܘܐܬܚܝܠ ܥܡܝܢܐܝܬ ܐܦ ܒܡܢ ܒܡܘܬܗ.
ܘܒܝܘܡ ܐܪܒܥܬܐ ܒܐܝܪ ܬܫܪܝ ܪܒܐ ܕܫܢܬܐ ܡܠܝܢܐܝܬ
ܐܬܦܬܚ ܠܗ. ܘܒܗ ܒܝܘܡܐ ܕܗܘ̈ܕܪܐ ܗܘ ܦܘܬܝܐ ܐܗܬܠܩ ܘܠܐ
ܗܘܐ ܒܠܘܕܘܗܝ ܢܦܩ ܗܘܐ ܠܗ ܒܪ ܒܢܝܐ ܗܓܢܐ ܕܢܬܠܝܐ
ܘܡܢ ܥܠܝܐ ܦܘܡܕܢܐ ܕܥܕܬܐ ܐܫܬܪܝ ܕܩܕܝܫܘ ܕܒܗܝܟܠܬܐ
ܘܒܡܘܪܝܢܐ ܐܫܬܒܩܘ ܒܡܠܟܐ. ܘܐܝܠܝܢ ܕܠܒܒܕܐ ܠܐ ܢܫܝܢ
ܕܢܬܦܠܓܘܢ ܒܡܟܐ ܐܬܥܒܕ ܒܠܗܘܢ ܐܚܪܢܐ ܐܢ̈ܫܝܢ ܒܡܫܢܐ
ܗܘ̈ܕܐ ܕܐܠܗܐ ܒܫܪ ܡܘܟܐ ܢ̈ܦܫܬܗܘܢ ܐܬܦܫܩܘ. ܗܟܢܐܗܘܢ
ܕܝܢ ܕܗܠܝܢ ܐܬܩܫܘܢ ܗܘܘ ܐܚ̈ܙܩܐ ܢ̈ܦܫܬܗܘܢ ܕܝܢ ܘܡܒܕܪܢܘܬܗܘܢ
ܕܗܠܝܢ ܐܚܝܕܘܗܝ ܗܘܐ ܗܘ ܗܢܐ ܗܘܕܪܐ ܐܦܣܘܩܐ ܕܗܘ̈ܕܪܐ
ܗܠܝܢ ܦܘܪܩܢܐ ܒܥܕܢܐ ܘܟܕ ܐܝܢܐ ܣܓܝܐܐ ܕܐܠܗܐ ○○○○

ܘܒܬܪ ܕܫܠܡ ܒܙܡܢܐ ܠܗܪܟܐ ܒܟܠܗ̇: ܢܙܕܒܢܘܢ ܕܠܒܢܐ
ܒܟܘܪܐ ܡܢ ܗܠܝܢ ܡܕܒܪܢܐ ܪ̈ܚܡܐ ܐܠܗܐ ܐܬܚܝܡ. ܘܡܛܠ ܗܢܐ
ܒܢܝܐ ܕܫܠܝܛܘܬܗܘܢ ܡܗܝܡܢܘܬܗ ܡܠܟ. ܗܘ ܒܪ ܕܟܠ ܗܠܝܢ
ܡܕ̈ܒܪܢܐ ܕܐܠܗܐ ܒܒܪܢܫܘܬܐ ܐܝܟ ܣܘܓܐܐ ܒܝܫܬܐ ܡܫܬܡܠܝܐ
ܗܘܐ. ܡܛܠ ܒܢܝܐ ܒܢܝܐ ܗܟܢ ܗܘܐ ܘܒܗܡܘܬܐ ܐܘܪܚܐ
ܕܚܝܠܬܐ ܦܓܥܬܐ ܒܦܘܡܕܢܐ ܕܗܘ ܕܫܠܝܛ ܗܘܐ ܒܟܠ ܕܒܢܝܐ ܐܟܘ
ܘܫܪܟܐ ܕܟܠܗܘܢ ܒܡܟ̈ܬܐ ܕܝܗܒ ܒܗܘܢ ܡܛܘ. ܘܡܛܠ ܒܢܝܐ
ܕܕܡܝܢ ܗܘܘ ܠܡܟܠܬܗܘܢ ܦܬܠܐ. ○○○

ܗܠܝܢ ܡܛܠ ܕܐܣܬܪܒ ܒܟܠܗ ܘܒܢܐ ܕܐܪܕܘܦܝܐ ܒܒܥܘܬܐ
ܕܠܘܦܠܝܢܐ ܒܚܡ ܐܦܘܕܡ. ܘܗܠܝܢ ܒܠܗܘܢ ܐܬܚܝܡܘܢ ܡܢܗܪܐ

ܕܬܠܬܝܢ ܡܢܗܝܢ ܢܫܐ ܘܡܫܡܫܢܝܗܘܢ ܠܐܬܪ̈ܘܬܐ ܐܚܪ̈ܢܝܐ ܫܢܝܘ.
ܘܗܕܝܢ ܡܢ ܬܡܢ ܕܟܠܗܘܢ ܠܘܬ ܐܪ̈ܥܐ ܡܫܡܫܢܝܗܘܢ ܬܡܢ
ܕܐܦ ܒܡܬܢܬܪ̈ܘܬܐ ܐܬܡܫܚܘ ܗܘܘ. ܡܛܠ ܕܟܠܗܘܢ ܢܦܠ
ܠܐܝ̈ܕܝܐ ܕܒܢ ܒܥܘܠܐ ܣܪܒ ܠܗܘܢ. ܘܐܦ ܡܫܡܫܢܘܗܝ ܠܐ
ܡܬܪܡܝܢ ܗܘܐ ܐܬܥܒܕ ܕܢܬܐ ܕܠܐ ܙܡܘܬܐ. ܕܠܝܬ ܡܢܗܘܢ ܒܢܝܐ
ܘܡܫܚܐ ܐܝܟ ܕܢܘܪܐ. ܘܠܗ ܠܗܢܐ ܡܕܝܢܬܐ ܠܡܕ̈ܝܢܬܐ ܡܢ̈ܝܢܐ
ܕܐܠܗܐ ܐܫܠܡ ܗܘܐ. ܘܒܪ ܠܫܠܡܘܬܐ ܐܬܡܪܒ ܒܗܘܢ ܠܟܠ
ܡܢ ܫܠܡܘܬܐ ܢܦܫܗܘܢ ܥܒܕ ܕܠܐ ܕܚܠܐ. ܘܐܦ ܡܢ ܒܗܠܝܢ
ܠܒܢܬܐ ܘܟܠ ܡܘܬ̈ܒܝ ܢܦܫܗܘܢ ܡܫܠܡܬܐ ܡܙܒܘ. ܘܐܬܪ ܡܢ
ܟܠ ܕܫܡܝܢ ܦܓܪ̈ܝܗܘܢ ܠܐܠܗܐ ܩܠܝܠܐ ܕܟܠ ܕܒܫܢܐ ܫܠܡܬܐ
ܐܫܬܘ. ܬܘܒ ܕܝܢ ܡܫܡܫܢܘܗܝ ܐܬܡܫܚܘ ܗܘܘ ܐܦܝܣܩܘܦܐ ܦܠܘܣ
ܘܢܝܠܘܣ ܘܬܘܒ ܡܛ̈ܪܢܐ ܕܝܪܝܐ ܦܪ̈ܡܣܬܐܘܣ ܘܐܠܘܝܐ ܦܢܝܣܐ
ܕܟܠܗܘܢ ܐܦܦܠܝܢܐ ܗܘܘ. ܡܫܒܚܢܐ ܗܘܘ ܓܒܪ ܕܫܡܗ ܕܝܢ
ܦܠܘܣܦܘܬܐ ܒܠܒܬ ܕܡܢ ܐܠܗܐ. ܘܦܩܕܘ ܒܥܡܘܕܬ ܕܡܫܐ
ܢܦܫܗܘܢ ܠܗܘܢ ܐܟܠܘ ܕܬܘܟܠܢ ܬܘܗ ܕܝܢ ܡܢ ܕܢܫܒ ܣܠܩܐ
ܠܫܡܝܐ ܘܠܡܩܒܠ ܒܐܚܕܐ ܐܝܟ ܒܫܒܝܐ ܠܬܘܗ ܒܫܡܝܐ
ܫܡܝܢܐ ܐܝܟ ܐܝܟ ܐܢܫܝܢ. ܘܒܡ ܒܢܝܐ ܕܩܠܝܠܐ ܥܠ ܐܝܟܢ ܀

ܡܟܬܒܢܘܬܐ ܕܦܠܘܣ ܘܕܬܢܝܘܗܝ ܕܒܟܡܗ. ܒܢܝܢ ܬܪ̈ܝܢܐ
ܕܕ̈ܘܦܫܐ ܕܒܢ̈ܝܡܬܐ.

ܡܢ ܒܬܪ ܕܝܢ ܢܦܩ ܗܘܐ. ܬܘ ܗܢܐ ܦܠܘܣ ܐܦܣܩܘܦܐ.
ܘܐܬܘܗܝ ܗܘܐ ܕܝܢ ܚܕ ܡܢ ܩܠܝܠܐ ܒܬܘܠܬܐ. ܘܒܪ ܐܬܡܪܒܠܬ
ܫܐܪܘܬܐ ܠܒܡܕܝܪܗ. ܬܘ ܠܢܦܫܗ ܦܠܝܐ ܦܛܪܐ ܕܡܫܝܚܐ ܒܒܪ
ܒܪ ܐܢܫܐ ܗܘܐ ܓܒܪ ܡܫܡܫܐ ܒܟܠ ܘܒܪ̈ܝܫܗ ܢܝܫܐ ܗܘܐ
ܘܡܫܡܫܢܘܬܗ ܦܫܝܛܬ ܘܕܒܐܝܬ ܐܬܡܫܚ. ܐܬܘܗܝ ܗܘܐ
ܕܝܢ ܡܢܫܐ ܕܒܕܬܐ ܕܦܪܐ ܡܕܝܢܬܐ. ܘܬܡܢ ܦܐܫܬ ܐܬܕܒܪ
ܗܘܐ. ܘܡܛܠ ܕܐܦܝܣܩܘܦܐ ܕܫܢܐ ܠܟܠܝܗܘܢ ܕܡܫܝܚܐ ܐܬܟܢܪ

ܕܡܢ ܐܪܥܐ ܐܬܐܟܠ. ܐܝܟ ܗܢܘܢ ܕܡܢ ܡܕܡܘܗܝ، ܣܥ. ܘܐܡܝܪܐ
ܕܟܠܗܘܢ ܗܢܘܢ ܕܒܣܘܪܝܐ ܐܣܛܪ ܗܘܐ. ܘܐܬܟܢܫ ܥܠܡ ܀

ܡܘܕܝܢܘܬܐ ܕܫܘܠܡܗ ܘܕܢܝܚܗ ܘܕܦܘܪܫܢܬܗ ܘܕܐܠܗܐ ܒܥܒܕ
ܥܒܕ ܕܐܪܙܘܦܐ ܕܒܝܥܬܗ

ܗܟܢܐ ܬܫܥܝܬܐ ܒܐܠܘܠ ܐܬܘܗܝ، ܗܘܐ. ܘܒܗ ܒܫܢܬܐ
ܐܬܟܢܫܬ ܬܫܡܫܬܐ ܕܗܘܪܐ ܕܐܠܗܐ ܘܣܝܡܬܐ ܙܒܢܬܐ ܐܬܒܢܝܬ
ܒܫܢܬ ܕܒܗ ܒܟܠܗ ܦܠܘܓܬܐ. ܘܟܠܗܘܢ ܐܣܛܪܛܝܓܐ ܗܘܘ ܒܚܒܪܐ.
ܐܬܟܢܫܘ ܗܘܘ ܕܝܢ ܒܡܚܝܠܐ. ܐܝܟ ܡܟܐܐ ܘܡܚܡܝܢ. ܘܩܛܠܐ
ܕܝܢ ܡܢܗܘܢ ܐܣܬܟܠܐ ܗܘܘ. ܘܟܠ ܡܟܐܐ ܬܘܒ ܒܒܝܬ ܗܘܘ.
ܘܗܢܘܢ ܗܢܘܢ ܠܗܘܕ ܚܝܠܘܗܝ ܕܡܠܟܐ ܘܦܠܓܘܗܝ ܕܗܦܠܐ
ܒܡܦܩܘܗܝ ܒܚܩܠܐ ܕܪܘܪܐ ܘܟܘܡܐ ܐܬܚܒܠ. ܘܬܘܒ ܒܬܪ
ܗܠܝܢ ܠܡܚܠܠܘ ܕܢܦܩܘ ܢܫܡܐ ܐܬܠܚܡܘ. ܘܗܢܘܢ ܬܘܒ
ܦܠܓܘܬܐ ܒܡܕܝܢܬ ܐܪܟܠܐ ܒܢܝܬܐ ܗܡܢܘ. ܒܪܡ ܕܝܢ ܒܟܠܗܘܢ
ܐܚܘܕܐ ܒܡܕܝܢܬܐ ܕܡܬܩܪܝܐ ܗܘܬ ܠܘܒܕܪܐ ܐܝܟ ܒܕܝܬܐ
ܕܐܪܥܐ ܗܦܟܐ ܐܬܚܒܠ. ܘܒܟܠܐ ܗܦܟܐ ܐܝܬ ܗܘܐ ܒܟܠܗܘܢ:
ܗܢܘܢ ܕܡܢ ܐܬܪܘܬܐ ܐܚܪܢܐ ܠܚܬܡܘܗܝ ܐܬܘ ܗܘܘ. ܘܗܦܟܐ
ܐܚܪܢܐ ܐܠܝܢ ܕܡܟܡܟܝܢ ܗܘܘ ܠܗܘܢ: ܒܟܐ ܕܢܣܟ ܗܘܐ ܠܗܘܢ
ܗܒܪܝܢ ܗܘܘ ܠܗܘܢ ܒܫܘܒܐ ܘܒܣܘܪܚܢܗܘܢ ܡܚܒܠܝܢ ܗܘܘ.
ܘܟܠܗ ܗܟܢܐ ܟܠܗܬܐ ܘܟܬܒܝܬܐ ܕܐܠܗܐ ܘܒܫܠܝܚܐ
ܘܒܢܝܢܐ ܡܡܟܡܝܢ ܗܘܘ. ܘܒܟܠܗܘܢ ܐܬܠܝܢܐ ܕܒܝܬܐ ܟܠܗܘܢ
ܐܝܟ ܒܗܡܟܐ ܣܡܝܟܝܢ ܗܘܘ ܠܗܘܢ: ܘܐܝܟ ܕܒܒܝܬܐ ܘܐܝܟ
ܕܒܥܒܕܐ ܒܟܠܗ ܘܒܝܬܐ ܗܘ ܡܬܪܒܝܢ ܗܘܘ. ܗܢܐ ܕܝܢ ܕܐܠܗܐ
ܘܣܗܕܐ ܒܥܒܐ ܠܡܗܡܒܪܘ ܗܠܝܢ ܠܐ ܐܫܟܚ ܗܘܐ ܘܒܪܫܬܗ
ܐܬܕܪ ܟܠܗܘܢ ܙܒܢܝܬܐ ܗܘ ܕܡܬܩܪܝܐ ܕܗܒܐ ܕܪܘܗܡܐܝܐ
ܘܠܗܘܢ ܦܪܫ ܐܝܟ ܣܝ ܡܢ ܣܝ. ܘܡܢܗܘܢ ܠܐܘܪܚܐ ܕܡܕܒܪܐ
ܒܚܕܬܐ ܐܬܚܙܝܘ. ܘܡܢܗܘܢ ܠܐ ܘܡܢܗܘܢ ܠܦܢܝܬܐ ܕܡܕܝܢܬܐ ܗ،

ܛܘܒܢܐ ܒܡܘܠܝܐ ܕܡܘܕܝܢܘܬܗ ܚܕܐ ܕܐܠܗܐ. ܐܚܪ̈ܢܐ ܗܟܝܠ ܐܢܫ̈ܝܢ ܩ̈ܠܝܠܬܗܘܢ ܒܟܘܡܪܢܐ ܕܦܪܢܣܘܗ ܗܓܡܘܢܐ ܦܓܪ̈ܐ ܡܛܠ ܒܟܘܠ ܕܗܘ̈ܪܐ ܕܐܠܗܐ ܡܐܟܘܠܬܐ ܠܚܝ̈ܘܬܐ ܗܘܝܢ ܗܘܘ. ܘܟܕ ܕܝܢ ܠܐ ܡܕܡ ܩܪܒ ܠܗܘܢ ܘܐܦܠܐ ܚܝܘܬ ܚܕܐ ܐܬܩܠܘ ܟܕ ܥܠܝܗܘܢ ܕܠܐ ܡܢ ܡܦܣܢܘܬܐ ܕܗܓܡܘܢܐ. ܘܠܐܬܪܐ ܕܙܕܩ ܗܘܐ. ܘܠܡܕܒܪܐ ܕܒܝܘܢܪܐ ܐܝܟ ܕܢܦܩ ܐܬܡܣܪܘ. ܘܟܬ̈ܒܐ ܕܢܡܘ̈ܣܐ ܐܬܬܗܝܒܘ ܘܒܫ̈ܝܠܐ ܕܥܠܬ ܠܘܬܐ ܠܒܘܪܐ ܕܠܐ ܡܬܦܠܓܐ ܕܬܫܡܫܬܗܘܢ ܡܢ ܐܢܫܝܢ ܐܝܟ ܕܐܬܚܙܝܘܢ ܒܒܝܬ ܕܐܠܗܐ ܐܫܬܠܡܘ. ○ ○ ○

ܡܘܕܝܢܘܬܐ ܕܗܕܪܝܢܘܣ ܘܕܐܘܒܘܠܘܣ ܒܝܘܡ ܫܒܬ ܕܐܝܪܘܕܘܦܝܐ ܕܩܣܪܝܐ ..○..

ܟܕ ܫܘܡܠܝܗ ܕܡܫܡܠܝܗܘ ܘܕܪ̈ܫܢܐ ܫܢ̈ܝܐ ܕܒܝܬ ܒܫܘܡܠܝܐ ܕܠ ܐܢܫ ܡܬܒܪ ܗܘܐ. ܘܗܕܪܝܢܘܣ ܘܐܘܒܘܠܘܣ ܡܢ ܕܒܬܐ ܕܡܬܩܪܝܐ ܕܟܢܝܫܐ ܠܗ ܫܪܒܐ ܕܡܘܕܝܢܐ ܐܬܗܕܪܘ ܠܩܣܪܝܐ. ܘܟܕ ܠܬܪܥܐ ܕܡܕܝܢܬܐ ܩܪܒܘ. ܕܡܛܠ ܐܝܕܐ ܥܠܬܐ ܐܬܝܘ ܐܫܬܐܠܘ. ܘܟܕ ܐܡܪܘ ܫܪܪܐ ܠܦܪܢܣܘܗ ܩܪܒܘ ܐܝܟ. ܗܘ ܕܝܢ ܒܡܕܡ ܠܐ ܐܗܡܝ. ܘܠܗܘܢ ܗܘܢܐ ܕܥܠ ܚܫܘܟܐ ܦܩܕ ܘܐܝܟ ܕܒܩܘܢܝܐ ܘܒܠܒܒܐ ܦܫܝܩܐܝܬ ܐܫܬܕܪ ܟܕ ܗܘ ܘܟܕ ܠܐ ܫܒܩ ܒܗܠܝܢ ܠܡܡܠܠܘ ܕܡܘܬܐ ܚܕ ܐܝܟܢ ܘܟܕ ܕܝܢ ܬܪ̈ܝܢ ܡܩܡ ܒܢܝܢܐ ܗܕܪܝܢܘܣ ܡܕܝܢܬܐ ܒܫܒܥܬܐ ܒܐܕܪ ܠܐܪܝܐ ܐܫܬܕܝ. ܘܠܢܝܫܐܝܬ ܠܡܓܘܣ ܫܠܡ. ܘܟܕ ܡܢ ܚܝܘܬܐ ܐܬܢܟܝܫ. ܠܣܝܦܐ ܐܬܬܫܠܡ ܘܐܬܩܛܠ ܘܐܘܒܘܠܘܣ ܠܝܘܡܐ ܐܚܪܢܐ ܒܬܪܗ ܒܐܕܪ ܕܝܢ ܐܝܟ ܚܠܘܗܝ ܗܘܐ ܗܘܢܐ ܕܝܠܗ ܘܐܦܢܝ ܠܗ. ܕܐܢ ܠܐܦ̈ܝܐ ܬܕܒܚ ܒܢܝܫܐ ܬܬܚܪܪ. ܘܗܘ ܕܝܢ ܒܠܗ ܚܡܝܪܐ ܕܕܒܚܐ ܒܒܝܬܐ ܐܡܪܝܢ ܗܘܐ. ܘܡܢܝܢܐ ܠܗ ܫܢܐ ܕܠܓܠܡ ܠܟܐ ܡܢ ܗܠܝܢ ܫܢ̈ܐ ܬܪ̈ܬܝܢ ܘܚܡܘܪܐ. ܘܗܕܝܢ ܠܐܪܝܐ ܐܫܬܕܝ. ܘܡܢ ܒܬܪ

ܐܬܬܦܝܣ ܘܡܚܒܒܢܘܬܐ ܕܠܐ ܚܘܣܟ ܕܒܗ ܠܦܪܢܣܐ ܕܐܠܗܐ ܗܘܬ
ܐܦ ܠܐܚܪ̈ܢܐ. ܘܟܡܟܡܗ ܕܝܢ ܕܦܠܘܡܘܣ ܬܕܒܠܘܦ ܕܒܢܐ
ܘܦܓܕܐ ܕܐܠܗܐ ܐܬܡܢܝ. ܐܚܘܗܝ ܗܘܐ ܕܝܢ ܦܟܐ ܕܒܠܗܘܢ
ܒܒ̈ܢܐ ܕܡܓܒܝܢܐ. ܕܡܢ ܒܠܗܘܢ ܡܛܠ ܐܘܟܡܢܗܝ ܘܥܒ̈ܕܘܗܝ
ܡܫܪ ܗܘܐ. ܘܡܛܠ ܕܐܟܢܐ ܕܬ̈ܠܬܐ ܕܝ̈ܢ. ܐܚܘܗܝ̇ ܗܘܐ ܘܬܒܥ
ܡܛܠ ܕܥܪܪܐ ܠܒܢ̈ܘܗܝ ܢܦܩ ܗܘܐ. ܠܐ ܪܚܡ ܒܠܗܘܢ ܒܠ ܕܥܒܕ
ܒܠܗܘܢ ܕܒܥܠܡܐ ܕܦܫ̈ܪܐ ܒܕܡܘܬ ܦܠܘܡܘܣ ܥܒܠ ܗܘܐ.
ܘܟܕ ܐܬܟܢܫ ܠܒܢܘܗܝ ܬܘܪܐܬ ܒܠܗܘܢ ܒܣܡܟܬܐ ܓܒ ܡܢ ܕܒܠ
ܐܚܪ̈ܢܐ ܐܬܘܒܕ. ܘܦܩܕ ܒܠܗܘܢ ܕܠܡܟܘܬܐ ܕܢܚܡܗ ܕܦܪܘܩ ܢܬܠܒ
ܠܡܕܝܢܘܬܐ ܕܒܝܬ ܘܡܦܩܐ ܟܬܪ ܗܠܝܢ ܕܝܢ ܣܕ. ܣܦܪ ܗܘܐ
ܕܡܚܝܢܐ ܕܬܪܥܣܪ ܢܥܠܡ ܗܘܐ. ܢܠܝܘܦ ܓܢܪ ܡܢ ܐܘܪܚܐ ܐܬܐ
ܗܘܐ. ܘܐܝܟ ܕܢܥܠܡܗ ܗܘܐ ܠܡܚܝܢܐ ܕܬܪܬܥܣܪܬܐ ܕܦܫ̈ܪܐ
ܘܟܕ ܒܟܬܘܬܐ ܕܐܬܐ ܟܕ ܒܕܒܝܠ ܠܡܕܝܢܬܐ ܠܐ ܓܠ ܗܘܐ.
ܒܪܟܬܗ ܡܢ ܐܘܪܚܐ ܡܢ ܐܝܟ ܠܦ ܗܘܐ ܒܠ ܥܪܒܐ ܕܡܕܝ̈ܢܬܐ.
ܘܪܗܛ ܗܘܐ ܠܚܝܬܐ ܕܡܕܝ̈ܢܬܐ. ܘܟܕ ܚܙܐ ܕܠܬܚܬ ܒܠ ܐܪܒܐ
ܦܓܪ̈ܝܗܘܢ ܕܣܗ̈ܕܐ ܦܫܝܩ ܗܘܘ. ܐܬܟܠ ܚܕܘܬܐ ܘܠܒܫ ܚܕ.
ܡܢܗܘܢ ܒܢܘܟܐ ܥܡܝܢܐ ܒܒܡ ܗܘܐ. ܘܟܕ ܢܥܡܬܐ ܒܥܠܡܐ
ܕܒܠܗܘܢ ܥܒܠ ܗܘܐ. ܘܟܕ ܒܕܒܝܠ ܗܠܝܢ ܦܟܪ ܗܘܐ.
ܘܕ ܒܡܗܘܢ ܠܐܟܘܣܕ ܒܓܐ ܗܘܐ. ܠܡܟܗܘܢ ܡܦܠܓܪ̈ܐ ܘܠܕ̈ܢܐ
ܡܟܗܘܢ. ܘܡܢ ܕܢܢܐ ܡܕܡ ܕܐܬܚܫܒ ܗܘܐ ܚܝܪܗ ܒܥܫܐ ܦܡܕ
ܘܠܝܘܪܐ ܢܛܪܬܐ ܐܦ ܠܚܢܐ ܐܥܠܡ ܗܘܐ. ܗܟܢܐ ܗܟܝܠ ܐܦ
ܗܢܐ ܢܠܝܘܦ ܟܕ ܕܐܬܝ ܗܘܐ ܘܣܕܐ ܒܡܠܐ ܪܡܐ ܠܐܠܗܐ ܗ̇ܘ
ܕܠܗܪܐ ܐܥܘܗܝ ܡܫܒܚ ܗܘܐ. ܘܟܡ ܒܢܫܐ ܕܡܕ̈ܝܢܬܐ ܢܥܡܗ
ܠܘܬ ܡܪܗ ܐܘܬܠܡܬ ܐܚܘܗܝ ܗܘܐ ܕܝܢ ܓܒܗ ܕܡܢܐ ܡܦܕܢܐ.
ܘܒܢܦܫܗ ܕܢܠܬܐ ܕܐܠܗܐ ܡܠܐ ܗܘܐ ܘܟܕ ܐܢܫܐ ܗܘܐ ܡܒܝܢܐ
ܘܒܢܘܢܐ ܘܡܟܠܗܝܢ ܓܦ̈ܬܐ ܢܦܝܠܐ ܗܘܐ. ܘܐܝܬ ܗܘܐ ܒܗ
ܪܢܐ ܥܡܝܩܐ ܕܪܘܚܐ ܡܕܥܬܐ. ܘܒܢܝܫܐ ܗ̇ܘ ܕܒܡ ܦܡܦܠܘܦ

ܡܣܪܗܒ ܗܘܐ. ܘܟܕ ܢܘܪܐ ܡܢ ܪܘܡܐ ܫܕܪܘܗܝ، ܡܬܓܘܠܐ
ܗܘܬ. ܡܟܐ ܘܡܟܐ ܠܫܠܡܘܬܐ ܕܣܗܕܘܬܗ ܫܠܛ ܗܘܐ. ܘܢܦܩ
ܠܗ، ܡܕܪܫܬܐ ܕܒܝܬ ܣܗܕܘܗܝ، ܡܣܪܗܒܐ ܗܘܬ ܐܝܟ ܗܢܐ ܗܘܐ
ܡܚܝܠ ܬܬܒܥܘܢ ܕܦܪ̈ܨܘܦܗ ܠܒܐ ܕܝܢ ܕܗܠܝܢ ܟܠܗܘܢ ܕܐܬܬܘܟܪ
ܒܦܪ̈ܨܘܦܗ ܐܘܟܝܠ ܣܠܩܘܗܝ ܠܣܩܘܠܦܘܣ. ܘܐܓܪܐ ܕܣܝܒܘܬܗ
ܕܣܠܩܘܗܝ ܡܢ ܐܠܗܐ ܐܬܝܗܒ ܕܐܦ ܗܘ ܒܟܢܫܐ ܕܣܩܘܠܦܘܣ
ܢܗܘܐ ܣܗܕܐ. ܡܢ ܕܒܟܬܗ ܓܝܪ ܕܐܫܬܟܚ ܠܣܩܘܠܦܘܣ ܟܠ
ܐܓܘܢܝ ܘܬܟܬܫܝ ܕܦܪ̈ܨܘܦܗ. ܘܫܐܠ ܒܫܠܡܐ ܕܢܚ ܡܢ ܣܗ̈ܕܐ
ܒܢܨܚܬܐ. ܠܒܟܘ، ܐܣܛܦܢܐ ܘܦܪ̈ܣܘܗܝ، ܠܡܓܒܘܢܐ ܗ̇ܘ ܕܝܢ
ܣܠܩܘܗܝ ܐܝܟ ܗ̇ܘ ܕܡܣܬܪܗܒ ܗܘܐ ܕܟܡ ܡܗ̈ܕܝܢܐ ܢܐܠ
ܒܠܗܬܐ ܘܕܢܫܩܠ ܪܫܐ ܐܬܦܣܩ ܒܠܚܘܕ. ܐܬܬܘܗܝ ܗܘܐ ܕܝܢ ܗܢܐ
ܣܠܩܘܗܝ ܡܢ ܐܪܒܐ ܕܡܫܕܘܢܐ ܘܢܝܚܐܝܬ ܒܦܠܣܛܝܢ ܡܬܕܒܪ
ܗܘܐ. ܘܟܪܙܘܬܐ ܕܐܘܢܓܠܝܘܢ ܫܒܩ ܘܐܠܗܐ ܕܟܐ ܐܝܟ ܗܘܐ.
ܘܠܐ ܒܠܚܘܕ ܐܠܐ ܐܦ ܗ̇ܘ ܘܡܫܬܡܗ ܒܪܒܘܬܐ ܕܦܓܪܐ
ܘܫܠܝܛܘܬܐ ܠܣܘܓܐܐ ܕܐܢܫܐ ܒܢ ܗܘܐ. ܘܫܡܗ ܠܟܠ ܐܢܫ
ܦܐܝܐ ܗܘܬ. ܘܒܫܪܘܫ ܕܪ̈ܘܚܐ ܒܡܣܟܢܘܬܐ ܕܪ̈ܘܚܐ
ܕܡܣܟܢܘܬܐ ܐܬܚܝܒ ܘܡܢ ܥܘܬܪ ܕܐܫܬܪ، ܡܢ ܦܠܣܛܝܢܐ ܡܠܠ
ܗܝܡܢܘܬܗ ܠܝܫܘ ܬܘܒ ܕܢܦܩ ܡܢ ܠܐ̈ܬܐ ܠܐ ܫܒܩܗ ܗܘܐ.
ܘܠܦܘܩܐ ܪܘܚܢܐ ܕܡܫܝܚܐ. ܕܢܦܫ ܐܬܦܪܢܣ ܗܘܐ. ܘܐܝܟ
ܗܘܪܐ ܕܬ̈ܘܒܐ ܡܫܘܕܥܐ ܘܕܐܪ̈ܝܡܬܐ ܡܬܪ̈ܓܬܐ ܘܕܘ̈ܝܐ
ܕܡܣܟܢܘܬܐ ܘܡܚܘܪܢܐ ܥܫܝܢ ܗܘܘ. ܐܝܟ ܗܘܪܐ ܘܥܠ
ܠܒܢܐ ܒܒܢ ܗܘܐ. ܘܒܕܡܘܬ ܐܒܐ ܡܪܚܡܢܐ ܠܐܒ̈ܐ ܕܒܗܘܢ
ܡܬܗܘܐ ܗܘܐ ܘܟܬܪ ܗܠܝܢ ܒܗܠܝܢ ܕܒܗܝܢ ܫܪܐ ܐܠܗܐ ܠܟ
ܡܢ ܕܒܝܫܐ ܘܡܦܪܐ ܘܡܠܦܢܐ ܕܒܣ̈ܡܐ ܕܢܬܡܠܠܐ ܒܡܗܕܝܢܘܬܐ
ܫܦܐ. ܘܗܢܐ ܗܘ ܐܬܠܛܠܐ ܒܣܘܪ̈ܢܐ ܕܪ̈ܘܚܐ ܕܡܢ ܠܟܠ ܒܬܡܝܢ.
ܕܟܡ ܒܢܡܘܣܐ ܒܟܢܘܢ ܐܫܬܒܠ ܘܐܬܟܠܠ ܘܐܝܟ ܕܕܡܣܐ
ܬܪܬܐ ܙܒܢܐ ܕܐܬܩܠܣܬܐ ܕܡܫܬܡܗܐ ܒܡܕܝܢܬܗ ܕܣܩܘܠܦܘܣ

ܚܠܝܐ. ܗܘ ܕܝܢ ܦܪܨܘܦܗ ܐܦ ܠܐ ܒܪ ܬܫܒܘܚܬܐ ܥܒ̈ܝܕ ܗܘܐ.
ܗܘܐ. ܘܒܝܘܠܦܢܐ ܘܒܡܟܝܟܘܬܐ ܣܓܝ ܗܘܐ ܘܒܢܟܦܘܬܗ
ܘܒܐܘ̈ܪܚܬܗ ܒܟܠ ܬܫ̈ܒܘܚܢ ܐܝܬܘܗܝ ܗܘܐ. ܗܘ ܗܟܝܠ ܓܠܝܢܐ ܕܗܘ
ܗܢܐ ܓܒܪܐ ܐܬܩܪܝ ܗܘܐ. ܒܪ ܡܢ ܓܪ̈ܕܝܢܐ ܕܢܩܡ ܒܠ ܡܪܘܗ.
ܡܢ ܡܫܪܬ ܒܢܝܐ ܡܒܐ. ܘܓܒܪܐ ܕܡܘܕܝܢܐ ܒܐܝܠ. ܗܘ ܕܝܢ
ܓܒܝܐ ܐܢܫܐ ܕܐܦ ܠܐ ܒܪ ܐܢܫܐ ܕܗܘ ܕܢܬܡܪܐ. ܐܠܐ ܚܘܬܐ
ܒܪܘܪܬܐ ܠܐ ܒܒܘܬܐ ܕܕܡܝܐ ܗܘܬ ܡܒܠ. ܐܦ ܠܐ ܒܠ ܗܘ
ܕܒܢ̈ܘܗܝ ܓܠܝܐ ܗܘܘ ܚܦ ܘܐܢܫ ܘܒܪ ܐܝܟ ܗܕܐ ܒܠܚܘܕ
ܕܪܘܦܠܝܢܐ ܗܘ. ܦܩܕ ܠܗܘܢ ܕܢܘܪܝܫ ܕܒܗ ܒܠܗ ܚܠܗܘܢ
ܢܦܘܩܘܢ܆ ܘܒܪ ܕܝܢ ܕܢܒܥܐ ܠܗܘ ܓܠܝܐ ܓܠܝܢܐ ܦܩܕ ܗܘܐ ܘܠܐ
ܐܬܬܒܥ ܠܐ ܐܝܟ ܕܒܓܒܪܐ ܕܒܪ ܐܢܫܐ ܐܬܢܨܚ ܗܘܐ. ܐܠܐ
ܐܝܟ ܕܒܡܫܚܐ ܘܐܝܟ ܕܒܟܐܒܐ ܕܠܐ ܢܦܫܐ. ܘܒܝܕܥܐ ܕܠܗܘܢ
ܠܓܪ̈ܡܐ ܘܠܓܘ̈ܫܡܐ ܢܚܠܘܢ ܕܢܦܬܪܘ ܦܩܕ ܗܘܐ. ܘܒܪ ܢܓܪܐ
ܗܠܝܢ ܒܒܪ ܗܘܐ. ܢ.ܒ ܕܦܪܘܐܬܠܝܐ. ܘܒܪ ܦܪܨܘܦܗ ܘܚܪܘܬܗ
ܒܓܠܝܢܘܬܗ ܗܘܐ. ܠܢܘܪܐ ܕܒܥܝܬܐ ܘܪܦܝܬܐ ܕܢܬܠܡ ܒܪ ܒܠܗܘܢ.
ܗܢܐ ܗܟܝܠ ܡܢܡ ܕܦܪܥܠܘܦ ܢܬܡܠܐ ܠܬܟܘܢܐ ܡܙܒ.
ܘܒܡܘܢܗ ܕܡܢ ܓܒܪܐ ܠܒܢܘܗ ܘܡܙܪܢܘܗ ܡܢܡ ܗܘܐ. ܡܬܚܙܐ
ܗܘܐ ܕܝܢ ܦܪܨܘܦܗ ܒܕܡܘܬ ܚܠܡܐ ܕܡܟܘܠ ܬܫ̈ܬܘܦܝܢ ܒܗܘܬܐ
ܐܬܠܝܒܗ. ܘܒܪ ܒܓܒܪܗ ܡܫܠ ܗܘܐ. ܒܦܪ̈ܝܘܦܗ ܦܓܝܫ ܗܘܐ.
ܘܒܪܚܡܢܐ ܠܒܢܒܐ ܕܠܐ ܕܚܠܐ ܒܐܘܪܚܐ ܕܡܘܬܐ ܙܕܐ ܗܘܐ.
ܘܒܫܪܪܐ ܪܘܚܐ ܕܡܘܕܝܐ ܓܠܐ ܗܘܐ. ܘܒܪ ܠܕܘܒܬܐ ܗ̇ܝ ܕܡܘ
ܡܘܬܐ ܡܓܒܠ ܗܘܐ. ܐܙܠ. ܒܕܡܘܬ ܦܠܘܣܦܐ ܢܒܠܕܗ ܒܪ ܒܬܦܗ
ܓܠܝܐ ܗܘܬ ܓܠܝܦ ܗܘܐ ܘܒܠ ܒܡܟܐ ܚܢܘܗܝ ܫܪܝ ܗܘܐ.
ܘܒܠ ܒܘܠܗ ܒܡܟܪܐ ܐܢܫܐ ܒܪܚܫ ܓܒܐ ܗܘܐ. ܘܒܢܦܫܐ
ܕܠܐ ܡܬܦܪܚܐ ܠܗܬ ܢܘܪܐ ܐܬܦܢܝܒ ܗܘܐ. ܐܝܟ ܐܢܫ ܕܒܕܡ
ܒܡܬܐ ܠܐ ܡܪܒܐ ܠܗ. ܘܒܪܚܡܐ ܒܢܪܐ ܕܠܐ ܡܒܒ ܒܠ
ܐܢܫܘܬܗ ܠܡܕܒܚܗ، ܦܩܕ ܘܡܒܠ ܠܗܬ ܐܠܗܐ ܕܒܓܠ ܢܐܠ

ܡܠܬܗ ܡܫܡܗܝܢܬܐ ܚܠܦ ܘܡܪܕܘܬܐ ܐܚܪܝ. ܘܬܘܒ ܒܗ̇ ܕܒܬܪܐ ܦܓܪܐܝܬܐ ܢܦܐܠ. ܕܟܕ ܗܝ ܘܟܐܢܐ ܐܪܥܐ ܐܝܬܝܗ̇. ܗܕܐ ܐܘܪܫܠܡ ܡܕܝܢܬܐ ܕܐܬܐܡܪܬ ܕܕܝܠܗܘܢ ܗܝ ܒܠܚܘܕ ܕܦܝܠܘܣܘܦܐ ܐܚܪܝ ܘܡܕܡܢܝܢܐ ܠܗ ܘܥܠ ܓܒܐ ܢܘܗܪܐ ܕܝܕܥܬܐ ܐܝܬܝܗ̇. ܘܗܘ ܗܢܐ ܬܘܒ ܟܕ ܗܠܝܢ ܐܡܝܢ ܕܡܕܡܝܐ ܕܠܗ ܐܝܬܝܗܘܢ. ܒܗ ܚܘܝܘ ܕܫܘܪܪܗ̇ ܒܦܪܘܫܐ ܐܚܝܕܐ ܒܗ. ܘܠܐ ܒܡܕܡ ܗܦܟܝܢ. ܘܐܝܟ ܗܘ ܕܗܠܝܢ ܦܪܝ ܐܝܬܝܗܘܢ، ܗܘܐ ܡܫܬܒܪ ܗܘܐ. ܗܘ ܕܝܢ ܕܢܐ ܒܪܚܡܬܐ ܐܫܬܡܥ. ܘܣܓܝ ܕܟܒܪ ܡܕܝܢܬܐ ܒܕܘܟܐ ܒܗ ܠܗܘܢ ܒܦܝܠܘܣܘܦܐ. ܘܣܓܝ ܐܬܐܡܪ ܒܗܘܢ ܒܥܕܬܐ. ܘܡܛܠ ܟܠ ܗܕܐ ܡܕܝܢܬܐ ܘܥܠ ܐܬܪܐ ܕܡܕܝܢܐ. ܒܗ ܕܝܢ ܠܚܠܝܡܐ ܗܘ ܒܡܫܘܚܬܐ ܢܓܕ ܗܘܐ. ܘܚܙܐ ܕܡܢ ܡܕܝܢܬܐ ܕܐܡܪ ܠܐ ܡܫܬܟܚܐ ܗܘܐ. ܟܕ ܕܒܢܐ ܕܡܘܬܐ ܦܓܪ ܟܠܗܘܢ ܕܪܫܡ ܢܬܝܠ. ܠܥܕܟܐ ܕܝܢ ܕܐܫܠܡܬ ܒܬܫܥܝܬܐ ܕܕܡܢ ܠܗܢܐ ܟܣܪ ܘܠܗܘ ܡܕܡܝܢܗܘܢ ܒܡܕܝܢܬܗܘܢ ܫܠܡܘ. ○ ○ ○ ○ ○ ○

ܘܗܕܝܢ ܡܢ ܒܬܪ ܗܠܝܢ ܟܠ ܕܒܢܬ ܦܝܠܘܣܘܦܘ ܥܠ. ܘܠܘ ܕܐܦ ܡܢ ܡܕܡ ܗܢܐ ܕܒܢܐ ܒܥܕܬܐ ܦܝܠܐܬܐ ܐܬܦܫܘ ܘܐܬܪܒ ܕܦܠܐ ܗܝ ܕܗܢܘܢ ܒܗ ܗܢܘܢ ܥܕܬܐ ܚܕܬܐ ܟܠܗܘܢ ܘܠܐܐ ܦܪܘܐܝܬ. ܘܗܕܐ ܟܠܗܘܢ ܢܦܠ ܐܢܘܢ ܕܐܢ ܡܬܦܠܣܦܝܢ ܗܘܝܢ. ܒܗ ܡܢ ܚܕ ܚܕ ܡܢܗܘܢ ܒܪܬ ܘܠܐ ܕܡܕܝܢܬܐ ܫܒܩ ܗܘܐ ܐܝܟ ܕܠܗܘܢ ܕܡܢ ܡܕܡܝܢܗܘܢ ܚܕ ܐܢܘܢ ܦܓܪ ܕܒܢܐ ܕܢܬܝܠ ܪܫܡܘ ܦܓܪ ܟܠܗܘܢ ܘܒܗ ܕܝܢ ܒܡܠܬ ܡܠܬܗ ܠܐ ܐܬܐܡܪܬ ܗܘܬ. ܡܢ ܒܬܪ ܐܢܫܐ ܦܠܐ ܚܕ ܓܒܪܐ ܕܦܝܠܘܣܘܦܐ ܡܢ ܡܕܝܢܬ ܒܢܝܐ ܗܘ ܕܠܚܡܬ ܕܢܐ ܚܕܪ ܗܘܐ ܓܒܐ. ܘܠܡܕܝܢܬܐ ܬܘܒ ܦܪܒ ܗܘܐ. ܘܟܠܗܘܢ ܪܒܐ ܬܘܒ ܡܓܐ ܗܘܐ. ܐܝܟ ܕܢܦܩ ܦܪܘܫܐ ܕܐܬܦܪܫ ܦܪܝܫܘܢ ܕܡܕܝܢܬܐ. ܐܝܬܘܗܝ ܗܘܐ ܕܝܢ ܗܢܐ ܦܪܣܘܦ ܦܘܠܚܢܐ ܬܪܝܢܘܬܗ ܫܡܥܘܬܐ ܕܦܝܠܘܣܘܦܘܬܐ ܒܬܪ

ܕܒܢ̈ܝܐ ܕܡܕܝܢܬܗ ܐܬܦܠܓܬ. ܘܟܕ ܒܗܠܝܢ ܒܥܬ ܣܘܥܪܢܐ ܐܝܟ
ܬܪ̈ܬܝܢ ܥܡܝܢ ܐܫܬܘܝܘ ܥܠܬܐ ܕܡܕܝܢܬܗܘܢ ܗܕܐ ܗܘܬ.
ܡܐܬܝܬܐ ܕܐܦܝܣܩܘ̈ܦܐ ܗ̇ܢܘܢ ܕܐܦ ܗ̣ܢܘܢ ܒܥܡܗܘܢ ܒܡܕܝܢܬܐ
ܐܫܬܡܠܝܘ. ܟܕ ܠܗܘ ܚܙܝ ܠܗ̇ܘܢ ܕܠܡܫܠܡܘ ܕܥܠܝܡܐ
ܐܬܓܕܪܘ. ܕܒܫ̈ܢܝܐ ܢܘܟܪ̈ܝܐ ܗܘܘ. ܘܡܛܠܗ ܐܝܟ ܕܢܐܠܨܘܢ
ܠܐܬܪ̈ܗܘܢ ܘܟܕ ܟܠܗ ܒܬܪܥܐ ܕܗܘܪܝܐ ܡܕܝܢܬܐ ܕܡܢ ܐܢܘܢ
ܘܡܢ ܐܡܪܝܐ ܐܬܘ ܐܫܬܐܠܘ. ܘܠܐ ܓܒܘ ܫܪܪܗܘܢ. ܐܠܐ
ܐܡܪܘ ܕܒܝ̈ܣܦܢܐ ܐܢܫܝܢ. ܘܒܐܘܡܢܘܬܐ ܕܒܢ̈ܝ ܒܝܬܐ ܠܒܒܗ
ܐܢܘܢ ܐܫܬܡܥܘ ܗܘܘ ܕܝܢ ܒܡܕܝܢܬܐ ܣܓܝܐܐ. ܘܟܕ ܐܬܦܪܣܘ
ܠܕܝܢܐ ܘܡܕܡܘܗܝ ܒܦܪܘܣܐ ܟܠܗ. ܒܪܫܝܬܗ ܠܒܬ ܣܘܥܪܢܐ
ܐܫܬܠܡܘ. ܠܒܬܪܗ ܕܝܢ ܕܗܘܝܐ ܒܫܬܘܬܐ ܒܢܝܢ ܥܒܕ ܠܗܘܢ
ܠܗܠܝܢ ܒܡ ܕܒܝܬ ܦܠܚܝܢܘܣ ܘܡܢ ܦܪܟܝܢܘܣ ܡܪܟܘ. ܗܘ ܕܝܢ
ܡܚܒܢܐ ܠܐܦܝܣܩܘ̈ܦܐ ܠܗܘܡ ܢܣ ܗܘܐ. ܘܟܠ ܕܚܙ̈ܘ ܕܫ̈ܢܝܐ
ܒܙܪ ܐܢܘܢ. ܘܠܡܕܡܘܗܝ ܐܢܬ ܠܡܝܬܬܐ. ܘܕܐܡܪܝܢܐ ܗܘ
ܫܡܗ ܫܐܠܗ. ܘܢܠܦ ܗ̇ܘ ܫܡܥܐ ܫܪܪܐ. ܫܡܥܐ ܕܒܢܝܐ ܫܡܥ
ܡܢܗܘܢ. ܐܦ ܗ̇ܢܘܢ ܫܪܟܐ ܕܐܦܝ̈ܣܩܦܐ ܕܒܡܗ ܢܠܦ ܗ̇ܢܘܢ
ܫܡ̈ܗܐ ܕܟܠ ܫܡ ܦܬܓܡܐ ܘܡܚܐ ܠܗܘܢ ܐܒܗܝܗܘܢ ܗ̇ܢܘܢ
ܫܡ̈ܗܐ ܕܢܒ̈ܝܐ ܠܒܥܝܗܘܢ ܘܡܚܐ. ܐܝܟ ܗܠܝܢ ܫܡ̈ܗܐ ܐܠܗܝܐ
ܐܪܡܝܐ ܐܫܟܢܐ ܫܡܘܐܝܠ ܕܢܝܐܝܠ ܘܟܕ ܐܝܟ ܗܢܐ ܫܡܥܐ
ܡܢܗܘܢ ܕܗܘ̈ܕܐ ܕܢܝܐ ܫܡܥ ܗܘܐ. ܠܐ ܐܬܟܢܝ ܒܢܝܐ
ܕܡܠܬܗܘܢ ܘܕܬ̈ܪܬܝܢ ܐܬܘܝܢ ܕܡܢ ܗ̇ܝ ܡܕܝܢܬܗܘܢ ܫܐܠ ܐܢܘܢ
ܗ̇ܘ ܕܝܢ ܡܠܬܐ ܕܕܡܝܐ ܠܗ̇ ܡܕܝܢܬܐ ܐܡܪ. ܘܐܡܪ ܕܐܘܪܫܠܡ
ܗܝ ܡܕܝܢܬܝ. ܠܗ̇ ܚܙܝ ܡܕܝܢܬܐ ܢܪܒ ܗܘܐ. ܗ̇ܝ ܕܐܡܪ ܥܠܝܗ̇
ܦܘܠܘܣ. ܕܗ̇ܝ ܐܘܪܫܠܡ ܥܠܝܬܐ ܚܐܪܬܐ ܗܝ. ܘܗ̇ܝ ܐܡܢ ܕܐܘܕܝ
ܒܗ̇ ܒܪܬܐ ܡܕܝܢܬܐ. ܘܟܠܠܝܬ ܗ̇ܘ ܡܚܒܢܐ ܒܠ ܗܕܐ
ܒܡܒܘ. ܘܗܕܝܢ ܐܢܬ ܒܠܝܢܘܢ ܦܘܪܣܐ ܘܒ̈ܢܝܐ ܕܢܘܪܐ. ܗ̇ܘ ܕܝܢ
ܟܕ ܐܢܕܘܗܝ ܠܒܣܬܪܗ ܐܬܦܟܪ ܘܬ̈ܠܝܘܗܝ ܒܡܚܠܝܢܘ ܐܬܦܫܩ. ܟܠ

ܘܒܟܕ ܥܠܡܐ ܒܗ ܟܠ ܐܢܫ. ܗܘ ܕܐܝܬܘܗܝ ܗܘܐ ܙܒܢܬܐ
ܕܒܝܬܐ ܕܦܘܪܫܢܐ. ܡܛܠ ܕܐܦ ܥܠ ܒܘܪܟܐ ܕܡܫܝܚܘܬܐ ܢܛܪ
ܗܘܐ ܘܙܒܢܬܗ ܘܐܙܠܦܬ ܡܢܗ ܠܡܫܡܫܬܐ ܕܬܡܢ. ܐܦ ܒܥܠܡܗܘܢ
ܕܒܢ̈ܘܗܝ، ܐܠܗܐ ܐܝܬܘܗܝ ܗܘܐ. ܘܠܪܘܚܐ ܕܐܠܗܐ ܥܠ ܒܢ̈ܘܗܝ،
ܡܫܘܬܦ ܗܘܐ. ܡܛܠ ܕܒܡܘܡܪܗ ܡܬܪܐܝܬ ܐܬܝܠܝܕ ܗܘܐ.
ܐܪܫ ܒܪ ܘܐܘܠ ܘܫܪܐ ܒܬܪܐ ܦܓܪܢܝܘܬܐ ܘܢܦܫܗ ܠܟܠܬܐ
ܕܐܠܗܐ ܝܗܒ ܗܘܐ. ܟܠ ܡܕܡ ܒܪ ܕܡܢ ܐܒܘܗܝ، ܐܬܝܗܒ
ܠܗ. ܘܟܕ ܗܘܐ ܠܒܪܢܫܐ ܘܠܒ̈ܢܝܐ ܘܠܡ̈ܠܐܟܐ ܦܠܓ ܗܘܐ. ܗ̣ܘ
ܕܝܢ ܒܡܡܠܐ ܡܦܘܪܫܐ ܕܠܐ ܡܫܚܐ ܗܘ، ܘܒܝܘܦܢܐ ܡܫܝܒܪܢܐ
ܕܦܠܘܣܘܦܘܬܐ ܐܠܗܝܬܐ ܡܬܒܪܒ ܗܘܐ. ܢܦܩ ܗܘܐ ܗܟܝܠ ܡܢ
ܒܪܗ ܡܕܝܢܬܐ ܗ̇، ܕܒܗ̇ ܒܡܘܡܬܗ ܘܡܒܪܕܘܬܗ ܐܬܝܕܥ
ܡܬܪܟܐ ܗܘܐ. ܘܡܛܠ ܕܝܕܥܬܗ ܘܪܚܡܗ ܠܐܢܫܐ ܡܬܠܒܒܐ
ܢܦܩ ܗܘܐ. ܥܕ ܡܢ ܫܒܝܚܬܐ ܐܢܫܘܬܐ ܘܠܟܠܬܐ ܐܠܗܝܬܐ ܐܝܟ
ܗܘܐ. ܘܐܫܟܚܟܐ ܥܡܝܩܐ ܕܢܦܫܐ ܢܦܩ ܗܘܐ ܘܒܡܕܝܢܬܐ
ܐܬܟܠܠ ○ ○ ○

ܘܕܬܪܝܢ ܒܬܪܗ ܠܐܝܓܘܦܛܐ ܐܬܦܪܒ. ܘܠܘ ܗܘ ܕܫܒܝܚܘܬܐ
ܥܒܝܕܬܐ ܡܚܘܪ ܗܘܐ. ܒܝܕܗ ܒܪ ܫܒܐ ܗܘܐ ܕܒܢܐ
ܘܡܕܝܢܐ ܘܠܐ ܗܘܐ ܠܒܝܫ ܒܡܠܝ ܡܚܘܪ ܗܘܐ. ܐܠܐ ܐܦ
ܝܘܒܢܐ ܗܘܐ ܕܬܘܒܢܐ ܐ̈ܠܗܝܐ ܗܘܢܐ ܒܪ ܒܡܠܗ ܒܡܗܕܝܢܐ
ܕܬܘܒܢܐ ܡܠܐ ܗܘܐ. ܐܝܟܢܐ ܕܐܠܗܘܢ ܠܬܘܒܢܐ ܕܐܠܗܐ ܡܢ
ܦܘܡܗ ܬܢܐ ܗܘܐ ܠܗܘܢ. ܘܐܝܟ ܗܘ ܕܒܡܗܕܝܢܗ ܒܥܠܡܗܘܢ
ܬܘܒܢܐ ܦܫܝܛܝܢ ܗܘܘ. ܘܡܫܡܫܢܐ ܕܒܝܬܐ ܕܐܠܗܐ ܐܝܬܘܗܝ،
ܗܘܐ ○ ○ ○

ܘܕܬܠܬܐ ܡܬܕܒܪܢܐ ܡܬܦܪܫܐ ܗܘܐ ܒܗܘܢ ܦܠܘܣ. ܒܪ ܐܢܫܐ
ܕܒܪܘܚܐ ܕܐܠܗܐ ܪܕܝ ܗܘܐ. ܐܝܬܘܗܝ، ܗܘܐ ܕܝܢ ܡܢ ܡܕܝܢܐ
ܡܕܝܢܬܐ ܘܗܘ ܗܢܐ ܐܦ ܡܢ ܡܕܝܢܬܗ ܒܡܫܡܫܢܘܬܐ

ܘܡ̈ܠܠܬܐ ܘܡܗܝܪܘܬܐ ܘܫܦ̈ܝܪܬܐ ܘܡܗܝ̈ܡܢܬܐ ܐܟܣܢ̈ܝܐ ܘܥܩ̈ܒܐ ܘܡܫܟ̈ܢܢܐ ܥܡ ܡܣ̈ܟܢܐ ܠܟܠܗܘܢ ܐܝܟ ܕܗܘ ܚܕ. ܣܒܝܪ ܒܟܠ ܡܠܬܐ ܫܪܝܪܐ ܕܐܠܗܐ. ܡܬܬܟܠܐ ܐܢܬ ܐܬܠܘܝܘ. ܘܡܬܝܪܘܬܐ ܕܫܠܡܐ ܕܒܗܘܢ܆ ܚܕ ܚܕ ܡܢܗܘܢ ܒܡܫܡܫܢܘܬܐ ܕܥܢ̈ܘܝܐ ܗܘ܆ ܘܠܡܫܡܫܬܐ ܕܡܫܡܫܢܘܬܐ ܥܒܝܕܬܐ ܒܗܬ ܕܝܠܗ ܦܬܚܘ. ܘܠܐ ܕܝܢ ܕܢܬܕܟܪ ܐܦ ܒܡܫܝܚܘܬܗܘܢ ܕܐܢܫܐ ܕܒܡܫܡܫܬܐ ܕܟܢܫܐ ܘܕܥ̈ܠܝܡܐ ܐܬܡܢܝܘܢ ܗܘܘ ܬܕܒܝܪ. ܘܠܐ ܙܕܩ ܕܢܦܩܐ ܐܦ ܠܐ ܫܠܝܛܘܬܗܘܢ ܡܫܡܫܝܢܬ ܥܠ ܕܚܕ ܚܕ ܡܢܗܘܢ ܒܡܫܬܘܬܗ. ܘܦܪ̈ܝܫܐ ܕܥܠ ܓܢܒܗܘܢ ܘܡܫܡ̈ܫܢܘܬܗܘܢ ܕܠܐ ܡܬܬܐܡܪ ܘܥܝܢ̈ܝܗܘܢ ܕܟܠ ܐܢܫܝܢ ܘܡܬܦܠܓܢܐ ܐܠܝܨ ܗܘܘ ܠܡܕܒܪܐ ܕܢܥܒܕܘܢ ܗܘ ܡܕܡ ܕܠܟܠܗܘܢ ܡܗܠܓ ܗܘܐ. ܘܡܢܐ ܡܬܬܒܥܐ ܕܢܐܡܪ ܒܬܪ ܩܠܝܠܗܘܢ ܐܠܗܘܬܐ. ܫܦܝܪ ܕܐܝܟ ܠܐ ܡܕܡ ܡܫܒܚܝܢ ܗܘܘ ܠܗܘܢ ܣܦ̈ܪܐ ܕܒܦܪ̈ܨܘܦܐ ܦܪܝܫܐ ܕܕܘܪ ܗܘܐ. ܫܘܐܠܗܘܢ ܕܕܪ̈ܫܐ ܡܦܢܝܢ ܗܘܘ. ܘܒܗܘܢ ܒܢ̈ܝܢܐ ܫܠܝܛܐܝܬ ܡܬܚܫܒܝܢ ܗܘܘ. ܘܒܪ ܬܘܒ ܥܠ ܐܝܠܝܢ ܕܡܢ ܐܡܟܐ ܐܬܝܗܘܢ܆ ܥܒܕܘ ܕܢܐܡܪܘܢ ܒܠ ܡܕܢܚܬܗܘܢ ܕܟܐܪܟܐ. ܘܒܠ ܗܘ ܡܕܢܚܬܗܘܢ ܐܢܕܐ ܕܟܢܫܐ ܐܢܬܘܢ ܡܕܒܪܝܢ ܗܘܘ ܘܕܐܡܪ ܗܘ ܐܘܪܫܠܡ ܒܠܚܘܕܐ ܕܟܢܫܐ ܐܢܬܘܢ ܐܡܪܝܢ ܗܘܘ. ܘܕܠܗ ܬܘܒ ܡܦܪܫܝܢ ܗܘܘ ܕܐܝܠܝܢ ܡܕܝܢ ܗܘܘ. ܘܡܛܠ ܗܠܝܢ ܡܬܪܐܝܬ ܐܬܝܒܬ ܠܟܠܗܘܢ ܕܢܐ ܘܐܬܬܒܥܬ ܠܟܠܗܘܢ ܒܝܕܪܐ ܡܫܝܚܐ. ܐܝܟ ܕܢܬܦܪܫ ܒܗܘܢ ܓܝܢܐ. ܘܒܪ ܡܢ ܗܟܢܐ ܢܦܠ ܠܗ ܠܡܬܬܐ ܒܠ ܚܕ ܡܢܗܘܢ ܕܢܗܘܐ ܒܠܝܠܐ ܕܒܗܬܐ ܦܡܕ. ܘܐܦ ܐܘܟܠܣܐ ܒܪ ܕܡܬܬܝܗܘܢ ܒܟܠ ܒܗ ܐܢܬܘܢ ܗܘܘ. ܬܪܝܢ ܒܪ ܡܢܗܘܢ ܥܒܕ̈ܐ ܐܢܬܘܢ ܗܘܘ. ܘܒܡܫܡܫܢܘܬܐ ܕܒܗ ܢܘܪܐ ܒܠܚܘܕ ܒܡܬܬܝܗܘܢ ܒܥܒܕܘ. ܘܐܫܬܢܝ ܡܢܗܘܢ ܠܝܠܒܟܐ ܕܦܬܘܪ ܐܥܠܬܗܘܢ. ܘܗܘ ܥܒܕܐ ܕܡܬܝܪܐܝܬ ܫܒܝܚ ܒܠ. ܕܒܗܬܐ ܕܡܫܠܡܐ ܡܢ ܕܗܠܝܢ ܢܘܪ ܦܦܫܠܗ ܒܪ ܐܢܫܐ ܕܫܪܪܐ ܢܣܒ ܐܠܗܐ.

ܒܪܒܝܗ ܕܐܒܗܬܗ ܐܬܘܪ̈ܝ ܗܘܐ. ܘܕܪܒܐ ܡܢ ܗܠܝܢ ܩ̈ܛܝܠܐ
ܡܪܕܘܬܐ ܘܐܘܪ̈ܚܬܐ ܕܒܝܫܐ ܐܝܬ ܗܘܐ ܠܗ. ܗ̇ܘ ܕܝܢ ܒܡܗܝܡܢܘܬܐ
ܕܐܠܗܐ ܡܫܠܡ ܗܘܐ. ܐܢܬܬܗ، ܗܘܐ ܕܝܢ ܡܫܡܠܝܘܬ ܒܢܦܫܗ
ܡܢ ܐܢܫܐ ܬ̈ܡܝܗܐ ܘܡܕܒܪ̈ܢܐ ܕܐܬܪܗ ܐܝܟ ܕܬܟ̈ܝܠܐ ܐܬܕܪܬ ܐܦ
ܫܠܡܘܗܝ ܒܥܘܠܝܢܐ ܕܫܠܝܘܬܐ ܐܬܬܘܗܝ ܗܘܐ. ܘܡܫܝܚܘܗܝ
ܒܡܗܡܢܐ ܡܢ ܟܢܫܐ ܕܓܒܐ ܐܬܬܘܗܝ ܗܘܘ. ܐܦ ܒܓܒܗ ܬܘܒ
ܫ. ܕܡܫܡܠܝܢܐ ܠܫܘܕܐ ܪܘܚܬܐ ܒܡܫܚܘ ܐܬܬܪ̈ܝ ܗܘܐ.
ܘܦܪ̈ܝܫܝ ܗܘ ܕܒܒܪܗ ܕܦܫܝܠܘܬ ܡܫܬܒܪ ܗܘܐ. ܒܫܘܒܚܐ
ܕܝܢ ܕܐܠܗܐ ܘܒܡܘܕܝܬܗ ܬܡܗܬܐ ܐܫܘܗܝ، ܐܬܬܘܗܝ، ܗܘܐ
ܘܬܬܪܐܬ ܐܝܟ ܒܪܐ ܫܒܝܚܐ ܠܦܫܝܠܘܬ ܒܒܢܝ ܗܘܐ.
ܘܒܠܒܕܡ ܠܡܪܒܝܘ ܕܒܟܐ ܗܘܐ ܘܐܒܝܢܐ ܐܝܟ ܢܐܡܪ ܒܠ
ܒܢܫܐ ܕܒܠܝܘܢ ܐܠܐ ܕܕܡܘܬܐ ܡܠܐܟܝܬ. ܕܒܢܫܐ ܕܒܕܬܐ
ܐܬܬܘܗܝ ܗܘܘ. ܘܠܐ ܗܘܐ ܠܒܪ ܡܢ ܦܪ̈ܝܫܬܐ ܐܚܪ̈ܢܐ ܐܢܫ.
ܒܡܫܝܚܘܬܐ ܓܒܪ ܡܗܝܪ ܗܘܐ ܒܗܘܢ ܡܫܡܠܝܘ ܘܟܠܦܣܐ
ܕܡܫܬܡܫܢܘܬܐ ܘܠܘ ܐܬܬܘܗܝ ܗܘܐ. ܘܟܠܦܣܐ ܕܦܪ̈ܘܫܐ ܐܝܬ
ܗܘܐ ܡܢܚܘܢ ܐܢܫ̈ܐ ܘܒܡܫܒܕܢܘܬܐ ܘܒܡܫܡܫܢܘܬܐ
ܕܡܫܘܬܐ ܫܦܝܪܬܐ ܐܦ ܡܢ ܡܕܡ ܥܘܠܡܢܐ ܕܡܫܒܕܢܘܬܗ
ܫܠܡܘܗܝ ܐܬܬܝܗܒ ܘܕܝܢܬܐ ܡܢ ܥܘܠܝܢܐ ܕܥܠܝܘܬܐ ܫܠܝܚܐܝܬ
ܦܟܠ. ܘܥܘܪܒܐ ܕܐܫ̈ܝܢܐ ܒܬܪ ܗܠܝܢ ܥܒ̈ܗܕܐ ܘܢܦ̈ܝܫܐ
ܐܬܬܘܗܝ ܗܘܘ ܘܡܛܠ ܕܡܗܘܬܐ ܕܡܠܟܐ ܠܒܘܪܐ ܕܒܕܬܐ
ܦܘܠܝܬ ܐܢܫܘܬܐ ܥܠܡܘ. ܘܗܝܢܐ ܗܟܠ ܠܒܝܬܐ ܬܡܗܬܐ
ܕܦܬ̈ܐܕܐ ܗܠܝܢ ܠܟܠܗܘܢ ܘܕܐܝܟ ܗܠܝܢ ܫܘܡ ܒܪ ܗܐ ܠܐ ܗܘܐ
ܦܬܓܡܐ ܗܘܘ ܒܡܫܝܢܐ. ܒܪܡ ܕܝܢ ܒܕܡܘܬ ܒܢܝܐ ܦܠܓ ܐܢ̈ܫܐ ܕܡܢ
ܬ̈ܒܥܐ ܕܠܐ ܕܡܢ ܠܫܪܕܐ ܐܬܡܢܥ. ܩܛܝܠܬܐ ܘܡܒܪ̈ܬܐ ܘܪ̈ܦܩܬܐ
ܘܡܬܚܫ̈ܒܬܐ ܘܡܬܦܢ̈ܝܬܐ ܕܢܦܫ ܐܬܪܒܝ ܠܗܘܢ ܒܐܘܡܢܘܬܐ
ܕܡܫܦܪܘܬܐ ܐܬܬܚܡܕ ܕܗܘܝܐ. ܕܡܫܬܐ ܐܦ ܒܡܘܗ ܐܝܬ
ܗܘܐ ܬ̈ܠܡܝܕܐ ܐܚܝܕܐ ܘܗܦ̈ܟܐ ܘܡܚܝ̈ܕܐ ܒܡ ܒܢܝ ܫܪܪܐ

ܕܒܗܡ ܐܫܬܡܠܝܘ ܒܡܗܝܡܢܘܬܐ ܐܢܫܐ ܬܡ̈ܝܗܐ ܘܫܠܝ̈ܛܐ ܕܬܬ̈ܘܒܥܐ ܦܓ̈ܪܝܐ، ܒܐܘܡܢܘ̈ܬܗܘܢ ܣܠܩ ܦܓܪܬܐ ܕܐܠܗܐ ܢܦܫܗ. ܦܓ̈ܪܝܐ ܓܝܪ ܐܝܬ ܗ̇ܢܘܢ ܕܟܡܝܢܐ ܙܕܘܦܩܐ ܕܡܢ ܐܢܫܝܢ ܐܬܢܣܝܘ. ܐܠܐ ܠܐ ܒܟܠ ܐܝܟ ܗܠܝܢ ܕܒܗܠܝܢ ܟܠܗܘܢ ܡܫܬܒܚ ܐܢܫ. ܒܝܫ ܕܒܗܘܢ ܡܠܟܘܬ ܒܗܠ ܕܗ̈ܢܘܢ ܕܡܦ̈ܩܬܐ ܕܦܓ̈ܪܐ ܘܕܕܘܒܪ̈ܐ ܕܢܦ̈ܫܬܐ ܘܬܪܒܝܬܐ ܘܕܡܦ̈ܩܬܐ ܕܫܢ̈ܝܐ ܡܦ̈ܩܬܐ ܕܟܝܢ̈ܬܐ ܡܫܬ̈ܠܡܬܐ ܕܡܗܝܡܢܘܬܐ ܡܫܡܠܝܬܐ ܐܝܠܦܢܘܬܗ. ܡܬܚܙܝܢ ܗܘܘ ܓܝܪ ܒܠܗܘܢ ܟ̈ܠܝܠܐ ܘܬ̈ܠܡܝܕܐ ܡܢ ܗ̇ܢܘܢ ܐܠܦ̈ܢܐ ܕܒܗܘܢ ܘܐܝܟܢܐ ܓܢ̈ܘܕܐ ܕܐܦ ܦܓܪܗܘܢ ܒܗܘܢ ܗܘܐ. ܘܦܘܠܘ ܕܒܢ̈ܝܢܗܘܢ ܘܒܦܓ̈ܪܝܗܘܢ ܣܠܝܩܝܢ ܗܘܘ. ܦ̇ܘܠܘ ܕܒܟܠ ܦ̇ܘ ܥܡܐ ܕܣܒܝܒ ܟܠ. ܒܡܚܠܗ ܘܦܘܠܚܗ ܕܡܢ ܡܕܝܢܐ ܘܦܘܠܚܗ ܘܦܘܠܚܢܗ ܕܬܪܝܢܘܬܗ ܡܢ ܐܪܒܥܐ ܕܡܦܩ̈ܢܘܬܐ ܐܬܘ. ܐܝܬ ܗܘܐ ܒܗܘܢ ܘܐܦ ܦܢ̈ܝܬܐ ܥܒܝܫܬܐ ܕܒܗܝܡܢܘܬܐ ܒܡܘܡܬܐ ܡܒܝܢܝܢ ܗܘܘ. ܘܠܗ ܡܫܡܫܢܐ ܕܒܕܬܐ ܕܐܘܪܫܠܡ. ܘܗ̇ܘ ܐܡܪܢܐ ܐܢܫܐ ܕܠܫܡܗ ܫܠܡ ܗܘܐ. ܬܐܕܘܠܘܦܘܣ ܐܝܟ ܗܡܢܐ ܗܒܠ ܐܬܬ̇ܠܝ ܗܘܬ ܐܦ ܡܦܬܒܘܬܐ ܕܡܘܗܒܬܗܘܢ. ܘܒܕܘܒܪܐ ܛܘܒ ܕܡܫܡܗܘܢ ܡܫܠܡܝܢ ܗܘܘ. ܡܛܠܗܘܢ ܓܝܪ ܪܒܝܢܐ ܒܫܦܠܐ ܘܫܝܡܐ ܐܝܬ ܗܘܐ ܠܗܘܢ ܒܕܡܘܬ ܬ̈ܠܡܝܕܐ. ܘܡܛܠܗܘܢ ܪ̈ܒܝܢܐ ܒܡܬܘܩܐ ܘܒܢ̈ܕܪܐ ܫܠܝܛܐ ܩܢܝܢ ܗܘܘ. ܐܝܬ ܗܘܐ ܒܗܘܢ ܕܡܢ ܕܐܦ ܒܢܘܠܦܢܐ ܐܠܗܝܐ ܥܦܪ ܡܦܣܝܢ ܗܘܘ. ܣܠܝܩܘܬܐ ܕܡܢ ܥܒܝܕܬܐ ܕܒܗܠܝܢ ܡܬܝܕܥܐܝܬ ܐܬܝܗܝܢ ܗܘܬ. ܘܒܕܡܘܬ ܥܒܕܐ ܡܗܝܡܢܐ ܕܐܫܬܡܥ ܒܫܘܬ ܒܡܒ̈ܛܢܐ ܦܐܝܬܘܗܝ ܕܡܪܝ، ܒܡܦܠܗܘܢ ܒܡܪܟܒܬܐ ܕܒܠܗܘܢ ܕܚܝܠܐ ܗܘܬ. ܠܐ ܓܝܪ ܡܕܡ ܐܝܬ ܙܕܩ ܠܝ ܕܐܫܬܥܝܘܗܝ، ܠܗܘ ܐܠܗܐ ܘܦܠܚܝܢܐ ܒܡܦܠܗܘܢ ܐܠܐ ܐܢ ܕܐܡܪܝܘܗܝ، ܡܪܝ، ܗܘ ܕܠܡܬܕܪܘܬܐ ܗ̇ܝ، ܕܒܝܬ ܢܘܚܐ ܡܬܕܡܪ ܒܗ̇. ܠܐ ܒܝܙܚܐܝܬ ܦܓܥ ܗܘܐ. ܘܡܬܬܒܥܘܬܐ ܕܡܢ ܢܘܚܐ ܕܐܠܗܐ ܘܬܫܒܚܬܐ ܕܢܘܗܪܐ ܐܠܗܐ ܠܝܬ ܗܘܐ ܐܢܫ

ܘܕܝܢܘܗܝ ܥܠ ܦܠܝܘܬܗ ܘܥܠ ܡܘܥܕܗ ܡܫܬܪܪ ܗܘܐ ܠܗ. ܟܕ ܪܕܝܦ ܠܥܘܠܐ ܗܘ، ܕܡܬܕܪܐ ܡܬܥܕܪ ܗܘܐ ܠܗ. ܘܡܬܢܛܪܘܢ ܡܢ ܢܘܪܐ ܗܕܐ ܕܡܬܚܙܝܐ ܡܬܚܫܒ ܗܘܐ ܠܗ. ܡܬܢܛܪܘܢ ܡܢ ܗܘ ܕܢܝܐ ܡܘܬܐ ܡܬܚܝܡ ܗܘܐ ܠܗ. ܘܡܬܢܛܪܘܢ ܥܠ ܗܘ ܕܢܝܐ ܕܥܠܝܗܘܢ ܕܝܢܐ ܡܬܥܕܪ ܗܘܐ ܠܗ. ܡܬܢܛܪܘܢ ܒܫܢܝܐ ܒܥܘܪܐ ܡܫܬܪܪ ܗܘܐ ܠܗ. ܘܡܬܢܛܪܘܢ ܕܢܘܗܪ ܒܟܠܝܠܘܬܐ ܕܫܡܝܐ ܡܬܩܝܡ ܗܘܐ ܠܗ. ܐܝܟ ܕܟܕ ܡܬܝܢܐ ܐܬܝܗܘܢ ܗܘܐ ܠܗܘܢ ܕܬܒܥܐ ܦܪܩ ܗܘܐ ܠܗ. ܘܐܝܟ ܕܟܕ ܗܘܠܐ ܐܬܝܗܘܢ ܗܘܐ. ܕܐܬܒܪܝܬܐ ܢܘܗܪ ܡܬܩܝܡ ܗܘܐ ܠܗ. ܗܘ ܕܝܢ ܒܠܚܘܕܝܗ ܒܡܘܥܕܗ ܥܒܝܕ ܗܘܐ ܘܫܠܝܛܐ ܒܟܠܗ ܘܢܛܘܪܐ ܘܫܠܝܛܐ ܒܦܓܪܗ. ܘܗܢܐ ܕܗܒܢܐ ܐܬܘܗܝ، ܗܘܐ ܒܕܡܘܬ ܕܗܒܐ ܗܘܐ ܒܝ: ܒܢܘܪܐ ܘܢܘܪܐ ܕܒܢܘܬܗ ܗܘ، ܗܘܐ ܘܦܠܓ ܡܢ ܫܢܝܐ ܕܐܒܝܐ ܒܥܘܪܐ ܡܕܝܢܬܗ ܕܒܦܪܘܩ ܐܝܟ ܗܘܐ. ܒܗ ܕܝܢ ܒܝܕܐ ܢܘܪܐ ܐܬܦܢܝ ܗܘܐ ܒܥܡܗ ܚܝ: ܐܝܟܢܐ ܕܡܢ ܦܠܓܘܬܐ ܕܡܬܪܢܝܢ ܐܬܘܗܝ، ܗܘܐ. ܘܐܦܩܘܦܐ ܢܦܩܗ ܦܪܐ ܗܘܐ. ܘܐܝܟ ܕܦܠܓܐ ܕܐܝܢܬܐ ܢܦܩܗ ܠܗܕܐ ܢܗܒ ܗܘܐ. ܐܠܐ ܠܐ ܠܐ ܗܘܐ ܒܝܕ ܚܕܬܐ ܥܠܝܬܐ. ܒܗ ܗܢܐ ܘܗܕܐ ܕܐܠܗܐ ܒܢܘܪܐ ܐܘܟܕ ܗܘܐ. ܗܢܐ ܕܝܢ ܘܗܕܐ ܦܪܫܐ ܕܐܡܪܢ ܠܥܠܡ، ܐܬܘܗܝ، ܗܘܐ ܡܢ ܐܒܐ ܦܪܝܬܐ ܕܡܬܚܙܝܢܐ ܕܒܪܬ ܠܓܒܝܢ ܘܒܗܢܐ ܥܠܡܐ ܕܐܡܪܝܢ ܒܐܦܘܢܐ ܕܒܘܬܐ ܫܡܝܬܐ ܕܗܘܕܐ ܕܡܫܝܚܐ ܐܬܬܒܥ ܘܐܬܒܠܠ ○○ ○○

ܡܕܝܢܬܐ ܕܡܩܒܠܢܘܬܗ ܘܕܒܠܗ. ܘܕܝܠܘܦܗ ܘܕܩܘܠܣܗ. ܘܕܦܪܨܘܦܗ ܘܕܬܘܩܒܠܗ ܘܕܡܠܝܘܬܗ. ܘܕܐܠܦܠܓܐ ܚܝ: ܕܗܘܝ ܒܡܫܝܚܐ ܬܫܒܚܬܐ ܒܫܢܝܬ ܥܣܪ ܕܕܪܘܦܐ ܕܒܝܘܡܬܐ.

ܒܬܪ ܗܠܝܢ ܡܫܠܡ ܒܗܕܐ ܦܪܐ ܠܝ ܕܢܝܚܬܐ ܪܒܬܐ ܕܐܬܗܦܟܬ ܢܬܒܥܐ ܕܡܩܒܠܢܘܬܗ ܗܕܐ ܦܪܫ ܒܟܠ. ܘܕܝܢܘܢ ܐܝܟ

ܐܢܘܢ ܘܡܛܠ ܕܢܘܒܠܘܢ ܗܕܪܬܐ ܠܡܕ̈ܝܢܬܐ ܕܡܫܝܚܝܘܬܐ ܐܪܕܘ ܘܐܬܘ ܡܢ ܐܬܪܗܘܢ. ܐܘܕܝܘ ܘܡܕܡ ܕܢܗܘܐ ܐܝܟ ܕܠܟܒ̈ܕܝ، ܒܢ̈ܬܐ ܦܪ̈ܚܐ ܐܢܘܢ ܡܕܡܟܘܗܝ، ܢܛܪ̈، ܛܘ̈ܪܚܐ ܕܡܢ ܕܡܕܝܢܬܐ ܐܢܫܐ ܒܪ̈ܒܢܐ ܐܬܚܙܝܘ ܗܘܘ. ܕܠܗܠܝܢ ܗܕ̈ܪܐ ܠܓܒܘ ܗܘܘ. ܘܡܕܡ ܦܪ̈ܝܫܘܗ ܡܟܝܕܢܐ ܐܦܠܐ ܐܢܘܢ: ܘܡܛܠ ܕܒܟܠ ܟܠ ܒܣܒܐ ܕܦܘܠܚܢܐ ܐܬܚܙܝ، ܗܘܐ. ܘܡܣܡ ܒܪ̈ܢܫܐ ܡܢܝܐ ܦܘܕ ܒܠܝܗܘܢ: ܘܥܠ ܡܢܗܘܢ ܦܘܕ ܕܒܢ̈ܝܗܘܢ ܘܬ̈ܠܝܗܘܢ ܒܢܘܪܐ ܘܦܪ̈ܥܠܐ ܢܬܚܠܘܢ: ܘܡܢܗܘܢ ܠܡܘܬܐ ܕܗܘܦܐ ܢܬܠܡܘܢ: ܚܕ ܡܢܗܘܢ ܕܝܢ ܗ̇ܘ ܕܐܪܘܗ ܫܡܗ ܗܘܐ. ܒܢܘܪܐ ܚܝܦܬܐ ܡܕܝܢܬܗ ܐܫܬܠܝܛ. ܘܦܪܢܡܘܗ ܘܐܠܝܢ ܒܫܦܐ ܪܢܝܢܘܢ ܐܬܦܫܘ. ○ ○ ○

ܡܕܝܢܬܐ ܕܦܠܪܘܗ ܗ̇ܘ ܕܡܬܟܢܝܐ ܗܘܐ ܒܟܫܠܟܐ. ܒܢܝܬ ܥܠ̈ܝ ܕܪܘܦܝܐ ܕܒܢܘܡܝܬ ܕܫܡܘܪܐ ܡܕܝܢܬܐ ○ ○ ○

ܒܘܡܟܐ ܒܣܘܪܬܐ ܒܢܝܫ ܒܢܘܢ ܐܢܫ، ܦܠܪܘܗ ܗ̇ܘ ܕܡܬܩܪܝܐ ܗܘܐ ܒܟܫܠܟܐ ܡܕܝܢܬܐ ܫܒܝܚܐ ܕܦܠܚܘܬܗ ܕܐܠܗܐ ܐܬܝܗ، ܗܘܐ. ܘܡܢܝܐ ܐܦ ܒܬܒܬܥܡܗ ܕܢܠܦ ܗܘܕܬܐ ܕܐܠܗܐ ܐܬܒܪܝ. ܘܡܢܝܐ ܐܬܝܗܝܢ ܒܐܝܩܘܢܐ ܕܡܕܝܢܬܗ. ܐܡܝܢܐ ܕܐܦ ܠܗ ܠܓܢܒܐ ܒܬܘܪܐ ܢܡܘܣܘܗ، ܘܠܐܢܘܢ ܕܥܠ ܓܒܗ ܦܢܝܢ ܗܘܘ ܙܘܒܢܐ ܐܬܒܥܝܬ ܐܬܡܟܝܢ ܗܘܐ. ܘܟܕ ܕܝܢ ܐܬܒܥܘܬ ܠܗ ܕܥܠ ܢܦܫܗ ܢܐܣܘ. ܘܟܒܫ ܣܘܥܪܢܐ ܥܠ ܓܒܫܡܗ. ܘܡܢ ܒܢ̈ܬܐ ܕܥܠܘܗ، ܦܢܝܢ ܗܘ، ܢܬܘܪܒ. ܘܥܠ ܥܠܡܝܢ ܬ̈ܠܝܗܘܢ ܙܒܢܗ ܡܫܡܥܐ ܗܘܐ. ܘܡܢܗܘܢ ܕܠܗ ܚܙܝܢ ܗܘܘ. ܠܐ ܒܠܚܘܕ ܡܬܢܗܪܝܢ، ܐܠܐ ܐܦ ܐܝܠܝܢ ܕܠܐ ܚܙܝܢ ܗܘܘ ܠܗ ܬܒܥܝܢ ܗܘܘ ܠܘܬܗ، ܘܚܕ ܚܕ ܡܢܗܘܢ ܐܝܟ ܕܠܒ̈ܢܝܐ ܕܦܫܝܩܘܢ ܡܢܗ ܒܗܝܢ ܗܘܘ. ܘܠܗ ܠܛܘܒܢܐ ܡܬܒܥܝܢ ܗܘܘ. ܘܡܢܗܘܢ ܠܓܒܗ ܗ̇ܘ ܛܒܐ ܡܫܝܠܝܢ ܗܘܘ. ܘܡܢܗܘܢ ܪܦܝܬܐ ܒܬ̈ܠܝܗܘܢ ܒܠܒܗ، ܡܒܠܝܢ ܗܘܘ.

ܐܝܠܝܢ ܕܒܡܫܡܫܢܘܬܗܘܢ ܢܛܪܝܢ ܗܘܘ ܠܗ ܥܠ ܗܠܝܢ. ܕܒ̈ܢܝܗܘܢ ܒܝܕ
ܗܘܘ. ܒܗܕܐ ܘܒܪܘܚܬܐ ܪܒܬܐ ܟܠܗ ܐܝܟܢ: ܫܒܝܚܐ ܗܘܬ ܠܒܪ
ܡܕܡ ܛܘܪܚܢܗ ܕܡܕܝܢܬܐ ܚܝܠܬܐ ܕܐܝܠܝܢ ܦܓܪ̈ܐ ܕܟܠ ܐܢܫܐ ܒܗ.
ܡܬܐܟܠܝܢ ܡܢ ܚܢܘܬܐ. ܒܗ ܕܝܢ ܡܫܬܡܬܐ ܦܓܪ̈ܐ ܒܡܝܐ ܐܘܩܝܡܐ
ܗܠܝܢ ܩܝܡܝܢ ܗܘܘ. ܬܕܡܘܪܬܐ ܐܝܕܐ ܕܠܐ ܡܬܫܥܝܢܐ ܒܟܠܗ
ܡܕܝܢܬܐ ܠܒܗܕ. ܢܦܫܐ ܗܘܐ ܒܝܬ ܘܐܝܟܐ ܦܪܝܫ ܗܘܐ. ܘܡܢ
ܥܠܝܗ ܦܓܥܐܗܘܢ. ܕܐܦܝܛܪܘܦܐ ܕܡܕܝܢܬܐ ܒܐܦܝܣܩܘܦܐ
ܕܕܡܐ ܐܝܟ ܢܘܦܬܐ ܥܫܝܢ ܗܘܘ. ܘܡܬܡܩܢܐ ܘܩܠܝܠܬܐ ܐܝܟ
ܕܒ̈ܢܝܐ ܐܬܘܠܝܘ ܘܐܬܛܠܩܘ ܒܗ. ܐܦ ܠܐ ܚܕܐ ܢܦܫܬܐ ܡܢ
ܥܡܐ ܚܒܫܬ ܗܘܬ ܘܒܟܘܡܐ ܕܥܠ ܐܝܟ ܗܕܐ ܡܬܡܠܠܐ
ܗܘܬ. ܕܟܐܦܐ ܕܢܒܥ ܘܐܪܥܐ ܒܗܘܢ. ܟܐܦܐ ܓܝܪ ܕܠܐ ܙܓܪܬܐ
ܘܐܪܥܐ ܕܠܐ ܫܝܢܐ ܚܕܕܐ ܠܗܕܐ ܘܒܪܕܝܢܐ ܠܐ ܫܡܥܬ.
ܘܕܡܐ ܗܘ ܕܡܢ ܟܐܦܐ ܢܕܐ ܗܘܐ ܘܐܪܥܐ ܕܠܐ ܡܦܠܐ ܡܢ
ܠܡܥܒܪ ܒܕܘܟܬ ܕܬܡܗܐ ܥܝܠܐ ܗܘܬ. ܘܠܟܠܗܘܢ ܗܢܘܢ
ܕܕܠܐ ܐܝܠܗ ܠܗܘܢ ܡܟܦܝܐ ܗܘܬ. ܘܒܪ ܡܬܥܝܢܐ ܠܗܢܘܢ ܕܠܐ
ܗܘܐ ܒܒ̈ܢܝܗܘܢ ܒܝܘ ܗܠܝܢ ܕܒܬܪ. ܕܫܒܝܚ ܕܗܠܝܢ ܕܐܬܬܪܝܡ
ܕܫܒܝܚܬܐ ܗܝ ܕܢܘܒܪܐ ܠܫܪܪܐ ܫܘ. ܐܠܐ ܠܗܢܘܢ ܐܝܠܝܢ ܕܒܗ
ܒܕܒܪܐ ܡܝܬܝܢ ܗܘܘ ܫܪܪܗ ܕܡܠܬܐ ܡܕܡ ܕܐܬܬܪܝܡ ܐܬܚܝܕ.
ܕܟܢܝܫܝܢ ܡܝܬܝܢ ܐܝܟܢ ܐܦ ܒܕܡܐ ܠܡܦܠܗܢܐ. ܗܢܐ ܗܟܝܠ
ܫܠܡܐ ܗܘܐ ܒܗܕܐ ܡܕܝܢܬܐ ܕܐܠܗܐ ܐܝܠܝܢ ܕܐܬܒܪܝܟܘܢܗܘܢ
ܘܬܬܘܥܝܗܘܢ ܕܠܗܘܢ ܠܚܘܒܬܐ ܡܕܡ ܒܢܝܢ ܐܬܡܗܪܘ. ...

ܡܕܝܢܬܐ ܕܐܪܗܝ ܘܕܦܪ̈ܝܡܘܣ ܘܕܐܠܝܐ. ܒܫܢܬ ܬܩܝܓ ܕܝܘܢܝܐ
ܕܒܝܘ̈ܡܬܗܘܢ ܕܐܡܠܟܘܢ.

ܒܬܪ ܕܝܢ ܡܕܡ ܕܐܬܪܘܡܐ ܒܗ ܗܝܕܝܢ ܒܗܕܐ ܗܘܢܐ
ܘܐܪ̈ܐ ܕܐܠܗܐ ܐܬܦܠܓܝܢ ܡܢ ܡܛܪ̈ܢܗ ܕܡܕܝܢܬܐ ܐܝܟܠܘܢ
ܐܬܠܒܟܘ. ܘܟܠܠ ܕܐܝܬܝܠܗ ܕܝܢ ܐܝܟܢ ܘܐܘܕܝܘ ܕܒܪ̈ܝܫܢܐ

ܡܕܝܢ̇ܗ. ܦܠܛܝܢܐ ܕܡܠܟܐ ܘܫܠܝܛܘܬܐ ܕܡܢ ܩܕܝܡ ܡܕܒܪܢܘܬܐ ܐܬܬ
ܗܘܬ. ܠܐ ܗܘܐ ܕܝܢ ܗܘ ܡܬܪ̈ܥܝܢܘܗܝ ܕܫܠܝܘܗܝ ܕܚܣܡܘܗܝ ܐܘܕܝܬ
ܗܘܬ. ܡܛܠ ܕܡܫܠܛܢܐ ܗܘ ܩܕܝܡ ܐܝܬܘܗ̇ܝ ܘܡܕܒܪܢܐ ܘܦܩ̈ܕܐ
ܡ̈ܠܟܐ ܘܦܩܕܬܗ. ܡܢ ܕܝܢܐ ܡܕܡ ܕܐܬܬܚܝܒ. ܚܕ ܕܝܢ ܡܢ ܗ̇ܢܘܢ
ܕܡܫܡܫܝܢ ܗܘܘ. ܒܬ ܥܘܩܒܐ ܕܡܕܒܪܢܘܬܐ ܐܝܬܘܗܝ، ܗܘܐ ܡܫܪܝܢܐ
ܕܒܢ̈ܝܬܐ ܘܫܡܗ ܗܘܐ ܡܩܕܘܢܝܣ ܘܕܒܪ ܗܘ ܡܢ ܫܡܗ ܠܘܬ ܟܠ
ܐܢܫ ܡܕܒܪ ܗܘܐ. ܘܠܗ ܠܗ̇، ܦܘܩܕܢܘܬܐ ܐܫܠܡ ܗܘܐ. ܘܡܢ
ܡܫܩܠܢܗ̇ ܘܠܘܬܗ ܒܠܚܘܕ ܡܕܡܘܟܐ ܗܘܬ. ܐܝܟ ܕܒܫܪܟܐ
ܕܗܪܡܝܢ ܒܢ̈ܝܢܘܗܝ، ܙܢ̈ܝܬܐ ܢܬܒܥܐ ܘܒܠܠܗ ܡܕܒܪܢܘܬܐ ܒܕ
ܒܪ̈ܡܫܐ ܡܬܒܪܐ ܗܘܬ ܡܕܒܪ ܗܘܐ ܠܗ. ܗܢܘܢ ܠܒܝܫ ܕܡܬܚܙܝܢܐ
ܡܪܟܢ. ܘܬܡܢ ܒܦܪܗܣܝܐ ܒܡܕܒܪܢܘܬܗ ܕܒܪܘܦܠܛܝܢܬܐ ܗܝ،
ܐܘܕܝܬ. ܘܫܠܝܛܘܬܗ ܘܡܬܡܕܒܪܢܘܬܗ ܠܘܩܒܠ ܟܠ ܕܩ̈ܢܘܢ ܕܒ̈ܢܝܐ
ܬܡܢ ܢܩܝܬ ܘܕܒܢܘܪܐ ܬܐܡܪ܃ ܡܢ ܡܬܚܙܝܢܐ ܐܫܬܠܚܬ. ܗܘ ܕܝܢ
ܗܢܐ ܕܝܢܐ ܒܠ ܝܘܡ ܒܝܘܡ ܒܠ ܡܫܘܬܗ ܡܗܘܦ ܗܘܐ. ܘܠܐ
ܡܪܚܡܢܘܬܗ ܘܡܒܪܝܢܘܬܗ ܡܢܝܘܐ ܗܘܐ. ܘܠܒܪ ܡܢ ܢܡܘܣܐ
ܕܒܝܢܐ ܡܬܕܒܪ ܗܘܐ ܗܒܝܢܐ ܕܐܦ ܒܠ ܓ̈ܠܕܐ ܕܠܐ ܢܦܫܐ
ܕܪ̈ܘܦܠܛܝܢܐ ܢܦܩ ܗܘܐ ܘܡܬܠܒܫ. ܐܝܟ ܕܠܐ ܢܬܡܕܪ ܘܕܠܗ̇
ܬܘܒ ܕܗܕܐ ܦܠܛܝܢܐ ܕܐܬܒܬܒܬ ܕܪ̈ܝܫܘܗܝ ܕܒܗ ܒܝܘܡܐ
ܒܡܕܝܢܘܬܐ ܐܫܬܡܠܝ ܦܪ̈ܨܘܦܘܗܝ ܡܢ̈ܬܐ ܕܢܬܐܒܠܘܢ ܡܢ
ܣܘܬܐ ܐܬܟܡܪ ܘܕܢܬܦܪܥܘܢ ܒܦܠܛܝܬ ܒܠܠܝܐ ܘܒܐܝܡܡܐ
ܐܝܟ ܕܡܢ ܦܠܛܐ ܢܬܐܒܠܘܢ ܢܦܘܪ̈ܐ ܕܝܢ ܡܢ ܙܘܥܐ ܠܗܢܐ
ܦܩܕܢܐ ܒܪܟܪܐ ܡܫܠܡܝܢ ܗܘܘ. ܘܕܠܐ ܢܬܦܪܥܘܢ ܡܢܝ
ܦܪ̈ܨܘܦܘܗܝ ܕܡܕ̈ܝܢܬܐ ܡܪܕܝܢ ܗܘܘ. ܣܘܬܐ ܗܒܠ ܕܒܢܪܐ
ܘܩ̈ܠܒܐ ܐܦ ܦܪܝܫܬܐ ܕܫܡܝܐ ܒܗܘܪܐ ܕܒܢ̈ܝ ܐܢܫܐ ܠܒܐ ܘܠܗܠ
ܡܬܬܥܝܡ ܗܘܘ. ܐܡܒܝܐ ܕܐܦ ܒܓܘܗ̇ ܕܡܕܒܪܢܘܬܐ ܒܪ̈ܡܫܐ ܦܓ̈ܪܐ
ܕܒܢ̈ܝ ܐܢܫܐ ܐܬܬܟܝܒܘ. ܘܒܠ ܐܢܫ ܒܠ ܗܠܝܢ ܐܟܠܐ ܠܒܝܫ
ܗܘܐ. ܕܠܐ ܡܢ ܡܬܬܘܡ ܐܝܟ ܗܠܝܢ ܒܢ̈ܝܬܐ ܐܬܦܪܢ ܗܘܘ، ܐܦ

ܐܬܝܗܒܘ ܗܘܘ. ܘܕܘܟܣ ܗ̇ܘ ܕܪܒ ܚܝܠܐ ܕܪ̈ܗܘܡܝܐ ܐܬܝܗܘܗܝ، ܗܘܐ. ܘܡܛܠ ܗܠܝܢ ܕܓܕܫ ܠܠܓ̈ܝܘܢܐ ܕܡ̈ܕܝܢܬܐ ܘܠܐܘܦܪ̈ܟܝܐ ܘܠܓܘܠܢܐ ܡܬܦܪܢܣܝܢ ܗܘܘ. ܐܡܝܢܐ ܕܣܓܝܐܬ ܗ̇ܘ ܡܕܡ ܕܡܢ ܟܠܬ ܦܬܟܪ̈ܐ ܢܦܠ ܢܟܝܘ. ܘܟܠܗܘܢ ܒ̈ܢܝ ܐܢܫܐ ܥܡ ܢ̈ܫܝܗܘܢ ܘܒ̈ܢܝܗܘܢ ܘܒ̈ܢܬܗܘܢ ܐܦ ܚ̈ܠܫܐ ܕܥܠ ܬ̈ܪܥܐ ܢܦܫܗܘܢ ܘܢܦܩܘ ܠܬ̈ܪܥܐ ܘܕܒܐܠܝܢ ܐܝܟܢ ܕܐܦ ܡܢܗܘܢ ܕܕ̈ܘܫܐ ܢܐܟܠܘܢ. ܘܟܠ ܡܕܡ ܕܡܬܕܒܪ ܒܥܘܡܩܐ ܐܬܦܢܝ ܕܢܬܠܦ ܡܢ ܢܘܡܐ. ܘܡܢ ܦܘܡ ܕܚܝܐ ܕܕ̈ܘܫܐ. ܒܪ ܗܠܝܢ ܡܛܠ ܡܢܝܢܐ ܡܣܬܒܪܝܢ ܗܘܘ، ܐܦ ܥܠ ܫܬܦܐ ܗ̇ܢܘܢ ܕܕܠܐ ܡܫܘܚܬܐ ܐܬܝܗܒܘ ܗܘܘ. ܘܡܦܪ̈ܢܐ ܕܐܝܠܝܢ ܕܗ̇ܘ، ܗܘ، ܐܬܢܕܪܘ ° ° °

ܡܣܬܒܠܐ ܡܛܠ ܪܟܐ ܘܕܠܘܫܐ ܕܐܟܘܬܗ ܐܦܠܐ ܡܟܬܒܬܡ ܗܘܐ. ܘܠܟܠܗܘܢ ܗܠܝܢ ܕܠܐ ܡܢ ܟܠ ܕܘܟܐ ܐܬܝ ܗܘܐ. ܘܢܦܩ̈ܬܐ ܕܡܘܠ ܐܢܫ ܒܐܘܠܨܢܐ ܘܒܦܘܪܣܐ ܡܢܝܢ ܗܘ،. ܐܠܐ ܚܝܠܐ ܐܠܗܝܐ ܡܛܠ ܗܠܝܢ ܕܓܕܫ ܗܘ،. ܠܡܫܘܬܐ ܠܥ̈ܝܢܘ ܕܕܝܠܗ ܐܬܝܗܒܘ ܗܘܘ ܢܗܒ ܗܘܐ. ܐܝܟ ܕܢܕܘܥܘܢ ܠܡܫ̈ܟܢܝܗܘܢ ܕܕ̈ܘܫܐ ܘܠܬܫ̈ܡܫܬܗܘܢ ܢܗܦܟܘܢ. ° ° °

ܐܢܫܐ ܕܝܢ ܩ̈ܠܝܠܐ ܡܢ ܥܡܐ ܕܡܕܝܢܬܐ. ܕܡܘܬܢ̈ܐ ܕܓ̈ܒܪܐ ܚܠܝܨܝܢ ܗܘܘ. ܐܦ ܒܫܓ̈ܪܬܐ ܕܐܠܗܐ ܢܦܫܗܘܢ ܡܛܝܒܐ ܗܘܬ. ܘܦܝܣܘ ܠܢܦܫܗܘܢ ܐܬܘ. ܘܒܪ ܡܦܚܡܢܐ ܠܡܬܟܪ̈ܐ ܒܟܪ̈ܟܬܗ ܕܡܕܝܢܬܐ ܡܚܝܒܐ ܗܘܐ. ܡܢ ܥܠܬܐ ܓܒܘܪ ܟܠܗܘܢ، ܘܕܝܢܠܐ ܡܢ ܠܡܚܝ ܡܟܗ ܟܠܗܘܢ،. ܠܝܬ ܠܢ ܠܡܐܡܪ ܐܫܘܢܐ ܠܒܪ ܡܢ ܚܕ ܐܠܗܐ ܒܟܘܕܐ ܘܒܪܘܚܐ ܕܟܘܠ. ܒܪ ܐܫܬܐܠܘ ܕܡܢ ܐܝܢܐ ܐܘܕܝܘ ܕܒ̈ܘܠܝܢܐ ܐܬܝܗܒܘ. ܘܒܚܕܐ ܕܡܠܬܗܘܢ ܒܪ ܕܝܢܐ ܕܡܕܝܢܬܐ ܡܓܠ ܗܘܘ. ܘܕܝܠܝܐܝܬ ܕܠܐ ܒܥܒܪ ܠܗܘܢ ܗܘ ܕܐܘܕܝܘ ܒܗ ܐܪܕܘ. ܘܡܕܡܢܬܗܘܢ ܒܪ ܥܒܕܗ ܗܘܐ ܐܝܠܘܢܝܘܣ ܘܐܫܪܝܢܐ ܡܬܦܪܐ ܗܘܐ ܘܒܝܢܐ. ܘܥܒܕܗ ܕܗ̇ܘ ܕܬܠܬܐ ܓܪܡܒܝܘܣ ܘܟܬܠܬܒܘܪܐ ܒܪܝܕ ܬܥܪ، ܐܫܪ، ܗܠܝܢ ܐܬܦܬܪ ܗܘ،. ° ° ° °

ܗܘܬ ܠܗܘܢ ܕܝܢ ܒܪܬ ܠܡܬܐ ܒܗ ܒܫܒܬܐ ܚܕܐ ܒܬܠܬ

ܕܗܠܝܢ ܡܕܝܢܬܐ ܐܬܝܗܘܢ ܗܘܘ. ܐܝܟ ܕܢܬܒܢܘܢ ܠܡܕܝܢܬܐ ܕܥܪܒܝܐ ܡܠܝܐ ܗܘܬ. ܐܦ ܡܢ ܗܢܘܢ ܕܡܕܝܢ ܗܘܘ ܠܗ ܠܐ ܐܫܟܚ. ܐܦ ܒܠܚܘܕܝܗܘܢ ܟܠ. ܐܘ ܠܡܬܕܡܟܢܘܬܐ ܕܠܐ ܡܬܬܡܠܠܐ. ܕܐܦ ܝܠܦ ܗܘ ܕܝܢܐ ܕܡܘܬܐ ܓܪ ܒܠܘܗܝ. ܘܝܠܦ ܒܠܗܘܢ ܡܕܒܪܢܐ ܕܒܟܠ ܕܘܟܐ ܡܠܝܐ ܗܘܬ. ܘܠܐ ܒܠܚܘܕ ܝܠܦ ܗܠܝܢ ܐܠܐ ܐܦ ܝܠܦ ܗܘ ܩܘܪܢܝܐ ܕܪܫܗ ܦܬܘ ܡܢܗ. ܘܟܕ ܡܢ ܐܠܗܐ ܒܥܐ ܗܘܐ. ܩܘܪܢܝܐ ܒܐܪܒܥܝܗܘܢ ܥܒܕܝܢ ܗܘܘ. ܒܕ ܒܠܚܘܕܝܗܘܢ ܡܠܝܐ ܗܘܬ. ܘܕܠܐ ܢܫܒܘܩ ܠܗܘܢ ܐܠܗܐ ܡܕܝܢ ܕܒܕܘ ܒܗ ܡܬܒܥܐ ܗܘܐ. ܘܟܕ ܝܠܦ ܟܠ ܐܢܫ ܒܒܪܬ ܩܠܐ ܫܪܝܬܐ ܡܠܝܐ ܗܘܐ ܠܟܠܗ ܒܢܫܐ ܕܫܪܝܐ ܕܡܕܝܢܬܗ܆ ܦܐܡ ܗܘܐ ܠܒܪܢܫܐ ܘܠܡܕܝܢܬܐ ܐܝܬ ܗܘܐ. ܘܗܕܝܢ ܗܘ ܒܝܢܬܗܘܢ ܡܡܠܠܝܢ ܐܢܝܢ ܘܥܡܗ ܟܠܦ ܕܡܢ ܗܕܐ ܬܫܥܝܬܐ. ܘܒܫܒܬܐ ܘܒܝܘܡ ܒܬܪܗ ܢܚܬܐ ܬܬܘܒܗ ܕܗܘܝܐ ܘܒܗܐ ܐܫܬܠܡ.

ܡܕܒܪܢܘܬܐ ܕܐܦܝܣܩܘܦܘܬܗ ܘܕܝܪܝܐ ܘܕܪܝܫܢܘܬܗ ܘܡܫܝܚܘܬܗ.
ܒܫܢܬ ܬܫܥ ܕܪܘܡܝܐ ܕܝܘܢܝܐ ܒܣܘܪܝܐ.

ܘܟܕ ܕܝܢ ܕܚܝܠ ܐܦܝܣܩܘܦܐ ܒܟܕ ܗܘܐ ܡܢ ܒܬܪ ܗܠܝܢ ܕܐܫܬܡܥ ܬܘܒ ܡܢ ܐܪܥܐ ܕܐܦܝܣܩܘܦܐ ܘܕܘܟܝܐ ܐܪܥܢܝܐ ܕܬܪܝܢ ܕܘܡܝܐ ܕܐܠܗܐ ܕܐܬܝܗܘܢ ܗܘܘ ܡܟܐ ܘܬܠܬܝܢ ܒܡܕܝܢܬܐ ܠܬܪܬܝܢ ܐܫܬܪܪܘ ܘܬܘܒ ܐܦ ܗܠܝܢ ܒܠܚܘܕ ܫܝܢܐ ܫܘܝܐ ܕܘܡܝܐ ܕܘܡܝܗܘܢ ܒܒܢܝܗܘܢ ܘܒܬܠܡܝܕܘܗܝ ܘܡܕܪܐ ܘܗܕܝܢ ܡܢܗܘܢ ܠܟܠܗܘܢ ܕܐܦܝܣܩܘܦܐ ܐܫܬܪܪܘ ܘܡܢܗܘܢ ܠܫܝܢܐ ܕܝܢܐ ܕܒܐܦܝܣܩܘܦܐ ܐܝܟ ܕܢܬܪܪܘܢ ܒܫܢܬܐ ܕܒܥܝܬܐ ܘܐܦܢܐ ܐܫܬܪܪܘ ܗܘܘ. ܒܗܠܝܢ ܕܝܢ ܡܢ ܩܕܡ ܒܪܘܚܗ ܕܪܘܡܝܐ ܘܡܢ ܕܒܗ ܕܘܡܝܐ ܡܕܝܢܐ ܦܘܩܐ ܦܠܚ ܘܢܫܐ ܒܚܪܐ ܘܚܝܠܐ ܠܪܘܡܝܐ ܕܒܫܢܬܐ ܝܚܝ ܗܘܐ ܘܬܒܥܝܬܐ ܡܫܝܚܘܬܐ ܕܐܠܗܐ ܟܠ ܡܫܡܫܢܘܗܝ ܦܪܘܫܐ ܒܟܠܐ ܐܫܬܪܪܬ ܕܒܠܚܘܕ ܒܢܝܬܐ ܕܡܕܝܢܬܐ ܡܫܝܚܐ ܘܡܫܬܡܫܢܐ ܫܪܝܪܐ ܡܦܪܫܢܐ ܕܐܬܪܘܬܐ

ܫܠܝܚܘܬܐ ܕܪ̈ܒܝܢܘ ܫܡܥܬ ܘܟܠܝܠܬܗ ܠܟܠܗܝܢ ܟܢܫ̈ܬܗ ܘܐܬܗ̈ܬܝܣܬ ܘܠܘܪܐ ܕܠܟܠ ܡܢܗ ܕܠܐ ܗܘܬ ܒܕܝܪܬ. ܗܘ ܕܝܢ ܡܬܟܬܒܢܐ ܡܛܠ ܗܠܝܢ ܒܗܠܝܢ ܕܒܓܕܬ ܕܠܐ ܕܫܠܝܐ. ܫܡܥܬܗ ܐܝܟ ܕܫܡܥܬ ܥܢܐ ܐܘܪܕܘܬ. ܘܒܣܘ̈ܪܐ ܕܢܣܬܒܪܘܢ ܒܗ ܕܠܐ ܕ̈ܫܒܝܢ ܦܓܕ ܗܘܐ ܐܡܝܢܐ ܕܡܬܟܬܫܝܢ ܫܕ ܡܢ ܒܬܪ ܐܢܫܐ ܠܐ ܐܫܬܪܝ ܡܝܢܐ. ܘܫܒܪ ܐܢܫܐ ܕܐܠܘ ܡܫܚܠܦܐ ܗܘܬ ܕܬܗܘܐ ܡܢ ܒܣܘܪܗ ܕܛܠܝܬܐ ܐܟܠ ܗܘܐ. ܘܟܕ ܫܠܡܬܗ ܒܫܢܬܐ ܕܕܒܟܐ ܘܒܟܬ. ܘܒܒܕܪܐ ܘܒܟܠܗܝܢ ܡܠܦ ܕܐܡܝܢ ܗܘ ܢܦܠܐ ܐܠܗܐ ܗܘ ܕܠܐ ܡܬܕܒܪܐ. ܗܘ ܕܐܦ ܠܛܠܝ̈ܬܐ ܘܒܡܘܪ̈ܕܝܐ ܒܫܠܝܚܘܬܐ ܕܡܬܬܪܘܬܐ ܡܟܝܠ ܘܡܫܠ ܗܕܝܢ ܠܬܪܬܝܗܝܢ ܛܠܝ̈ܬܐ ܠܫܬܐ ܘܠܛܠܝܘܬܐ ܥܡܐܝܬ ܒܝ̈ܢ ܘܡܬܟܬܐ ܕܒܝܕ ܢܘܪܐ ܒܠܒܗܝܢ ܦܓܘ. ܥܡܗ ܕܝܢ ܕܡܬܒܛܠܬܐ ܐܬܘܗܝ ܗܘܐ ܫܬܐ. ܘܒܫܬ ܐܟܘܗ ܒܐܪܥܐ ܕܓܢܐ ܐܬܘܗܝ ܗܘܐ. ܘܗܝ ܐܫܬܪܬܐ ܡܢ ܦܘܪܐ ܡܕܝܢܬ ܐܢܕܐ ܕܐܦ ܠܦܓ̈ܢܐ ܐܝ̈ܕܝܐ ܘܥܡܗ ܘܠܛܠܝܐ ܘ.ܘ.ܘ.

ܡܢ ܒܬܪ ܗܠܝܢ ܕܝܢ ܦܠܘܗ ܡܘܕܝܢܐ ܠܐܓܘܢܐ ܐܬܘܣܪ. ܘܫܠܝܚܘܬܐ ܐܦ ܗܢܐ ܐܬܟܬܫ. ܘܟܕ ܫܡܥܬܐ ܡܢ ܕܢܝܐ ܒܗܠܐ ܐܬܢܣܒ. ܕܢܬܓܠܠ ܦܓܪ ܕܝܢܐ ܕܗܘܦܐ ܕܫܒܩ ܪܫܐ ܡܓܠ. ܘܟܕ ܕܝܢ ܠܕܘܟܬܐ ܗܝ ܕܒܗܕܢܝܗ ܕܦܘܠܚܢܐ ܬܡܢ ܡܩܦܐ ܗܘܐ. ܡܢ ܡܦܠܘܢܪܐ ܗܘ ܕܪܥܗ ܫܒܠ ܗܘܐ. ܟܕ ܗܘܐ ܕܒܕܝܢܐ ܡܠܠ ܪܘܫܐ ܝܗܒ ܠܗ. ܘܟܕ ܝܒܫܢܐ ܗܘܐ ܡܦܠܘܢܪܐ ܒܓܕ ܠܗ. ܒܟܠܗ ܒܡܬܟܬܐ ܘܫܒܫܬܐ ܦܕܡ ܒܠ ܡܕܝܢ ܬܘܕܝܬܐ ܘܫܓܕܬܐ ܘܬܫܒܘܚܬܐ ܘܝܩܪܐ ܠܐܠܗܐ ܗܘ ܕܠܗܕܐ ܘܒܗܕܐ ܐܫܘܝܗ. ܡܫܡܫ ܗܘܐ. ܘܗܝܕܝܢ ܫܠܦ ܦ̈ܬܐ ܒܢܝ ܥܢܫܐ ܘܟܠܢܟܐ ܟܠܝܗܘܢ ܦܕܐ ܗܘܐ ܘܕܒܟܠ ܢܛܠ ܠܗܘܢ ܐܠܗܐ ܒܦܘܪܢܐ ܡܬܝܒܝܢ ܗܘܐ. ܘܒܬܪ ܗܠܝܢ ܫܠܦ ܡܗܘܪ̈ܐ ܒܟܠܕ̈ܒܒܐ ܡܛܠܐ ܗܘܐ. ܦܓܪ̈ܐ ܢܝܪ ܡܫܝܚܘܢ ܒܗܘ ܒܕܝܢܐ ܒܪܝܟ ܗܘܘ ܠܗ. ܘܟܕ ܢܫܬ ܬܘܒ ܒܟܠܗܘܢ ܐܦ ܒܠ ܫܒܪ̈ܐ ܝܠ ܘܒܠ ܐܝܠܝܢ ܕܡܢ ܒܒܝܬܐ

ܗܘܬ ܒܒܪܝܬܐ ܐܝܬܝܗ̇ ܗܘܬ. ܘܒܡܘܡܪܗ ܗܘܬ ܒܬܘܠܬܐ
ܗܘܬ ܘܠܘܫܡܥܐ ܕܐܢܫܘܬܐ ܕܒܐ̈ܕܢܝܗ̇ ܫܡܥܬܐ ܗܘܬ ܠܐ ܗܦܟܬ.
ܘܒܪ ܥܒܕܗ̇ ܢ̈ܟܠܐ ܡܥ̈ܒܕܬܐ ܒܠ ܢ̈ܟܠܐ ܦܪܘܫܐ ܐܝܟܢܐ ܗܘܬ.
ܒܠ ܕܒܘܠܠܝܢܐ ܠܕܝܢܐ ܦܠܓܐܐ ܘܪܥܝܢܐ ܝܗܒ ܗܘܐ. ܡܛܠ ܗܢܐ
ܗܝܠ ܠܘܩܕܡ ܒܒܝܫܘܬܐ ܠܟܘܠܗ ܦܓܪܗ ܣܒܠ ܗܘܐ ܘܗܘܝܢ
ܐܬܬܠܝܬ ܦܓ̈ܥܝܗ̇ ܐܘܬܪܘܗ. ܠܐ ܗܘܐ ܣܓܝ ܕܝܢ ܐܝܠܐ ܬܪ̈ܬܝܢ
ܘܬܠܬ ܕܫ̈ܢܝܢ ܒܣܓܝ ܥܒܕܐ. ܘܦܓܪܐ ܦܓܥܐ ܘܐܦ ܕܫ̈ܢܬܐ
ܦܓ̈ܥܬܐ ܒܒܥܕܐ ܕܗܘܝܢ ܕܗܘܝܢ ܗܘܘ ܠܗ̇ ܠܐܘ ܘܐܬܦܫܝܘ.
ܘܐܬܚܠܡ ܒܠܒܗ̇ ܐܣܝܐ ܘܡܢ ܦܘܪܥܢܗ ܕܡܫܒܚܘܬܐ ܦܘܪܐ
ܡܢܐܝܬ ܐܫܬܘܕܝܘ ܒܗ̇. ܒܪܒܪܐ ܗܘܘ ܒܝܫ ܗܘ̈ܝܢ ܕܐܢܫܐ
ܒܐܘܪ̈ܚܬܗܘܢ ܘܒܠܒ̈ܒܐ ܒ̈ܝܫܬܗܘܢ ܘܒܪ ܣܠܝܗ̇ ܗܘܐ
ܠܛܠܝܬܐ ܒܬܥ̈ܒܕܘܗܝ، ܗܘ ܗܝܢܐ ܕܝܢܐ ܣܓ̈ܝܐܐ. ܦܓܥ ܘܛܠܝܬܐ
ܐܫܬܪܝܬ ܐܝܕܐ ܕܦܓܪܗ̇ ܒܝܪܐ ܗܘܬ ܘܒܥܒܗ̇ ܚܠܝܬܐ ܗܘܬ.
ܢܟܝܢܐ ܕܝܢ ܙܒܢܐ ܐܝܢܐ ܕܠܒܝܪܘܬܐ ܕܦܓܪܗ̇ ܡܣܝܒ ܗܘܐ ܐܝܬ
ܗܘܐ ܠܗ. ܘܒܥܒܘܬܐ ܘܠܐ ܡܪܚܒܘܬܐ ܕܗܠܝܢ ܕܒܫܘܬܗ
ܡܫܘܬܦܝܢ ܗܘܘ، ܠܐ ܗܦܟܬ. ܘܡܢ ܡܢܝܢܬ ܟ̈ܠ ܐܢܫܐ ܦ̈ܓܥܐ
ܕܗܝܟ ܡܫܒܚܢܐ ܡܣܝܡ ܗܘܘ ܡܢܬ ܒܗ ܡܫܒܚܢܐ ܘܐܡܪܐ.
ܕܒܗܡܐ ܠܐܡܬܝ، ܠܫܬ، ܗܒܢܐ ܡܢܐܢܬ ܕܠܐ ܕܝܫܡ ܗܘܪ ܐܝܬ.
ܘܒܪ ܗܠܝܢ ܒܪܟܝܢܘܗ ܙܒܢܐ ܥܒܕ ܗܘܐ. ܡܪܢܐܝܬ ܡܫܬܒܝܢ
ܗܘܐ. ܘܕܝܬܘܬܗ ܡܪܡܘܡ، ܠܛܠܝܬܐ ܗ، ܕܒܓܝܢ ܐܝܟܐ ܕܘܠܛܠܝܐ
ܥܒܕܗ̇ ܗܘܐ. ܦܩܕ ܗܘܐ ܕܒܪ ܡܬܬܠܝܡ ܒܗ̇ ܠܡܓܒܬܗ̇
ܕܕܡܦܠܓܝܢ ܐܝܬܘܬܗ̇، ܕܝܢ ܒܥܒܕܗ ܕܐܡܪ ܦܓܪܐ ܡܬܦܠܓܐ
ܗܘܬ. ܘܡܫܒܚܢܐ ܡܦܠܠܐ ܒܫܒܬܗ ܕܬܒܥܐ ܦܩܕ ܗܘܐ ܠܗ.
ܗ، ܕܝܢ ܛܠܝܬܐ ܘܠܛܠܝܐ ܐܦ ܠܒܪܬ ܡܠܗ ܕܡܥܒܕܢܐ ܒܥܘܪܬ.
ܘܦܩܕ ܠܗܘܢ ܕܢܓܒܘܢ ܡܫܒܚܝܢ ܗܘܘ. ܕܒܦܠܝܪܐ ܒܬܬܠܝܢ ܒܗ
ܒܛܠܝܬܐ. ܘܒܠ ܓܒܝ ܒܠܬܐ ܫܬܘܬܗ. ܐܡܒܝܐ ܕܐܬܗܬܒ
ܒܕܘܒܫܝܐ. ܗܕܝܢ ܛܠܝܬܐ ܢܓܫܬܐ ܒܒܕܝܐ ܗܘ ܕܐܪܗܘܒܘܬܐ

ܙܒܢܘ ܠܗܘܢ ܐܒܗ̈ܝܗܘܢ ܕܢܣܒܘܢ ܠܒ̈ܢܝܗܘܢ ܒܥܡ̈ܡܐ ܕܢܟ̈ܪܝܐ ܥܒ̈ܕܐ ܘܫܠܡܘ ܠܗܘܢ ܗܘܦܪ̈ܢܝܗܘܢ ܠܡܫܥ̈ܒܕܢܝܗܘܢ. ܘܒܗܘܢ ܘܒܡܫܥ̈ܒܕܢܝܗܘܢ ܘܒܬ̈ܠܝܗܘܢ ܘܒܒ̈ܢܝܗܘܢ ܡܬܬܐܪܟܝܢ ܡܘܪ̈ܕܝܐ ܬܡܢ̈ܝܢ ܗܘܘ. ܘܒܫܥܒܘܕܗܘܢ ܘܒܡܪܕܘܬܗܘܢ ܡܬܒܣܪܝܢ ܗܘܘ. ܘܐܝܟܢܐ ܡܫܟܚ ܐܢܐ. ܕܠܐ ܗܘܐ ܟܠܗ ܡܢ ܝܡܝܢܐ ܕܐܠܗܐ ܐܬܬܚܝܪ ܗܠܝܢ. ܒܬܪ ܕܝܢ ܡܢ ܒܬܪ ܒܘܚܪܢܐ ܗܢܐ ܒܒ̈ܢܝܐ ܕܗܘܐ ܕܥܠ ܡܣܩ̈ܢܝܗܘܢ ܐܬܬܗܘܒܝܘ ܡܢ ܬ̈ܠܝܗܘܢ ܕܗܘܡܠܐ ܚܠܦ ܐܢܘܢ. ܘܬܘܒ ܒܒ̈ܢܝܗܘܢ ܕܗܢܘܢܐ ܒܗܦܟܐ ܒܐܝܕ ܗܘܐ ܠܗܘܢ. ܘܗܕܝܢ ܒܚܪܬܐ ܒܗܢܐ ܡܬܚܫܒܝܢ ܗܘܘ. ܘܗܠܝܢ ܗܦܟܘ ܠܐ ܗܘܐ ܒܠܚܘܕ ܒܬ̈ܪܐ ܐܠܐ ܐܦ ܬ̈ܠܝܐ ܒܥܕܪܐ ܘܗܦܟ̈ܝܐܬܐ ܡܢ ܢܫ̈ܐ ܘܒܬܪ ܗܠܝܢ ܠܡܦܠܠܘ ܕܢܫܡܐ ܐܝܟ ܕܢܦܘܩܘܢ ܒܫ̈ܢܬܐ ܐܦܬܠܡܘ. ܢܫܘ ܕܝܢ ܕܕܒܝܢ ܠܗܠܝܢ. ܒܬܪ ܟܠܟ ܘܒܢܐ ܐܦ ܬܠܬܐ ܒܬ̈ܪܝܢ ܡܢ ܦܠܘܛܝܢܐ. ܗܢܘܢ ܕܡܢ ܩܕܡ ܟܠܟ ܐܡܪܢ ܒܠܝܗܘܢ ܦܢܘܢ ܕܠܡܦܬܐ ܕܠܘܕܘ ܐܬܬܒܝܘ ܗܘܘ. ܡܛܠ ܕܠܐ ܗܦܟܬܐ ܡܢ ܠܦܘܢ ܒܝܠܗ ܗܘܘ. ܘܐܦܠܐ ܠܢܘܡܣܐ ܘܠܢܘܠܦܢܐ ܕܡܬܒܥܐ ܗܘܐ ܠܠܕܪܘܬܐ ܡܝܟܐ ܢܦܫܗܘܢ. ܘܒܫ̈ܢܬܐ ܗܦܟ̈ܝܐܬܐ ܐܝܠܝܢ ܕܠܐ ܗܦܩܝܢ ܐܝܟ ܕܢܬܘܒ ܐܝܟ ܗܦܟܘ. ܒܚܪܬܐ ܕܝܢ ܕܒܠܝܗܘܢ ܐܘܠܝܬܝܗܘܢ ܗܢܐ ܡܫܡܫ ܒܪܫܐ ܡܦܢܐ ܗܦܟܘ ܗܘܘ. ܐܚܪ̈ܢܐ ܕܝܢ ܒܝܕܐ ܡܕܢܚܐ. ܟܕ ܒܝܠܘܬܐ ܒܢܫܝܢ ܗܘܘ. ܘܒܡܪܢܐ ܕܒܬ̈ܪܐ ܐܠܗ̈ܐ ܐܡܝܢ ܗܘܘ. ܐܬܠܒܒܘ ܘܐܒܟܬܗܘܢ ܕܦܢܘܢ ܣܟܐ ܕܒܪ̈ܝܗܘܢ ܒܬ̈ܠܝܗܘܢ ܘܒܒ̈ܢܝܗܘܢ ܗܦܟܘ ܐܘ̈ܠܝܐ ܐܚܪ̈ܢܐ ܕܝܢ ܘܐܦ ܒܟܬ̈ܒܘܢܐ ܕܪ̈ܘܪܒܝܢ ܡܢ ܗܠܝܢ ܡܟܐ. ܘܒܪ ܒܬ̈ܠܝܗܘܢ ܘܒܒ̈ܢܝܗܘܢ ܢܫܘ ܐܦ ܒܗܘ̈ܪܐ ܡܫ̈ܢܐ ܒܟ̈ܒܢܝܗܘܢ ܐܬܗܪܘܒ. ܘܬܘܒ ܐܚܪ̈ܢܐ ܡܬܪ ܡܢ ܗܠܝܢ ܠܗ̇ ܠܗܕܐ ܡܬܗܪܘܬܐ ܪܬܐ ܐܬܘ ܘܒܬܪ ܒܠܗܘܢ ܐܦ ܟܡ ܡܟܬܐ ܐܬܒܨܪܘ ○ ○ ○

ܘܬܘܒ ܟܕ ܡܢ ܗܠܝܢ ܥܕ ܗܘܐ. ܐܬܬܐ ܠܗ ܠܡܟ̈ܝܢ ܠܫܕܐ ܐܢܕܐ ܕܐܦ ܟܦܘܫܡܗ ܐܝܬܝܬܐ ܗܘܬ. ܐܠܐ ܒܪܚܝܢܐ ܚܠܬܝܢܐ ܕܡܢܝܐ

ܐܬܢܩܦ ܗܘܐ. ܐܡܬ ܕܝܢ ܕܡܫܠܡܬܐ ܫܢܬܐ ܩܕܡܝܬܐ. ܦܓܥܬ
ܒܐܢܩܘܬܐ ܒܐܪܥܐ ܕܦܠܘܓܝܐ ܘܒܥܠܡܗܘܢ ܒܒܘܪܝܗ ܡܘܬܢܐ
ܗܘܐ. ܘܡܬܬܘܪܐ ܒܠܫܢܐ ܐܪܡܝܐ ܠܗ. ܘܡܢܐܝܬ ܡܬܬܘܪܐ
ܕܒܣܘܪܐ ܘܠܗ ܠܡܕܝܢܬܐ ܗ̇ܝ. ܦܪܨܘܦܗ ܕܓܕܒܢܐ ܐܝܟ.
ܘܒܢܫܐ ܒܗܠܝܢ ܕܗ̇ܢܘܢ ܡܕܝܢܝܐ ܡܟܐ ܐܝܬ. ܠܘܬܢ. ܫܢܬܐ
ܗܘܬ ܠܢ ܝܘܡܬܐ ܗ̇ܝ ܗܕܐ. ܐܝܕܐ ܕܫܘܐ ܗܘܬ ܕܒܗܕܢܐ
ܒܬܪܒܐ ܢܦܩܐ ܠܗ. ܡܘܬܢܐ ܗܘܐ ܕܝܢ ܣܓܝܐ ܕܗܘܢܐ ܐܓܘܢܐ
ܬܚܝܬܐ ܘܡܢ ܒܠ ܚܝܠܢ ܠܚܒܬ ܕܗܢܐ ܒܢܝܢ ܗܘܘ. ܘܠܡܗܘܢܘܬܗܘܢ
ܗܠܝܢ ܒܢܝܢܗܘܢ ܫܝܢ ܗܘܘ. ܟܕ ܦܓܥܐ ܕܒܠܗܘܢ ܡܗܘܢܝܐ
ܒܬܘܒܠܝܐ ܦܓܥܐ ܘܒܠܝܘܬܐ ܕܠܐ ܡܗܘܢܝܐ ܒܡܥܝܢܗ
ܕܐܠܗܐ ܡܩܕܡ ܗܘܘ. ܘܡܘܬܢܐ ܗܢܘܢ ܕܠܗܘܢ ܡܥܝܢܐ ܕܐܬܦܪܩ
ܐܬܓܙܪ ܠܗܘܢ ܡܢ ܢܦܫܐ ܘܦܓܪܗ ܠܗܘܢ ܐܒܗܝܗܘܢ ܟܕ ܐܬܐ
ܠܐ ܡܓܠܗܘܢ. ܐܟܣܢܝܐ ܕܝܢ ܗܢܘܢ ܕܡܢ ܡܕܝܢ ܒܒܠܕܒܒܐ
ܕܐܠܗܐ ܐܝܬܝܗܘܢ ܗܘܘ. ܗܢܘܢ ܗܠܝܢ ܒܐܠܗܐ ܡܕܝܢܐ ܕܒܠ
ܘܒܕܝܢܐ ܕܡܕܝܢ ܒܫܕܘܬܗܘܢ ܒܡ ܐܘܠܨܢܗܘܢ ܡܩܕܡ ܗܘܘ.
ܘܐܟܣܢܝܐ ܕܡܢ ܐܒܗܝܗܘܢ ܕܢܦܩܘ ܠܬܬܪܐ ܒܠܫܘܕ ܢܦܫܘ
ܗܘܘ ܕܠܐ ܢܦܩܘ ܠܬܬܪܐ ܒܗ̇ܘ ܕܒܢܐ ܒܦܘܪܥܢܐ ܕܒܢܝܢܗܘܢ
ܡܬܬܚܥܝܢ ܗܘܘ. ܘܡܘܬܢܐ ܗܢܘܢ ܕܡܢ ܢܦܫܐ ܒܠܝܘܡ ܡܫܝܢܗܘܢ
ܒܦܓܪܬܐ ܕܒܬܪܐ ܡܬܐܓܠܝ ܗܘܘ. ܫܕܝܢ ܗܘܘ ܘܡܢܚܝܢ ܘܫܢܝ
ܘܥܒܕܝܢ. ܟܕ ܒܦܪܝܢ ܐܟܣܢܝܐ ܒܐܠܗܐ ܕܐܒܗܝܗܘܢ ܘܡܒܕܝܢ
ܒܗܘ ܐܠܗܐ ܕܐܦ ܗܢܘܢ ܡܒܕܝܢ ܒܗ. ܘܡܣܬܒܪܝܢ ܫܠܡ ܗܘ
ܐܢܫܐ ܕܐܘܪܚܬܐ ܦܓܥܬܐ ܒܦܪܘ ܒܗ. ܦܓܥܝܢ ܗܘܘ ܕܝܢ ܠܦܢܝܐܬ
ܘܢܦܩܘܗܘܢ ܒܓܠܓܝܢ ܗܘܘ. ܟܕ ܥܒܕܝܢ ܠܒܪܘܢܐ ܕܡܓܕܠܢܐ
ܕܦܟܝܢ ܘܡܥܡܕܘܬܐ ܒܒܬܪܐ ܠܐܟܣܢܝܐ ܦܪܝܢ ܗܘܘ. ܘܒܒܘܢܐ
ܕܢܦܫܐ ܠܗܘܢ ܡܥܡܕܝܢ ܗܘܘ. ܒܝܘܡܐ ܓܝܪ ܟܕ ܦܓܥܐ ܗܘܐ
ܠܗܘܢ ܦܪܐ ܗܘܐ ܘܐܡܪ. ܐܠܗܐ ܐܫܟܚܐ ܐܪܡܝܐ ܕܒܝܬܐܠ
ܘܐܝܫܝܐ ܕܒܐܘܣܛܝܘܢ ܠܗܠܝܢ ܕܝܢ ܗܘܘ. ܕܡܢ ܒܝܬ ܒܒܪܝܐ

ܐܝܟ ܕܒܗܠܝܢ ܢܗܒ ܕܠܡܟܬܒܬܐ ܗܘܬ ܕܐܬܟܬܒܬܐ ܕܐܠܗܐ ܗܝ ܕܠܗ ܝܠܦܬܐ ܠܣܘܪܝܝܐ. ܡܛܠ ܗܝ ܕܠܗ ܒܫܘܬܗ ܘܠܐ ܡܬܚܫܒܘܬܗ ܕܠܘܬ ܒܢ̈ܘܗܝ ܕܐܠܗܐ ܀ ܀ ܀

ܡܬܗܦܟܐܝܬ ܕܝܢ ܐܫܬܟܚ ܗܠܝܢ ܐܝܟ ܕܠܡܬܪ̈ܓܡܢܐ ܐܠܝܢ ܕܐܦ ܡܢܗܘܢ ܫܡܥܝܢ ܒܕܡܐ ܠܒܢܝ ܒܗ ܡܫܡܥܝܢ ܐܢܫܝܢ ܡܢ ܕܝܬܒܐ ܒܐܢ̈ܛܝܘܟܝܐ ܕܦ̈ܠܘܫܐ ܕܐܒܝܢ ܒܠܘܗܝ. ܕܒܫܘ̈ܩܬܐ ܘܒܡܕ̈ܝܢܬܐ ܐܝܟ ܕܠܡܗܘܕܢܐ ܢܝܫܘܥ ܐܚܝ ܠܗܠܝܢ ܠܐܠܝܢ ܕܐܬܝܢ ܒܬܪ݂ ܢܫܘܐ ܕܝܢ ܕܒܢܐ ܕܣܪ̈ܛܘܗܝ ܘܡܦܫܩܬܘܗܝ ܕܐܢܫܐ ܪ̈ܫܝܐ ܗܘܘ ܕܠܘܩܒܠ ܒܢܝ ܐܬܪ̈ܘܗ. ܕܒܗܠܝܢ ܝܬܒܐ ܀.

ܡܕܪܫܘܬܐ ܕܦܘܠܘܣ ܘܕܝܘܠܝܢܐ ܘܕܝܫܘܥ. ܒܫܢܬ ܬ̈ܪ ܕܐܪܕܘܫܐ ܕܒܢ̈ܘܗܝ ܒܡܫܪܝܐ.

ܒܕܡܐ ܠܫܢܬ ܫܬ ܕܐܪܕܘܫܐ ܕܒܢ̈ܘܗܝ ܘܡܫܬܠܡܐ ܕܠܦܘܠܘܣ ܘܫܘܪ ܗܘܐ ܢܫܒ ܗܘܐ ܘܦ̈ܢܝܐ ܒܢ̈ܝܐ ܕܡܕܪ̈ܫܝܐ ܒܡܛܠܬܗ ܐܬܬܣܝܡܘ ܗܘܘ ܗܘ̈ܢܐ ܕܡܬܬܩܝܡ ܗܘܘ ܦܪܘܣܘܦܘ ܒܐܪܒܐ ܕܪ̈ܒܢܐ ܗܝ ܕܐܫܬܦܩ ܥܠ ܝܕܝ ܐܦܝܣܩܘܦܘ. ܘܡܛܠ ܫܒܝܐ ܕܐܪ̈ܦܘܢܐ ܕܐܫܬܘܗܝ ܒܐܪܒܐ ܗܘ ܐܬܘܣܦ ܫܡܥܐ ܐܦ ܠܐܝܠܝܢ ܕܟܠܝܢ ܠܗ ܕܢܫܬܪܘܢ ܦܪܘܣܘܦܘ ܗܘܝܐ ܗܘܐ ܫܡܥܐ ܡܛܠ ܠܡܠܦܢܘ ܒܢ̈ܝܐ ܦ̈ܢܝܐ ܕܡܕܪ̈ܫܝܐ ܕܐܬܬܣܝܡܘ ܒܥܠܡܐ ܐܪܒܐ ܕܐܦܠܘܣ ܘܬܡܢ ܒܝܬ ܐܬܬܣܝܡܘ ܗܘܘ ܡܟܐ ܫܡܥ ܘܠܠܬܐ ܗܘܕܝܢ ܘܐܫܬܕܪܘ ܒܪܒܐ ܒܡ ܢ̈ܫܐ ܩܠܝܠܐ ܡܕ̈ܪܫܝܐ ܠܡܬܒܩܝܐ ܕܐܬܐ ܗܘܐ ܒܡܠܘܦܢܐ ܕܐܬܬܣܝܡܘ ܗܘܐ ܫܡܥܗ ܦܪܡܠܝܘܣ. ܗܘ ܕܒܗ ܒܪܒܢܐ ܠܐܪܒܢܝܘܣ ܡܬܒܩܝܐ ܡܢ ܫܘܠܛܢܗ ܐܬܢܒܪ ܗܘܐ ܐܬܬܣܝܡܘ ܗܘܐ ܒܬܪ ܒܪܒܐ ܐܢܫܐ ܕܡܢ ܫܢܝܐ ܙܢܝܫ ܗܘܐ. ܒܪܒܗ ܗܘܐ ܒܬܪ ܒܪܒܝܪܘܬܗ ܠܗܘ ܕܡܢ ܦܕܡܘܗܝ، ܡܛܠ ܕܡܢ ܐܦܝܣܩܘܦܐ ܕܡܬܪ̈ܒܝܢܐ ܐܬܬܣܝܡܘ ܗܘܐ. ܘܡܬܪܒܝܬܐ ܕܡܕ̈ܪܫܝܐ

ܗܝܕܝܢ ܟܠ ܘܡܬܟܢܫ ܒܟܠ ܫܘܦܝ̈ܢ ܒܐܝܟܘܢܐ ܕܡܫܬܢܝܘܬܗ
ܐܬܟܢܫ. ܘܡܢ ܟܠܗܘܢ ܦܘܪ̈ܫܐ ܕܐܝܟܢ ܥܒܝܕ ܗܘܐ. ܡܛܠ ܕܗܘ ܡܢܗ
ܕܟܘܠܗܘܦܘܬܐ ܘܡܢܕܘܬܗ ܕܟܢ̈ܫܐ ܐܠܗܝܬܐ ܘܐܢ̈ܫܝܬܐ
ܡܫܬܟܚ ܗܘܐ. ܘܕܠܗ ܕܗܘܢܐ ܡܬܟܬܒ ܟܟܠ ܡܕܡ. ܠܗܘܢ
ܗܢܘܢ ܕܢܣܟܬܗ ܟܕ ܫܐ̈ܠܐ ܘܦܘܢ ܦܬܟܡܐ ܗܘ ܐܘܪܚܘܗ
ܢܘܒ ܗܘܐ. ܘܠܫܪܬܐ ܕܢܕܟܝ ܠܬ̈ܠܡܐ ܡܢ̈ܬܐ ܐܠܟܝܗ ܗܘܐ
ܟܠܘܢܟܐ. ܘܟܕ ܢܘܢܗ ܕܟܢ̈ܠܐ ܠܐ ܡܬܟܦܢ ܗܘܐ. ܘܫܢܐ
ܕܠܘ̈ܫܟܐ ܠܐ ܫܟܝܚܝܢ ܠܗ ܒܢ̈ܟܪܐ ܡܢ̈ܝܐ ܠܗܬܗ ܐܬܝܫܝܢ
ܘܡܟܐܢܬ ܟܟܢ̈ܘܗܝ ܦܪܘܗ ܗܘܐ. ܘܠܐ ܐܟܫܝܢ ܕܢܦܟܘܗ ܐܝܟ
ܕܦܒܪ ܗܘܐ ܘܪܢܐ ܟܬܪܟܝܬܗ ܕܢܐ ܒܘܠܐ ܕܟܗܪܐ ܢܫܝܒܘܗܝ
ܠܗܕܐ ܐܦ. ܟܕ ܒܡ ܫܢܘ ܡܟܪ̈ܢܐ ܕܟܟܝܬ ܐܘܪܚܐ ܕܡܢ
ܠܟܠ ܟܬܝܟܝܢ ܢܫܟܚ ܠܗܢܐ ܟܕ ܕܢܐ ܡܢܪܐ ܕܟܗܠܝܢ ܟܠܗܘܢ
ܝܬܒܬܐ ܟܝܢ̈ܬܐ ܠܗܡܟܠ ܡܟܪ̈ܢܐ ܕܐܠܗܐ ܐܬܝܫܝܢ. ܐܢܐ ܟܕ
ܦܘܪܟܢܐ ܘܡܗܘܡ ܟܪܫܐ ܢܗܘܐ ܠܗ. ܦܫܘܩܐ ܗܝ ܟܕ ܕܢܒܟ ܡܢ
ܗܠܝܢ ܕܟܬܝܟܝܢ ܐܢܫܝܢ ܀ ܀ ܀

ܘܠܠܐܝܬ ܟܕ ܘܟܪܫܟܬܗ ܘܠܐ ܗܘܐ ܠܟܝܟܪܐ ܦܝܫܐ ܡܛܠ
ܗܠܝܢ ܕܐܡܟܪܢ ܠܟܟܟ ܕܢܐ ܟܐܢܐ ܕܐܠܗܐ ܐܕܪܟܗ ܗܘܐ.
ܘܡܟܐܢܬ ܘܡܟܢܪܐܢܬ ܟܗ ܡܬܢܘܡ ܗܘܐ. ܘܟܘ ܕܟܠ ܟܢܡ
ܟܢܘܡܟܐ ܟܪܡܘܬܗ ܢܬܒ ܗܘܐ. ܘܟܦܠܚܐ ܕܡܕܟܘܗܝ ܦܐܡ
ܗܘܐ. ܡܫܬܟܚܪ ܗܘܐ ܘܟܠ ܟܠܗ ܟܟܐ ܕܟܠܗܦܢܐ ܡܫܬܘܠ
ܗܘܐ ܟܢܕ ܠܠܝܐ ܡܢ ܟܘܠܗ ܟܐܘܬܗ ܐܫܠܝܡܗ. ܘܡܢ ܟܠܗܘܢ
ܐܡܪ̈ܘܗܝ ܐܝܟ ܡܟܫܢܕܐ ܐܫܝܡܗ. ܘܟܕ ܟܡܫܪܐ ܡܕܢܝܬ
ܗ̇ ܕܟܢܗ ܗܠܝܢ ܟܠܗܝܢ ܟܢܝܫܬܐ ܕܡܢ ܠܟܠ ܟܬܝܟܝܢ ܦܓܪ ܗܘܐ.
ܟܝܪ ܕܢܐ ܕܡܟܡܡܟܝܢܘܦ ܪܫܟܐ ܕܐܟܘܬܗ ܠܟܘܬܐ ܟܝܫܐ
ܐܫܬܠܡ ܗܘܐ. ܘܝܟܪܐ ܠܗܘܕܡ ܘܡܟܟܟܐ ܕܟܝܫ ܡܢ ܟܠ ܡܟܝ̈ܬܡ
ܐܬܟܟܪ ܟܗ. ܐܟܢܐ ܕܟܝܢܬ ܩܠܐ ܕܢܘܕܐ ܕܬܫܐ ܘܝܘܫܥܬܐ
ܦܪܫܘܬܐ ܟܐܕܬܘܗܝ ܡܕܡ ܡܟܘܬܗ ܡܢ ܟܠ ܦܘܩܕܢ ܐܬܘܫܝܢ ܗܘ.

ܢܕܒ ܗܘܐ. ܒܠܚܘܕܝܐ ܗܘܐ ܓܝܪ ܕܒܡܘܡܬܗ ܙܟܐ ܗܘܐ ܘܦܐܐ. ܘܡܙܕܗܪܢܘܬܐ ܕܡܕܒܪܢܘܬܗ ܘܡܢܟܦܘܬܗ ܕܢܦܫܐ ܘܡܢܟܦܘܬܐ ܥܬܝܕ ܗܘܐ. ܕܡܬܢܝܚܘܬ ܕܝܢ ܢܦܫܗ ܗܘܐ. ܘܠܘܬ ܟܠܗܘܢ ܒܢ̈ܝ ܐܢܫܐ ܕܒܟܠܗ ܢܒܝܐ ܗܘܐ ܕܢܗܘܐ. ܘܗܘ ܗܢܐ ܡܢ ܕܢܫܬܒܚܐ ܒܡܕܒܪܢܘܬܗ ܒܡܫܠܠܘ ܕܢܫܐ ܐܫܬܪܪܘ ܒܗ. ܘܡܛܠ ܕܝܢ ܡܗܡܢܘܬܗ ܘܠܘܬ ܡܕܒܪܢܘܬܗ ܠܡܗܘܐ ܒܢܫܐ ܕܢܘܪܐ ܫܡܗ. ○ ○ ○

ܘܒܗ ܡܢ ܗܢܐ ܗܘܕܐ ܥܒܕ ܗܘܐ. ܗܘ ܗܢܐ ܕܢܨܐ ܫܟܝܚ ܒܡܫܝܚܘܬܗ ܠܐ ܓܝܪ ܙܕܩ ܕܢܬܦܪܫ ܫܘܬܦܐ. ܗ̇ܢܘܢ ܕܡܢܙܪܢܘܬܐ ܕܢܫܝܬܗܘܢ ܡܬܚܫܒܝܢ ܘܚܒܪܐ ܘܬܠܬܐ ܟܠܗܘܢ ܕܡܫܡܫܬܐ ܕܦ̈ܓܪܝܗܘܢ ܦܬܝܚ ܗܘܘ ܘܡܫܒ̈ܚܝܢ ܘܒܢܦܫܗܘܢ ܒܫܠܡܘܬܐ ܕܦܓܪܬܐ ܕܐܠܗܐ ܥܒܝܕܝܢ ܗܘܘ. ܘܐܝܟ ܕܒܗܘܢ ܒܫܦܝܪܘܬܗܘܢ ܠܠܒܘܗܝ ܐܬܩܢܘ. ܘܬܘܒ ܟܕ ܡܢ ܗܠܝܢ ܘܠܗܘܒܐ ܥܡܝܩܐ ܘܐܠܗܐ ܡܐܠܗܘܬܐ ܠܫܘܘܬܐ ܣܒܪ ܗܘܐ. ܘܬܘܒ ܡܢ ܗܢܐ ܗܟܢܐ ܗܘ ܥܢܝܐ ܥܕ ܗܘܐ. ܘܒܠ ܐܚܪܢܐ ܐܝܬܝܐ ܗܘܐ. ܘܕܗܘܦܟ ܒܕܪܬܗܘܢ ܦܡܪ ܗܘܐ. ܘܠܐܗܒܬܐ ܕܡܗܝܡ̈ܢܐ ܥܡܠܐ ܐܢܘܢ. ܘܦܩܕ ܬܘܒ ܐܦ ܡܢ ܗܠܝܢ. ܘܥܠ ܗ̇ܢܘܢ ܕܒܢܬ ܗܠܝܢ ܐܝܬܝܐ ܗܘܐ. ܗ̇ܘ ܕܐܦ ܗܘ ܓܒܪܐ. ܕܡܢ ܟܬܪ ܙܒܢ ܗܘܐ ܗܘܕܐ ܕܐܠܗܐ ܒܠܡܫܠܠܘ ܕܫܘܐ ܫܒܩ ܐܢܘܢ. ܘܬܘܒ ܡܢ ܗ̇ܢܘܢ ܥܒܕ ܗܘܐ. ܘܒܠ ܐܚܪܢܐ ܐܝܬܝܐ ܗܘܐ. ܘܒܝܬܐ ܠܗܘܢ ܝܗܒ ܗܘܐ. ܘܠܐ ܐܬܬܚܝܒ ܫܡܬܐ ܕܢܦܫܗ ܒܓܒܪܐ ܐܠܐ ܐܦ ܒܓܘܫܡܐ ܕܢܩܬܐ ܠܢܦܫܬܗ ܡܬܠܒܫ ܗܘܐ. ܘܬܠܬ ܬܠܬܐ ܠܝܒܪܐ ܕܦܓܪܐ ܠܪܘܚܐ ܐܫܠܡ ܗܘܐ. ܘܠܐܚܪܢܐ ܬܘܒ ܒܗ ܐܗܘܪܐ ܐܫܠܡ ܗܘܐ. ܗܘ ܕܝܢ ܕܢܐܐ ܫܟܝܚܐ ܗܠܝܢ ܒܠܗܝܢ ܕܒܬܒ ܒܫܪܪܐ ܫܟܐ ܗܘܐ ○ ○ ○

ܘܡܢ ܒܬܪ ܫܘܠܡܗܘܢ ܕܗܠܝܢ ܕܒܬܒ ܐܦ ܗ̇ܘ ܫ̇ܡܥܐ ܕܢܣܒ ܒܠ ܦܘܩܠܘܣ ܗܘܕܐ ܕܐܠܗܐ ܫܡܝܢܐ. ܗ̇ܘ ܕܐܬܝܗܒ ܗܘܐ

ܚܙܐ ܕܗܘܐ ܠܗ ܠܡܫܝܚܐ ܦܓܪܐ ܕܡܫܪܝܘܬܗ ܟܠܝܐܝܬ ܡܢܗ
ܥܠܘܗܝ ܕܡܫܝܚܗ، ܦܫܝܩ ܗܘܘ ܐܫܬܟܚ ܠܐ ܬܘܒ ܐܫܟܚ
ܕܫܢ̈ܝܐ ܙ̈ܘܓܐ ܐܝܟ ܡܕܢܚܐ ܠܘܬ ܦܠܛܝܐ ܢܗܪܐ. ܘܠܡܦܩܘܗ
ܕܡܠܐ ܕܬܟܠ ܒܓܙܪܬܗ ܫܡܫܗ ܗܘܐ. ° ° °

ܘܒܗ ܒܗ ܕܝܢ ܕܗܘܐ ܦܠܛܝܐ ܕܚܙܝܬܐ ܥܠ ܗܘܐ. ܐܬܐ ܠܗ ܠܟܠ
ܩܪܝܐ ܕܡ̈ܕܝܢܬܐ ܗ̇ܢܝܢ ܕܒܟܠܗܝܢ ܦܠܛܝܐ ܠܦܠܣܛܝܢܐ ܠܗܕܐ
ܦܠܛܝܬܐ ܐܬܦܪܫܬ. ܘܠܟܠܗܘܢ ܥܡܐܝܬ ܠܦܠܛܝܢ ܕܫܡܥܐ
ܕܐܝܬ ܒܦܠܣܛܝܢܐ ܐܫܬܘܕܥܘ ܗܘܘ. ܟܕ ܡܕܡ ܠܐ ܐܫܟܚ ܠܗܘܢ
ܐܦ ܠܐ ܐܘܠܨܢܐ ܕܬ̈ܓܪܐ ܐܝܬ، ܚܠܦܝܗܘܢ. ܗ̇ܝ ܓܝܪ ܒܠܚܘܕܬܐ
ܡܕܝܢܬܐ ܠܒܠܚܘܕܝܗܘܢ ܗ̇ܢܝܢ ܡܕ̈ܝܢܬܐ ܠܦ̈ܠܛܝܐ ܒܡܦܩܢܘܬܗ̇
ܕܠܡܦܠ ܦܠܛܝ ܡܕܝܢܬ. ܘܠܐܘܠܨܢܐ ܘܠܬܓܪܐ ܕܠܗܘܢ ܕܚܫܝܢ
ܗܘܘ ܒܦܓܪܗ̇ ܒܪܕܘܦܬ ܫܒܪܐ ܡܚܠܦܬ. ܘܠܒܥܠܕܒܒܐ ܗ̇ܘ
ܕܠܡܩܠܗܘܢ ܦܐܝܩ ܗܘܐ ܒܡܘܡܬܗ ܪܓܙܬ. ܘܠܕܝܢܐ ܦܪܟܐ
ܘܡܢܐ ܒܫܠܛܘܢܘܬܗ ܘܒܓܙܪܬܗ ܙܘܢܐ ܕܢܦܫܗ ܡܚܒܒ. ܘܠܘܬ
ܡܘܕ̈ܝܢܐ ܐܚܪ̈ܢܐ ܐܝܟ ܕܫܘܠܛܢܐ ܒܝܕܗ ܠܗܘ ܗܓܡܘܢܐ
ܚܕܝܐ. ܢܦܩܐ ܕܝܢ ܐܬܘܗܝ ܗܘܐ ܚܕ ܒܫܒܐ. ܗ̇ܘ ܕܒܗ ܡܘܕ̈ܝܢܐ
ܐܬܕܝܢܘ ܗܘܘ ܒܩܣܪܝܐ. ܘܒܝܘܡܐ ܗܢܐ ܕܡܢ ܠܟܠ ܐܬܚܒܫ.
ܘܒܫܢܬܐ ܕܡܢ ܐܬܦܪܣܬ. ܗܢܐ ܦܘܩܕܢܐ ܐܬܦܪܣ . ° .

ܡܘܕܝܢܘܬܐ ܕܕܘܡܢܝܢܘܣ. ܒܫܢܬ ܫܬ̈ܐ ܕܪܕܘܦܝܐ ܕܒܝܘܡܬܢ.
ܒܩܣܪܝܐ ܡܕܝܢܬܐ.

ܐܘܪܒܢܘܣ ܗܘܐ ܗܓܡܘܢܐ ܒܦܠܣܛܝܢܐ. ܘܗܘܐ ܚܕ ܒܬܪ،
ܐܚܪ، ܐܬܘܗܝ ܗܘܐ. ܘܗܘܐ ܗܘ ܡܢ ܗܝ ܒܫ̈ܢܝܬܗ ܡܬܕܝܢܬ
ܗܘܐ. ܘܒܥܒܕܘܬܗ ܕܠܡܦܠ ܒܟܠ ܥ̈ܡܢ ܡܬܦܠܛܝܢ ܗܘܐ ܘܕܝܢܐ
ܐܘܠܨܢܐ ܗܦܟ ܒܗܢܐ ܚܕ ܡܢܐ ܕܐܡܝܪܢ ܢܬܒܥܐ. ° ° °
ܒܗ ܗܟܝܠ ܒܙܒܢܐ ܡܢܐ ܕܐܡܝܪܢ ܠܘܗܝ، ܟܕ ܐܢܫܐ ܚܕ
ܕܟܠܗ ܒܡܦܪܥܗ ܡܬܠܒ ܗܘܐ. ܘܡܠܟܐ ܕܐܘܣܬܐ ܡܬܦܪܣܢܬ

ܐܬܦܪܥܬ ܘܟܠܗܘܢ ܫܠܡܐ ܗܘܬ. ܘܕܡܚܪܘܢ ܒܬܠܬܗܘܢ
ܡܢܗܘܢ ܒܝܫܐ ܗܘܬ. ܘܡܛܠ ܗܠܝܢ ܟܠܗ ܕܒܗܘܢ ܡܛܠܠܐ
ܗܘܬ. ܐܬܚܫܒܘ ܒܢ̈ܫܐ ܐܝܟ ܗܘ ܕܡܕܡ ܕܠܐ ܒܙܒܢܐ ܘܕܠܐ
ܒܥܠܬܐ ܒܒܪܬ ܗܘܬ. ܘܫܦܝܪܘܬܗ ܡܫܦܪܢܘܬܐ ܘܒܪܝܫܝܬܗ
ܠܐܘܪܚܢܘܬ ܡܠܟܘܬܐ ܡܪܟܒܐ. ܒܕܝܠ ܓܝܪ ܥܩܠܘܦܛܝܐ
ܕܩܠܘܦܛܝܐ ܠܒܝܫ ܗܘܐ. ܘܠܐ ܕܒܝܫܐ ܡܢܝܐ ܠܗ ܕܒܗ ܘܐܝܟ ܗܘ
ܕܗܦܟܐܐ ܡܢܗ ܕܠܦܠܛܐ ܐܬܚܙܝ. ܘܒܪܝܫܝܬܗ ܫܡܬܐ ܘܫܘܚܬܐ
ܕܠܝܗ ܐܬܡܛܠ ܘܥܒܕ ܠܗ ܠܦܠܛܐ ܕܐܬܒܫ. ܘܡܛܠ ܕܐܫܬܘܫ
ܟܕ ܦܠܛܐ ܗܝ ܐܝܟ ܒܪܢܫܐ ܠܘܡܠ ܥܘܡܕܐ ܕܟܠܗܘܬܐ
ܡܬܚܐ ܗܘܬ. ܐܬܝܪܬ ܕܝܢ ܗܠܡܘܢܐ ܥܘܪܐ ܒܗܘܪܐ ܡܢܝܐ
ܒܢ̈ܝܗ ܘܒܢ̈ܬܗ ܡܥܬܕ ܗܘܐ. ܒܕܡܐ ܕܐܬܚܙܝܘ ܡܢ̈ܐܠ ܠܗܘ
ܡܢ ܐܠܒܝܗ ܐܬܗܪܘܬ. ܘܡܛܠ ܕܗܝ ܦܠܛܐ ܗܘܢܐ ܡܗܡ ܒܪܝܐ
ܬܒܥܐ ܘܗܘܪܐ ܟܕ ܥܬܘܡܐ ܗܘܒܪܬ. ܘܒܕܒܠ ܒܝܫܐ ܗܘܬ.
ܘܥܒܕ ܠܗ ܕܐܬܒܫ. ܗܝ ܕܝܢ ܩܦܬܗ ܐܪܡܒܬ ܘܒܢ̈ܝܗ ܦܬܚܬ.
ܘܒܦܪ̈ܘܦܐ ܚܙܐ ܒܗܘ ܒܕܝܐ ܕܐܘܠܝܢܗ ܚܢܪܐ ܗܘܬ. ܠܓܠܐ
ܗܘܬ ܕܝܢ ܒܥܘܦܪܗ ܘܒܚܝܘܬܐ ܕܥܘܡܬܗ ܘܒܦܠܐ ܙܒܢܐ
ܠܡܠܟܘܬܐ ܐܫܬܪܝܬ ܗܘܬ. ܡܢܐ ܠܓܒܐ ܐܝܬ ܐܘ ܒܪ ܐܢܫܐ. ܘܠܐ
ܢܕܐܝܬ ܕܗܘ ܡܕܡ ܕܡܪܝܠܗ ܗܘܬ ܕܐܫܬܘܫ ܒܐܘܕܝܐ ܐܫܬܘܫܬܗ.
ܬܪܝܐܬ ܕܝܢ ܫܪܝܐ ܐܝܟܐ ܕܠܫܘܦܬܐ ܕܐܘܠܝܢܗܘܢ ܕܗܘܕܐ
ܕܐܠܗܐ ܥܒܕܬ ܕܐܬܗܘܦܟ. ܒܠܝܗ ܓܝܪ ܒܟ ܗܘܕܐ ܦܘܡܐ ܗܘܬ.
ܘܒܕܡܘ ܡܬܠܠܐ ܗܘܬ. ܕܟܫܕܐ ܡܢ ܦܘܪܗܝ ܠܐܘܠܝܢܗܘܢ
ܢܥܬܦܘܢ. ܐܝܟܢܐ ܕܬܬܦܠܓ ܠ ܒܥܡܗܘܢ ܡܢܬܐ ܐܦ
ܒܟܠܗܘܬܐ ܕܥܡܐ. ܠܐ ܓܝܪ ܡܥܡܝܐ ܗܘܬ ܟܕ ܪܘܫܐ ܐܢܐ
ܡܢ ܢܩܝܗܘܢ ܕܐܫܬܘܦ ܒܢ̈ܝܫܗܘܢ. ܘܫܝ ܗܘܫܐ ܕܡܛܠ
ܦܘܪܥܢܐ ܕܒܬܘܪ ܒܫܘܬܐ ܙܒܢܐ ܗܘܫܐ ܡܕܡܝܐ ܦܘܡܐ ܐܢܐ.
ܕܐܫܬܒܩܬ ܕܐܘܡܕܡ ܠܗܬ ܐܠܗܝ ܐܦ ܠܫܘܢܗ ܕܪ̈ܘܡܐ ܕܠܗܘܢ
ܦܬ̈ܘܝܐ ܡܕܡ ܥܠܠ ܒܒܝܐ ܗܘܬ. ܗܘ ܕܝܢ ܕܒܝܐ ܙܒܢܐ. ܟܕ

ܣܢܝ̈ܩܝܗܘܢ ܢܦܫܗܘܢ. ܘܟܠ ܥܕܢ ܢܦܩܘܢ ܐܝܟ ܕܠܦܠܚܘܬܐ
ܢܦܩܘܢ. ܠܥܒܕܘܬܐ ܢܥܒܕܘܢ ܘܠܗ̇ܘ ܚܢܐ ܕܡܫܝܚܐ ܢܫܬܥܒܕܘܢ.
ܘܡܢ ܡܛܠ ܟܪܝܐ ܕܥܒܕܬܐ ܠܐ ܢܫܠܘܢ. ܐܠܐ ܡܢ ܕܠܦܩܐ
ܕܒܘܪܐ ܫܘܒܗܘܢ ܕܠܚܠܡ ܠܐ ܕܚܕܝܢ ܢܫܠܘܢ. ○ ○ ○

ܘܟܕ ܫܠܡ ܗܘ ܣܘܥܪܐ ܕܐܠܗܐ ܒܛܠܝܐ ܙܥܘܪܐ ܗܢܐ ܕܝܢ. ܦܟܐ ܐܡܪ
ܗܘܐ. ܘܟܥܠܝܡܘܬܗ ܕܐܘܣܛܝܢܘܣ ܐܝܟ ܬܟܝܠܐ ܕܠܐ ܡܬܠܐ ܦܩܕ
ܗܘܐ ܣܓܝܬܐ ܘܦܓܪܐ ܦܓܪܢܐ ܒܥܐ ܐܬܦܠܓ ܗܘܐ. ܘܓܡܪ
ܕܫܘܬܐ ܢܥܡܘܢ ܒܠܘܗܝ. ܗܘ ܕܝܢ ܠܒܝܬܐ ܘܡܢܫܝ ܟܠ ܡܕܘܬܐ
ܠܡܫܝܚܐ ܘܠܡܥܒܕܐ ܠܐ ܐܦܩ ܗܘܐ. ܘܟܠܝܠܘܬܐ ܕܫܠܡܘܗܝ،
ܘܠܟܝܢܘܬܐ ܕܡܫܝܚ ܠܡܥܒܕܗ ܕܫܘܬܐ ܒܝܬܐ ܐܝܠ ܗܘܐ.
ܘܕܝܢܐ ܒܝܬܐ ܐܪܥܬܗ ܗܘܬ. ܘܟܬܝܒܢ ܠܗ ܡܟܣܟܣܐ ܗܘܬ.
ܘܟܕ ܒܕܒܠ ܢܦܫܐ ܐܝܟ ܗܘܬ ܒܗ. ܬܘܒ ܠܒܝܬ ܐܘܪܝܐ ܐܬܬܠܝܬ.
ܘܐܘܡܬܐ ܚܕ. ܬܡܢ ܚܕܐ. ܘܡܢ ܒܬܪܟܢ ܒ̈ܐܦܐ ܐܬܬܬܠ ܒܗ.
ܦܘܫܡܘܗ ܒܝܬܐ ܐܫܬܪܝ. ܢܦܫܗ ܕܝܢ ܕܦܘܠܚܢܐ ܐܦܘܗ ܒܐܐܪ
ܦܢܝܐ ܗܘܬ ܘܠܦܠܚܘܬܐ ܕܥܒܕܢܐ ܕܠܬܡܢ ܡܛܪܘܢܐ ܗܘܬ
ܐܝܠܬ. ܘܟܡ ܬܠܐܟܐ ܘܟܬܝܫܐ ܕܣܘܪܐ ܦܪܫܐ ܐܬܡܓܠܬ.
ܘܟܕܡܟܐ ܠܗܪܟܐ ܡܟܝܠ ܬܒܬܒܗ ܘܦܪܟܘܬܗ ܕܐܦܝܣ
ܘܟܠܐ ܗܘܐ. ○ ○ ○

ܡܕܒܪܢܘܬܐ ܕܬܐܘܕܘܣܝܐ ܒܡܠܟܘܬܐ ܕܐܠܗܐ. ܒܥܬ ܫܢ̈ܝܐ ܕܪܘܡܝܐ ܕܒܢܝ̈ܡܝܢ. ○.

ܒܙܒܢܐ ܠܒܬ ܫܢ̈ܝܢ ܪܘܡܝܐ ܒܢ̈ܝܡܝܢ ܐܬܡܒܝܢ ܗܘܐ.
ܘܪܝܫܐ ܐܬܘܗܝ ܗܘܐ ܢܝܫܐ ܘܡܘܟܐ ܬܪܝܢܐ ܒܗ ܒܢܝܫܐ.
ܘܦܠܠܬܐ ܫܢܐ ܐܠܗܬܐ ܘܦܪܫܬ ܒܟܠ. ܡܢ ܫܠܡ ܒ̈ܬܠܬܐ
ܕܒܢܗ ܕܐܠܗܐ ܕܒܝܘܪ ܡܕܝܢܬܐ. ܗ̇ܝ ܕܐܟܠܐ ܒܢܬ ܬܡܟܣܪܐ
ܒ̈ܢܝܢ ܐܬܝܗ ܗܘܬ ܘܡܫܘܟܐ ܕܝܢܐ ܕܠܘܬ ܐܝܟܢ ܕܡܦܠܘܠ
ܡܕܒܪܢܘܬܐ ܕܐܠܗܐ ܡܢ ܒܬ ܕܝܢܐ ܕܡܦܠܟܘܢܐ ܬܝܢ ܗܘܘ.

ܢܟܝܢ ܗܘܘ ܠܗ ܡܫܠܛ ܘܡܫܪܪܝܢ ܒܡܘܗܒܬܗ ܕܐܦܛܪܘܦ
ܒܒܘܝܐܐ ܠܗ ܠܦܛܪܝܪܟܐ ܐܟܘܬܗ. ܘܕܘܟܐ ܕܝ ܟܬܒ ܐܝܠ ܗܘܐ
ܡܕܡܕܡ. ܠܐ ܗܘܐ ܡܕܡ ܐܚܪܢ ܕܢܦܩܐ ܗܘܐ ܠܕܝܠܝܐ ܐܠܐ
ܒܠܫܘܕ ܕܒܪܘܦܛܝܢܐ ܐܚܝܕܘܗܝ، ܡܫܪܝܐ ܗܘܐ. ܘܡܕܝܢܬܐ ܕܝܢ ܚܕ
ܡܛܠܬܐ ܕܠܚܘܕܘܗܝ ܡܛܠ ܗܘܐ. ܒܥܡܗ ܒܢ ܫܘܒܚܐ ܕܐܠܗܐ ܥܠ
ܗܘܐ. ܘܬܪܝܨܘܗܝ ܫܘܐܝܬ ܚܕ ܡܢܘܢ ܒܪܝܫܐ ܡܟܠܘ. ܟܕ ܕܝܢ
ܕܡܟܐ ܗܘܐ ܫܟܐ ܗܘܐ ܠܫܡܗ ܕܦܪܘܩ. ܚܕ ܚܙܐ ܫܠܚ ܐܠܗܐ
ܕܥܠ ܡܫܡܫܢ ܗܘܐ. ܘܐܫܬܢܝܐ ܡܛܠ ܡܠܬܐ ܕܡܪܢܐ ܡܟܐܬ ܗܘܐ.
ܘܚܕ ܒܪܕܝܐ ܕܒܠܬܐ ܠܬܪܝܨܘܗܝ ܫܘܐܝܬ ܢܟܦ. ܗ̇ܘ ܕܝܢ ܗܘܢܐ
ܕܢܢܐ ܐܚܝܕܘܗܝ، ܗܘܐ ܐܘܪܚܢܘܗܝ ܡܫܡܗܘܢܐ ܡܛܠ ܕܒܕܒܠ
ܡܫܡܗܘܢܐ ܒܩܬܘܠܝܩܐ ܐܚܝܕܘܗܝ، ܗܘܐ. ܘܒܪ ܐܬܬܐ ܕܝܢ
ܡܫܡܫܢܘܬܐ ܠܗܕܐ ܚܕܬܐ ܕܡܢ ܠܟܠ ܐܬܬܟܒܬ. ܐܝܟ ܕܡܛܠ
ܫܠܝܚܘܬܗ ܕܐܘܪܚܢܘܗܝ ܒܩܬܘܠܝܩܐ ܕܒܫܢܬܐ ܐܘܦܩ ܠܗ. ܘܠܗܘ
ܡܛܠܬܐ ܕܡܛܠ ܡܪܢܗ ܡܢ ܡܘܬܐ ܚܪܢܗ. ܘܠܟܠ ܡܢ ܟܠ ܫܢܝܢ
ܒܒܕܗ. ܘܠܗܘ ܫܘܒܚܐ ܕܐܠܗܐ ܒܪ ܒܝܬܗܘܢ، ܚܙܐ ܗܘܐ. ܠܗ ܕܡܢ
ܫܘܬ ܥܢܐ ܡܬܐܒܠ ܚܕܐ ܗܘܐ. ܡܢ ܒܬܪ ܗܘܝܢ ܕܐܒܪܗܘܢ،
ܒܐܘܦܪܝܢ. ܡܕܡܕܡ ܐܫܬܐܠ ܗܘܐ ܫܘܒܚܐ ܐܟܘܬܗ ܕܐܢ̈ ܒܦܪ
ܒܐܠܗܗ. ܗ̇ܘ ܕܝܢ ܒܡܠܟܐ ܙܕܩܐ ܠܟܘܠܗ ܒܢܝܐ ܐܟܪܙ ܗܘܐ. ܐܘ
ܐܢܫܐ ܫ̈ܢܝܐ ܕܐܣܛܘܢܐ ܗܘܢܐ ܕܐܝܢܐ ܒܗ. ܠܐ ܗܘܐ ܡܛܠ
ܚܠܬܐ ܒܫܬܐ ܠܗܢܐ ܐܣܛܘܢܐ ܐܬܘܬ. ܫܘܒܚܐ ܐܢܐ ܚܙܝ
ܕܗܠܟܝܢ ܫܪܝܪܐ ܕܐܠܗܐ ܘܠܟܠܟܘܢ ܡܫܡܫ ܐܢܐ ܕܬܪܒܘܢ ܠܚ̣ܕ
ܐܠܗܐ ܒܠܚܘܕܘܗܝ، ܘܠܢܝܚܐ ܕܚܝܝܢ ܘܠܗܘ ܒܪܘܝܐ ܕܫܡܝܐ
ܘܕܐܪܥܐ ܬܪܒܘܢ ܘܬܫܬܒܚܘܢ. ܘܥܠ ܕܐܬܬܐ ܥܠ ܡܛܠ ܗܢܐ
ܫܡܝܐ. ܒܫܘܬܐ ܕܢܒܝܐ ܡܫܒܚ ܐܢܐ. ܠܐ ܗܘܐ ܚܙܝ ܒܡܛܪܬܐ
ܐܫܬܘܝ ܠܡܪܟܐ. ܐܠܐ ܐܢ ܢܟܝܢ ܒܪ ܫܪܪܐ. ܗ̇ܘ ܕܟܡ ܒܪܟܐ
ܠܡܘܬܐ ܡܛܡ ܐܢܐ. ܘܥܠ ܐܦ ܗܡܝܢܘܬ ܡܬܬܥܝܢܐ. ܕܐܬܐ
ܠܗܘܟܐ ܠܐܠܗܝ ܕܛܠܝ ܡܢܝ ܕܥܠ ܡܘܬܐ ܢܩܫܘܢ. ܘܒܬܪ

ܗܘܐ. ܗܘܕܐ ܕܝܢ ܐܚܪܢܐ ܕܒܠܘܩܝܢܐ ܒܬܪ ܐܦܣܩܘ ܐܓܦܘܣ
ܠܐܓܘܢܐ ܕܣܗܕܘܬܐ ܐܬܬܢܝ. ܘ . ܘ . ܘ

ܡܣܗܕܘܬܐ ܕܐܓܦܘܣ ܒܫܢܬ ܐܪܒܥ ܕܪܕܘܦܝܐ ܕܒܝ̈ܘܡܬܢ. ܘ.

ܒܫܢܬ ܐܪܒܥ ܕܪܕܘܦܝܐ ܕܒܝ̈ܘܡܬܢ. ܘܝܘܡܐ ܥܪܘܒܬܐ ܐܝܬܘܗܝ، ܗܘܐ ܒܥܣܪܝܢ ܒܬܫܪܝ ܐܚܪܝ. ܘܒܗ ܒܝܘܡܐ ܝܘܡܐ ܡܟܣܡܝܢܘܣ ܛܪܘܢܐ ܕܟܘܪ̈ܢܐ ܠܡܕܝܢܬܐ ܩܣܪܝܐ ܐܬܐ ܗܘܐ. ܘܡܫܬܒܗܪ ܗܘܐ ܕܡܕܡ ܚܕܬ ܢܚܘܐ ܠܟܠܗܘܢ ܫܢ̈ܝܐ ܕܡܠܟܘܬܗ ܡܬܒܥܝܢ. ܘܒܗ ܕܝܢ ܒܝܘܡܐ ܗܘܡܐ ܒܐܬܪܐ ܕܒܗ ܡܠܬܗ ܒܒܝ ܗܘܐ. ܘܡܬܒܥܐ ܗܘܐ ܕܒܡܐܬܝܬܗ ܕܛܘܪܢܐ ܡܕܡ ܕܡܬܒܪ ܡܢ ܐܝܠܝܢ ܕܒܥܕܐ ܡܬܒܥܐ ܗܘ، ܢܚܘܐ ܗܘܐ. ܘܡܕܝܢܐ ܗܘܬ ܒ ܗ̇ܝ، ܚܕܬܐ ܚܕܬܐ. ܐܠܐ ܕܗܘܕܐ ܕܐܠܗܐ ܠܡܒܣܠܬܐ ܕܣܗܕܘܬܐ ܐܬܚܙܝ، ܗܘܐ ܒܗ ܡܢ ܡܕܡ ܗܘܢܐ ܢܒܥܘܐ ܐܝܬ ܗܘܐ ܕܒܡܐܬܝܬܗ ܕܡ̈ܠܟܐ ܬܫܘܒܬܐ ܕܚܒܝܫܐ ܕܦܪܝܣ ܒܐܘܟ̈ܠܘܣܝܢ ܘܡܥܝܠܝܢ ܡܢ ܚܕ̈ܪܐ ܩܕܡ ܚܝ̈ܘܬܐ ܢܟܝ̈ܐ ܗܘܐ ܒܥܝ̈ܢܐ ܕܡ̈ܠܟܐ. ܘܒܥܡܡܐ ܕܗܟ̈ܢܐ ܚܕ̈ܬܐ ܘܢܘܟ̈ܪܝܐ. ܘܬܘܒ ܐܦ ܒܚܕܬܐ ܕܟܠ ܓܒܘ. ܕܚܝ̈ܘܬܐ ܘܒܚܝܠܬܢܘܬܐ ܕܓܒܪ̈ܐ ܐܬܠܝܛܐ ܘܦܘܪܓܝܐ ܘܚܙܝܐ ܦܓܥܐ ܢܗܘܐ ܠܚܙ̈ܝܐ ܘ ܘ ܘ

ܡܬܒܥܐ ܗܘܐ ܗܟܝܠ ܕܐܦ ܒܗܢܐ ܒܐܬܪܐ ܕܒܗ ܠܗ̇ ܕܡ̈ܠܟܐ ܕܡܕܡ ܪܒܐ ܘܡܫܬܒܪܐ ܢܚܘܐ ܒܗ ܒܐܬܪܐ. ܘܒܟܠܗܝܢ ܡܕ̈ܝܢܬܐ ܕܝܠܗ، ܠܗܘܢ ܡܕܡ ܚܕܬ ܠܐ ܒܒܝ ܗܘܐ. ܒܕܡܐ ܕܡܕܡ ܕܢܚܝܪ ܗܘܐ ܟܠܗܘܢ، ܘܡܫܒܠ ܗܘܐ ܒܠ ܦܘܪ̈ܢܝܐ ܪܒܟܐ. ܐܬܐ ܠܡܬܚܙܝܘ ܗܘܕܐ ܕܐܠܗܐ ܕܒܒܠܘܗܝ ܘܕܡܘܬܐ ܡܬܚܙܝܬ ܗܘܐ. ܘܡܬܒܥܝܢܘܬܐ ܕܒܡܕܝܢܬܗ ܦܟܐ ܗܘܐ. ܘܕܝܬܐܝܠ ܡܢ ܣܗܕܘܬܐ ܒܬܦܪܘ̈ܢ ܢܦܠ ܗܘܐ. ܥܒܕ ܕܝܢ ܐܝܬܘܗܝ، ܗܘܐ ܐܓܦܘܣ. ܗܘ ܕܟܠܗܘܢ، ܘܟܠ ܐܬܠܝܛܐ ܐܬܦܣܩ ܕܡܢ ܣܗܕܘܬܐ ܕܐܬܟܠܝ. ܘܒܥܕܢܐ ܐܚܪܢܐ ܥܒܕܗ ܥܒܪܐ ܕܬܘܠܝܛܐ ܐܬܦܪܥܬ.

ܕܐܘܪ̈ܗܝܐ ܕܐܟܢܐ ܦܓܥܐ ܠܗܘܢ ܠܟܠܠܗܘܢ ܕܢܫܒܐ ܗܕܐ
ܕܐܝܬ ܒܟܠܘܓܝܢܐ ܐܬܪ ܐܫܬܒܩ ܗܘܐ. ܘܡܢ ܒܬܪ ܕܟܒܪ
ܟܠܗ̇، ܬܘܒ ܒܫܢ̈ܬܐ ܦܓܥܢ̈ܝܬܐ ܘܐܫܬܪ،. ܐܙܠ ܠܐܠܟܣܢܕܪܝܐ
ܡܕܝܢܬܐ ܘܡܛܪܘܠܘܣ ܗ̇ܘ ܕܐܝܬ ܗܘܐ ܠܗ ܥܡ ܒܠܘܓܝܢܐ ܕܡܦܪܫܘܬܐ
ܟܠܗ̇ ܐܪܥܐ ܕܐܝܓܘܦܛܘܣ ܦܠܚ. ܘܣܢܝܗ̇، ܕܝ ܕܐܟ̄ ܡܫܝܚܝܬ
ܠܦ̈ܠܘܓܝܢܐ ܘܠܒܪ ܡܢ ܢܡܘ̈ܣܐ ܕܕܝܢ ܗܘܘ. ܒܫܘܪܐ ܕܐܠܗܐ
ܡܟܝܠ ܗܘܐ. ܘܬܫܠܡܬܐ ܦܪ̈ܫܬܐ ܕܐܠܗܐ ܠܢܫܘܬܐ ܘܠܝܚܝܕܘܬܐ
ܘܠܝܚܝܕܐ ܕܦܓܪܐ ܡܫܠܡ ܗܘܐ. ܘܟܕ ܗܠܝܢ ܩܕܡ ܒܢ̈ܘܗܝ،
ܕܐܬܠܝܛܐ ܠܒܢ̈ܝܐ ܡܬܦܪܢ ܗܘܘ،. ܠܗܘ̇ ܗܘܟܝܪܐ ܕܡܫܝܚ ܗܘܐ
ܠܐܚܘܗܝ، ܢܦܫܗ ܝܗܒ ܗܘܐ ܘܦܠܓܢܐ ܕܐܠܗܐ ܐܝܟ ܢܘܪܐ ܠܗ
ܡܫܬܘܠ ܗܘܐ. ܘܫܦܝܪܘܬܗ ܒܡܕܒܪ̈ܢܘܬܗ، ܐܝܟ ܕܒܫܒܬܐ ܢܛܝܪܬܐ
ܡܫܬܡܪܐ ܗܘܬ. ܘܒܝܬ ܢܦܫܬܐ ܠܘܬ ܡܛܪܘܦܘܠܝܣ ܗܦܪܟܝܐ ܒܘܠܐ
ܐܬܦܪܒ. ܘܒܬ̈ܠܐ ܫܒܝܚܬܐ ܘܒܟܬ̈ܒܐ ܕܥܢܘܬܐ ܠܗ ܡܚܒܫܬ
ܗܘܐ. ܘܒܐܢ̈ܫܘܗܝ، ܬܬ̈ܠܡܝܕܘܗܝ ܥܠ ܐܦܘܗܝ، ܡܫܒܚ، ܗܘܐ. ܘܥܠ
ܫܡܗ ܥܠ ܐܪܥܐ ܐܪܥܝܗ ܗܘܐ. ܘܟܕ ܡܕܪܟܝܢ ܗܘܘ ܠܗ
ܠܦ̈ܘܩܕܢܘܗܝ، ܕܢܕܪܘܫܘܢ، ܡܫܘܬܐ ܦܫܝܬܐ ܢܡܘܣ ܠܗ. ܟܕ ܐܡܪ
ܗܘܐ ܠܗ. ܕܠܐ ܠܒܪ ܡܢ ܒܢܝܐ ܥܠ ܒܢ̈ܝܘܗܝ، ܕܐܠܗܐ ܬܘܒܢܐ
ܠܦܠܝܓܘ. ܘܡܛܠ ܕܡܢ ܡܫܪ̈ܘܬܐ ܦܓܥܢ̈ܝܬܐ ܐܬܚܘܝ، ܗܘܐ. ܡܢ
ܢܡܘ̈ܣܐ ܐܦܝܣܗ. ܗܘܐ ܕܠܒܪ ܡܢ ܢܡܘ̈ܣܐ ܡܬܕܒܪ ܗܘܐ ∘ ∘ ∘

ܘܒܬܪ ܗܠܝܢ ܟܠܗܘܢ ܕܟܕ ܗܘܐ ܐܠܗܦܘ ܡܬܝܪܬ
ܒܡܫܡܫܢܘܬܐ ܦܓܥܢܝܬܐ ܫܢ̈ܝܐ ܕܦܓܪܗ ܐܬܟܬܒܘ ܗܘܘ ܦܘܩܕ
ܗܘܐ ܘܐܝܟ ܕܠܐܚܘܗܝ، ܒܢܝܬܗ ܘܒܝܬܢ̈ܘܗܝ، ܘܦܠܝܓܘ
ܘܒܡܕܝܢܬܗ ܕܒܝܬܐ ܗܘܐ. ܡܫܢܐ ܐܦ ܡܫܘܡ ܒܪ̈ܫܝܢ
ܠܢܓ̈ܪܐ ܕܒܝܬ ܗܘܘ. ܘܡܫܠܡܢܐ ܕܒܢܝܢܘܢ ܡܟܐ ܕܢܬܠܐ
ܠܬ̈ܢܝܢ ܡܢ ܐܝܟܐ ܕܢܝܢܐ ܡܟܠ ܗܘܐ ∘ ∘ ∘

ܗܢܐ ܡܛܠ ܟܒܪܗ ܕܢܦܩܒ ܒܐܠܟܣܢܕܪܝܐ ܡܕܝܢܬܐ ܬܬܘܒܐ
ܕܢܠܦ ܫܪܪܗ ܬܘܒ ܗܢܘ ܗܘܐ. ܘܟܠܠܠܐ ܕܟܘܬܐ ܬܘܒ ܐܓܠܝܬ

ܒܡܘܪ̈ܝܢ ܕܡܕܝܢܬܐ ܗܢܐ ܡܕܡ ܕܗܘܐ ܐܬܒܕܩ ܗܘܐ. ܘܒܪܘܠܐ ܐܚܝܕܐ ܒܗ̈. ܒܢ̈ܝܕܐ ܡܬܬܘܠܝܢ ܗܘܘ ܕܢܝܚܘܢ ܕ̈ܗܘܠܝܢ ܗܘܘ. ܘܛ̈ܠܝܐ ܘܒܬ̈ܘܠܐ ܘܣ̈ܒܐ ܐܚܝܕܐ ܘܒܠܗܝܢ ܡܬܥܢ̈ܝܬܐ ܕܢܦܩܬܐ ܒܕܡܐ ܕܐܦ ܬ̈ܘܠܬܐ ܢܦ̈ܩܬܐ ܕܡܬ̈ܦܠܘܢܐ ܡܬܬܦܠܝܢ̈ ܗܘܘ. ܠܚܝܬܐ ܗܕܐ ܢܚܘ. ܘܒܠܗ̇ ܡܕܝܢܬܐ ܒܡ ܬ̈ܠܕܝܢ ܫܘܐܬ ܬܫܡܫܬܐ ܠܐܠܗܐ ܕܒܪ̈ܘܦܠܝܢܐ ܒܠܥܕܘܗܝ، ܡܫܡܫܝܢ ܗܘܘ. ܘܒܠܗ̇ ܙܒܢܐ ܒܥܡܡܐ ܕܡܥܫܢܐ ܡܕܝܢ ܗܘܘ ܕܢܣܒ ܚܝܠܐ ܒܢ̈ܝܗܘܢ، ܕܗܘܢܐ ܕܢܨܒܪ ܐܟܠܝܢܐ ܘܒܡܕܝܢܬܗ ܢܗ، ܦܪ̈ܝܫܬܐ ܠܒܠܗܘܢ ܫ̈ܢܝܐ ܐܝܟ ܗܢܐ ܡܛܠ ܫܘܠܡܐ ܠܬܫܡܫܬܐ ܕܐܦܝܣܩܘܣ ܗܘܐ ܒܬ̈ܪܝܢ ܒܢ̈ܝܢ ܘܕܘܒܪ̈ܘܗܝ ܒܗܢܐ ܢܡܘܣܐ ܡܬܕܒܪ. . . .

ܡܕܒܪܢܘܬܐ ܕܐܠܘܣܣ

ܐܒܘܬܗܘܢ ܕܝܢ ܕܗܠܝܢ ܕܗܢܘܢ، ܒܐܦܝܣܩܘܣ ܣܗܕܐ. ܡܢ ܒܬܪ ܕܡܢ ܥܠܠ ܐܚܘܗܝ، ܒܪ ܐܒܘܗܝ، ܘܒܪ ܐܡܗ ܕܠܗ ܕܐܦܝܣܩܘܣ ܡܕܒܪܢܐ ܗܘܐ. ܕܥܒܕܗ ܗܘܐ ܐܠܘܣܣ ܒܪ ܒܢ̈ܝܠܐ ܕܐܠܗܐ ܠܗܘܒܠܗܘܢ ܡܩܪܒ ܗܘܐ. ܘܐܦ ܒܗܡܡܢܘܬܐ ܕܝܪ̈ܘܗ ܐܝܟ ܕܒܢܝܐ ܡܬܒܥܐ ܗܘܐ. ܐܦ ܗ̇ܢܘܢ ܠܗܘܒܠܗ ܒܛ̈ܒܘܬܐ ܘܒܬ̈ܟܝܠܐ ܒܒܗ ܡܬܓܬܥܝܢ ܗܘܘ. ܘܐܝܟ ܣܕܪܐ ܕܡܪܟܐ ܚܙ ܠܗܘܒܠ ܚܙ ܡܚܒܝܢ ܗܘܘ. ܘܕܐܝܢܐ ܡܢ ܓܒ̈ܐ ܢܫܒ ܘܒܘܬܐ ܡܬܬܬܥܝܢ ܗܘܘ. ܗܢܐ ܕܝܢ ܬܡܝܗܐ ܐܠܘܣܣ ܡܢ ܡܕܡ ܕܐܚܘܗܝ، ܢܛܠ ܢܦܫܗ ܠܐܠܗܐ. ܙܒܢܗ ܠܗܠܘܣܦܘܬܐ ܐܥܠܝܡ ܗܘܐ. ܘܒܟܠ ܒܘ̈ܩܝܢ ܕܬ̈ܟܠܐ ܕ̈ܐܒܢܐ ܙ̈ܘܪܟܐ ܡܚ̈ܝܣ ܗܘܐ. ܘܠܐ ܗܘܐ ܟܠܝܢ ܒܡܪܕܘܬܐ ܕܡ̈ܩܢܐ ܙܕܐ ܗܘܐ ܐܠܐ ܐܦ ܒܫܡܫܬܐ ܕܪ̈ܘܚܢܝܐ ܡܟܣ ܗܘܐ. ܘܒܚܝܢܐ ܕܡܣܒܠܢܘܣ ܣܗܕܐ ܘܕܢܐ ܦܓܪܐ ܐܬܝܗܘܗܝ، ܗܘܐ̇. ܘܒܡܠܒܠܐ ܐܠܗܐ ܡܢ ܠܗܬܗ ܐܝܟ ܕܒܐܪ̈ܓܘܢܐ ܕܚܝܫ ܠܬ̈ܠܒܘܬܐ ܐܬܓܒܝ ܗܘܐ. ܘܗ̇ܘ ܗܢܐ ܐܠܘܣܣ ܒܬܪ ܣܗܕܘܬܗ ܬܡܝܗܬܐ ܕܡܕܡ ܒܢ̈ܝܢ ܐܬܬܟܠܬ ܘܡܬܡܢܝܘܬܗ ܕܒܒ̈ܝܬܐ

ܘܕܠܐܠܗܐ ܐܒܗܘܗܝ، ܟܠܗܘܢ ܝܕܥ ܗܘܐ ܐܝܟܢܐ. ܘܟܕ ܠܐܢܘ ܠܗܘܢ ܡܫܟܠ ܘܐܙܕܒܢܘ ܘܢܦܩܘ ܡܢܗܘܢ ܕܒܟܗ ܡܬܬܚܡܝܢ ܗܘܘ. ܬܘܒ ܠܒܢܬ ܐܘܪܫܐ ܐܘܟܠܗܘܢ، ܘܠܘܡܐ ܕܒܬܪܗ ܡܕܡܘܢ، ܬܘܒ ܕܗܘ ܕܢܐ ܡܢܝܢܐ ܟܠܝ ܡܢ ܪܘܡܐ ܡܢܗܘܢ، ܗܘܘ. ܘܟܕ ܬܘܒ ܒܗܕܘܬܗ ܡܕܡܬܐ ܦܘ، ܗܘܐ. ܘܟܕ ܗܟܢܘܬܐ ܘܩܠܣܘܗܝ، ܘܟܠܗ ܠܟܘܐ ܕܡܥܡܥ ܗܘܐ ܠܒܝܬܗ ܣܒܘ. ܒܫܢܬܐ ܦܒܕ ܟܠܗܝ، ܕܒܒܗܡܘܢ ܕܡܟܐ ܢܕܘܢܝܗ، ○ ○ ○

ܬܕܡܘܪܬܐ ܕܝܢ ܐܚܪܬܐ ܕܡܢ ܟܬܪ ܗܢܐ ܫܘܒܪܢܐ ܗܘܬ. ܝܕܥ. ܐܢܐ ܕܠܐ ܡܬܡܨܝܐ ܠܗܘܢ ܕܠܐ ܗܘܐ ܒܫܘܬܐ ܕܒܢܝܢܫܐ ܐܟܘܬ، ܣܘܗܝ ܠܬܕܡܘܪܬܐ ܡܕܡ ܐܝܟ ܚܢܢ ܩܕ ܐܢܫܐ ܕܠܐ ܢܫܡܥܘܢ ܠܥܡܡܐ ܕܐܬܕܢܐ ܐܝܟ ܕܠܫܘܬܐ ܕܒܫܢܐ ܒܢܝܢ ܕܝܢ ܠܐ ܕܗܘ ܠܝ ܕܐܝܟ ܠܚܢܢܐ ܘܫܘܪ، ܗܡܫܘܢܝܬܐ ܢܗܘܐ ܐܦ ܐܢܫ ܬܕܡܘܪܬܐ ܐܚܪܢܐ ܕܒܡܘܢܝܢܗ ܕܫܘܕܪܐ ܕܐܠܗܐ ܐܘܬܒܬ ܘܫܘܕܪܐ ܕܗܠܝܢ ܕܐܬܬܟܝ ܠܗܘܢ ܠܟܠܗܘܢ ܒܡܘܪܝܗ ܕܫܘܕܪܐ ܒܡܕܝܢܬܐ ܡܢ ܐܢܫ. ܡܛܠ ܕܐܦܠܐ ܚܕ ܡܢ ܒܡܘܬܢܗ ܕܡܕܝܢܬܐ ܡܢ ܗܕܐ ܚܝܘܬܐ ܕܚܫܬܐ ܦܫܝ ܗܘܐ. ܒܕ ܓܝܪ ܒܡܘܬܢܘܗܝ، ܕܡܟܐ ܕܚܫܬܐ. ܒܪ ܐܢܫܐ ܕܐܠܗܐ ܐܫܬܕܪ، ܗܘܐ. ܘܒܐܦܐ ܒܬܠܝܗܘܢ، ܐܘܣܝ ܗܘ،. ܒܪܫܬܗ ܥܕܡܢܐ ܪܒܐ ܘܙܘܓܐ ܫܢܝܐ ܘܛܠܠܐ ܬܒܢܝܐ ܠܢܫܐ ܪܒܐ ܕܠܝܢ ܗܘܘ. ܘܙܘܓܐ ܡܫܢܐ ܐܦ ܠܗ ܠܡܕܝܢܬ ܡܪܟܠ ܗܘܘ. ܘܡܠܐܢ ܒܘܟܬܐ ܘܡܕܝܢܬܐ ܐܬܕܘܗܝ، ܠܥܡܡܐ ܦܫܝܛ ܗܘ،. ܡܛܠ ܕܗܟܢܘ ܕܐܬܬܐ ܒܟܠܗ ܟܡ ܒܡܘܬܢܗ، ܒܗ ܒܗܘܡܐ ܗܘ ܡܬܚܫܒ ܗܘܐ. ܘܟܕ ܒܕܢܐ ܗܘ ܦܓܪܐ ܡܢܝܐ ܕܫܘܕܪܐ ܕܐܠܗܐ ܐܝܟ ܗܘ ܕܐܦܠܐ ܕܫܦܝܪܘܗܝ، ܢܟܐ ܐܥܒܕ ܗܘܐ. ܦܓܘܢܝ، ܘܟܕ ܛܠܠܐ ܡܕܡ ܬܪܒܐ ܕܡܕܝܢܬܐ ܫܡܗ ܗܘܐ. ܘܟܕ ܒܕܢܐ ܗܘ ܐܘܠܝܢܐ ܘܙܘܓܐ ܬܒܥ ܗܘܐ. ܘܡܬܕܡܐ ܗܘܐ ܠܐܘܠܝܢܐ ܕܡܢ ܐܠܗܐ ܐܫܬܕܪ ܗܘܐ. ܘܟܝܘܢܐ ܫܢܝܐ ܟܠ ܒܟܠ ܐܢܫ ܡܬܠܒܫ ܗܘܐ. ܘܠܟܠܗܘܢ

ܥܠ ܗܘܐ. ܘܬܠܡܝܕܘܗܝ ܠܦܘܪܐ ܢܦܪܐ ܒܠܘܪܐ ܡܫܘܬܐ ܢܦܫܗ ܗܘ.
ܐܡܪܝܢ ܕܒܕܡܘܬ ܡܐܪܘܬܐ ܒܗܘܪܐ ܕܬܠܡܝܕܘܗܝ، ܢܥܠ ܒܫܘܒܠܗ
ܘܒܗܘܢ ܒܬܪܡܘܗܝ، ܐܝܟ ܕܒܦܫܝܐ ܡܢܝܢܐ ܢܘܪܐ ܡܝܬܐ ܗܘܬ
ܘܒܣܪܐ ܡܢ ܩܠܝܠ ܕܒܠܘܗܝ، ܒܒܪܢ ܗܘ. ܒܪ ܒܫܝܢܐ ܦܠܢܐܐ
ܐܬܘܗܝ ܗܘܐ. ܐܝܟ ܗܘ ܕܕܠܐ ܫܒܐ ܒܡܣܟܢܘܬܗ ܒܒܝܬ
ܗܘܐ. ܡܢ ܠܟܠ ܒܪ ܐܢܫ ܗܘܐ ܠܗ ܡܒܕܪܢܐ ܗܘ ܘܐܠܗܐ ܕܒܗ
ܒܒܪ ܗܘܐ. ܘܟܠܐܢܫ ܠܟܠ ܐܢܫ ܒܕܡܘܬ ܥܒܕܐ ܡܬܢܐ
ܗܘܐ. ܘܡܟܠ ܗܕܐ ܠܫܒܘܬܗ ܦܠܢܐܬܐ ܕܗܘ ܦܗܪܗ ܕܡܫܝܚܐ
ܐܦ ܒܦܘܪܦܠܢܐ ܦܠܢܐܐ ܐܬܒܢܝܘ ܠܫܡܗ. ܘܒܦܪܗܣܝܐ
ܦܠܢܐܬܐ ܡܢܝܢ ܗܘܘ. ܘܒܡܠܐ ܪܒܐ ܘܒܟܠܬܐ ܠܠܦܬܐ
ܒܗܕܘܬܗ ܕܒܐܠܗܐ ܡܒܪܐ ܗܘܐ. ܘܒܗܕܐ ܫܠܝܛܘܬܗ ܒܠ
ܫܠܡ ܒܗܠܐ ܕܢܦܫ ܡܒܪܝ ܗܘܐ. ܕܦܪܩ ܗܘ ܒܒܠܝܢ ܠܐܠܝܢ
ܕܠܘܬܗ ܐܦ ܗܢܘܢ ܡܬܦܪܢܝܢ

∘ ∘ ∘ ∘ ∘ ∘

ܘܗܕܐ ܒܠܚܘܕ ܫܪܝܬܐ ܕܡܟܝܢܘܬܐ ܐܦܒܝܫܘ ܠܝܘܫܒܐ. ܐܝܟ
ܕܐܬܐܦܪܘܢ ܢܗܝ ܗܘܐ. ܗܢܘܢ ܒܢܝ ܐܠܘܦܣܗ، ܕܡܕܒܪܢܐ
ܒܕܡܘܬ ܕܗܘܐ ܡܫܬܠܢܐ ܒܒܕܝܢ ܗܘܘ ܘܒܦܫܘܗܝ ܒܐܒܐ ܪܒܐ
ܡܬܡܒܪܝܢ ܗܘܘ. ܘܐܝܟ ܗܘ ܕܡܢ ܕܡܟܠ ܡܣܟܢܘܬܗ ܕܠܘܬ
ܡܠܦܢܐ ܕܒܪܗ ܐܝܟ ܗܘ ܕܗܢܘܢ ܗܘ ܢܝܫܘܗܝ ܡܬܠܡܕܝܢ
ܗܘܘ. ܘܒܪ ܒܒܐܒܐ ܡܬܢܐ ܢܝܫܝܢ ܗܘܘ. ܫܡܥܘܗܝ ܒܠܘܗܝ،
ܡܫܪܝܢ ܗܘܘ. ܘܒܬܚܫܘܗܝ ܒܠܘܗܝ، ܡܬܠܡܕܝܢ ܗܘܘ. ܘܕܢܐܡܪ
ܕܡܢ ܐܡܟܐ ܗܘ ܘܡܟܘ ܐܠܝܢ ܗܘܘ ܠܗ ܘܒܪ ܡܟܘ ܘܐܡܟܐ ܒܡܪ
ܡܟܐܠܝܢ ܗܘܘ ܠܗ. ܘܕܢܚܒ ܘܢܬܠܦܘܢ ܠܒܘܕܢܐ ܦܒܕܝܢ ܗܘܘ
ܠܗ. ܗܘ ܕܝܢ ܒܒܠܗܘܢ ܐܝܟ ܕܒܕܒܘܐ ܒܢܝܐ ܫܐܪ ܗܘܐ. ܘܐܝܟ
ܕܒܐܝܕܐ ܡܫܬܠܢܐ ܡܬܒܡܐ ܗܘܐ ܒܗܘܢ. ܘܦܬܟܪܐ ܠܢܕ
ܡܢܗܘܢ ܠܐ ܢܩܒ ܗܘܐ. ܘܒܠܗܘܢ ܒܗܕܐ ܒܪܬ ܡܠܐ ܡܬܢܒܫ
ܗܘܐ. ܒܪ ܡܒܕܐ ܒܡܒܫܢܐ ܕܐܠܗܐ ܗܘ ܘܒܪܐ ܐܬܘܗܝ، ܕܐܠܗܐ

ܕܕܒܪܐ ܒܗ ܦ̈ܠܚܐ ܕܡܫܡܫܢܘܬܐ ܒܕܡܘܬ ܥܒ̈ܕܐ ܠܡܪ̈ܘܬܗܘܢ
ܟܠܗ. ܘܥܠ ܐܦ̈ܘܗܝ ܠܐ ܡܣܒܝܢ ܗܘܘ. ܘܟܕ ܐܪܥܐ ܒܐܘܪܚܐ
ܕܬ̈ܠܡܝܕܘܗܝ ܠܐ ܡܣܬܟܠܝܢ ܗܘܘ. ܘܒܟܠܗܝܢ ܦܘܩܕܢܘܗܝ ܘܫܦܝܪ̈ܘܬܗ
ܡܬܪܥܝܢ ܗܘܘ. ܘܟܕ ܒܠܥܕܝ ܗܠܝܢ ܫܠܝܚܐܝܬ ܫܡܥܘܢ ܗܘܐ.
ܘܡܕܡܝܬ ܠܒܝܬ ܐܘܪܚܐ ܫܡܝܢܐ ܐܫܬܠܡ ܕܐܝܠ ܗܘܐ. ܘܠܠܐ
ܘܐܡܝܢܐ ܬܘܡ ܒܗܕܐ ܬ̈ܠܡܝܕܘܗܝ ܐܬܡܟܟܘ ܗܘܘ.. ܘܟܬܪ ܢܟܝܐ
ܐܝܢܐ ܠܒܝܬ ܕܢܗܐ ܠܐܦܝܣܘܗܝ ܠܟܠܗ ܓܒܪ ܫܠܝܐ ܐܬܘܗܝ،
ܘܬܡܢ ܐܘܪܒܢܘܗ ܡܫܡܫܢܐ ܬܫܡܫܬܐ ܕܒܝܬܗ ܘܕܚܘܣܝܢܗ
ܟܠܠܐ ܐܪ̈ܓܓܐ ܒܬܫ̈ܒܚܬܐ ܢܘܗ̇. ܘܟܠ ܕܩ̈ܠܐ ܕܬܫܒ̈ܚܬܐ ܒܗ
ܒܗܕܐ ܕܐܠܗܐ ܢܘܗ̇ ܗܘܐ. ܘܓܒܪ ܕܡܓܪ̈ܢܘܗܝ ܢܦܪܘܫܝܗܝ،
ܒܕܡܐ ܕܓܒ̈ܪܐ ܡܓܢ̈ܘܗܝ ܢܬܚܝܠ. ܘܡܚܝܘܬܐ ܥܠ ܐܦ̈ܘܗܝ،
ܘܥܠ ܡܕܠܗ ܫܡܥ ܗܘܐ ܐܡܝܢܐ ܕܡܠܠ ܡܚܝ̈ܘܬܐ ܡܢܝܚܬܐ
ܦܪܘܩܗ ܐܬܚܫܒ ܗܘܐ. ܐܡܝܢܐ ܕܐܦܠܐ ܚܕ̈ܝܘܗܝ، ܡܕܡ ܗܘܘ
ܠܗ ܡܢܗ. ܗܘ ܗܟܢ ܫܡܥܐ ܕܡܫܝܚܐ ܒܕܡܘܬ ܐܕܡܘܫ ܒܢܦܫܗ
ܘܒܓܢܪܗ ܐܬܚܫܠ ܗܘܐ ܘܐܬܢܪܐܬ ܒܡܘܬܒܐ ܕܥܠ ܐܠܗܐ
ܦܐܝܢ ܗܘܐ ܘܟܕ ܫܓܝܐܬܐ ܡܫܟܚ ܗܘܐ ܠܗ ܡܫܡܫܢܐ ܗ̇ܘ
ܢܛܪ ܡܢ ܗܕܐ ܕܢܣܒܪܘܬܐ ܐܢܬܘܗܝ، ܗܘܐ ܠܐ ܐܫܒܩ ܗܘܐ
ܘܬܘܒ ܡܫܟܚ ܗܘܐ ܠܗ ܕܒܪ ܡܢܗ. ܘܡܢ ܐܡܟܢܐ ܗܘ ܘܐܡܝܢܐ
ܓܒܪ ܗܘܐ. ܘܗܘ ܠܐ ܡܕܡ ܐܢܫ ܐܘܕ.. ܐܠܐ ܐܢ ܕܒܥܕܐ
ܗܘ ܕܡܫܝܚܐ. ܗ̇ܘ ܕܝܢ ܡܫܡܫܢܐ ܡܛܠ ܗܠܝܢ ܡܬܪܐܝܬ ܥܠ
ܫܝܘܬܗ ܡܗܦܟ ܗܘܐ ܘܡܬܪܐܝܬ ܒܡܝܬܘܬܗ ܦܓܪ ܗܘܐ. ܡܛܠ
ܒܪܬ ܡܠܬܗ ܕܗܘܕܐ ܕܠܐ ܡܕܒܪܢܐ ܗܘܬ ܘܓܡܪ ܬ̈ܠܡܝܕܘܗܝ،
ܒܟܬܒܐ ܕܝܠܝܕ ܒܡܫܝܚܐ ܢܬܒܥܘܢ. ܘܢܘܪܐ ܢܬܠܗܒ ܒܗܘܢ.
ܘܟܠܗܘܢ، ܕܝܢ ܕܕܒܪܐ ܡܕܡ ܕܐܬܦܩܕ ܠܗܘܢ ܥܠܝܗ. ܘܬܠܐ
ܗܘܐ ܗܘ ܫܡܗܐ ܒܢܘܡܐ ܫܓܝܐܐ ܐܝܟ ܕܒܝܬܐ ܕܫܠܝܬܐ
ܢܕܠ ܠܟܠܗܘܢ ܣܢܝܐ، ܒܕ ܒ̈ܢܝܗ، ܘܕܩ̈ܢܝܬܗ ܒܡܪܝܐ ܡܫܪܝܢ
ܗܘܘ. ܘܟܠܗ ܥܡܐܝܬ ܡܕܒܪ ܗܘܐ. ܘܕܡܘܬܐ ܐܝܪܬܐ ܦܪܘܩܗ

ܘܠܕ̈ܝܘܪܐ ܢܦܩܘܢ. ܘܟܠܗܝܢ ܡܕ̈ܝܢܬܐ ܒܝܘ̈ܪܐ ܣܚܦܬܗ ܩܕܡ
ܗܘܘ. ܕܒܒܪܐ ܗܘ ܢܥܡܪܘܢ ܘܢܚܝܘܢ ܠܡܕܝܢܬܐ ܕܡܬܒܪܐ
ܢܬܒܢܘܢ. ܘܠܟܠܝ̈ܬܐ ܘܠܡܫܬܪ̈ܘܬܐ ܟܕ ܡܬܒܪܝܢ ܒܒ̈ܬܐ
ܘܒܫ̈ܘܩܐ ܘܡܕܒܪܢܘܬܐ ܕܟܠ ܡܕܝܢܬܐ ܫܪܝܢ ܗܘܘ. ܘܗܕܝܢ
ܒܫܒܘ̈ܚܝܗܘܢ ܠܗܘܢ ܩܕܡ ܗܘܘ. ܘܐܡܝܢܐ ܕܐܬܦܢܝܘ ܗܘܘ
ܕܢܒܢܘܢ ܐܠܝܢ ܗܘܘ ܠܗܘܢ. ܘܟܕ ܗܢܐ ܡܫܬܠܡܐ ܕܠܐ ܦܟܐ
ܡܢ ܟܠ ܦܢܝܢ ܠܟܠ ܐܢܫ ܡܬܝܗܒ ܗܘܐ. ܗܘ ܕܝܢ ܟܠ ܐܦܣܩܘ
ܗܘܕܐ ܕܥܘܕܪܐ ܒܒܝܬܐ ܕܡܢ ܟܠ ܩܠܝܠ ܡܬܕܪ ܗܘܐ ܦܓܪ. ܟܕ ܐܢܫ
ܒܗܢܐ ܦܘܪܢܣܐ ܠܐ ܐܬܪܓܫ ܗܘܐ. ܐܦ ܡܢ ܕܝܠܗ ܕܒܝܬܗ ܒܒܝܬܐ
ܫܘܝܢ ܗܘܝ. ܒܪܝ ܗܘܐ. ܘܠܘܬܗ ܕܡܫܟܢܐ ܕܐܬܪܐ ܦܩܕ.
ܘܠܒܢܝܐܬܗ ܡܢ ܦܬܓܡܘܗܝ. ܘܡܢ ܟܠܗ ܫܘܠܛܢܐ ܕܠܘܬ ܡܫܟܢܐ
ܦܐܡ ܗܘܐ ܐܬܦܣܝ. ܘܠܐ ܗܘܐ ܠܟܠܗܘܢ ܟܕ ܠܘܬ ܡܫܟܢܐ
ܐܬܦܪܢܣ ܗܘܐ. ܘܟܕ ܗܘ ܐܦܘܪܝܣܛܘܣ ܡܟܝܢܐ ܗܘܐ. ܦܩܕ
ܘܠܐܢܫܗ ܕܡܟܝܢܐ ܠܒܝܬܗ ܗܘܐ ܘܡܢ ܢܘܡܝܐ ܫܠܝܐ ܕܡܬܒܪܐ
ܟܠܗܝ. ܘܒܐܣܟܡܐ ܡܬܒܪܐ ܘܡܟܝܢܐ ܒܗ ܒܣܘܡܟܬܐ
ܐܠܗܬܐ ܕܢܦܫܐ ܡܢ ܫܠܝܘܬܐ ܡܦܫ ܗܘܐ ܠܗ. ܟܕ ܐܡܪ ܠܗ
ܕܠܐ ܠܡ ܙܕܩ ܠܝ ܕܢܦܫܘܩ ܡܢ ܚܕ ܐܠܗܐ ܕܥܘܪܐ ܒܠܚܘܕܘܗܝ.
ܘܠܡܬܒܪܐ ܕܠܐ ܢܦܫܐ ܘܠܕ̈ܝܘܪܐ ܒܢ̈ܝܫܐ ܢܕܝܚ. ܗܘ ܕܝܢ ܕܫܠܝܬ
ܡܢ ܟܠ. ܡܫܡܠܝܘܬܗ ܕܠܘܬ ܬܘܪܟܐ. ܟܕ ܫܠܝܐ ܐܦܣܩܘ ܒܟܕ.
ܗܘܐ ܘܡܛܠ ܡܫܡܠܝܘܬܗ ܫܠܝܗ ܕܢܘܗܪ ܡܢ ܟܠ ܐܒܕ̈ܘܗܝ ܕܒܪܗ
ܗܘܐ. ܕܠܒܒܪܐ ܕܫܠܝܐܘܬܐ ܢܦܘܩ ܡܬܒܢܝܐ. ܘܟܠ ܠܘܩܒܠܐ
ܘܟܠ ܟܘܠ ܡܟ̈ܬܒܐ ܐܥܒܕ ܘܡܢ ܫܠܝܬܐ ܠܟܒܥܬܐ ܠܐ ܐܬܝܠܠ.
ܘܒܐܝܕܝܐ ܕܒܪܬܐ ܘܟܠܝܢܐ ܕܡܛܠܠ ܬܫܒܘܚܬܐ ܫܕܐܬ ܡܠܠ.
ܐܡܪܝܢܐ ܕܒܛܠ ܐܦ ܠܗܘܢ ܠܬܕܘܩܘܗܝ. ܐܢ ܡܫܒܚܝܢܐ ܗܘܬ
ܕܢܦܩ ܢܟܐ ܗܘܐ. ܘܕܢܝܚܘܢ ܡܢ ܫܠܝܘܬܗܘܢ ܡܠܦ ܗܘܐ.
ܘܠܦܪܘܣܐ ܕܟܘܪܐ ܘܠܗܘ ܡܫܝܚܝܐ ܕܒܗܠܐ ܘܐܠܗܐ ܢܕܒܢ. ܘܟܕ
ܗܠܝܢ ܗܘ ܗܘܕܐ ܩܕܫܐ ܕܐܠܗܐ ܦܩܪ ܗܘܐ. ܗܢܘܢ ܡܫܒ̈ܚܢܐ

ܕܓ̈ܠܝܢܐ ܐܬܦܪܫ ܗܘܐ ܘܒܣܘܪܥܢܘܬܐ ܘܒܥܝܕܐ ܕܩ̈ܕܡܝܐ ܐܒܘܗܝ،
ܗܘܐ. ܘܒܡܗܡܢ̈ܝܐ ܕܒܝܬܐ ܘܒܐܘܟ̈ܣܢܝܐ ܥܒܝܕ̈ܐ ܢܦܫܗ ܝܗܒ ܗܘܐ.
ܘܠܐ ܡܢ ܬܪܥܗ ܕܦܓ̈ܪܐ ܐܘܪܚ ܗܘܐ. ܐܦ ܠܐ ܡܢ ܡܫܪܘܬܐ
ܕܓ̈ܠܝܢܘܬܐ ܐܬܕܒܪ ܗܘܐ. ܘܐܝܟ ܫܬܐܣܬܐ ܕܥܠܡܝܢ ܓ̈ܠܝܬܐ
ܡܣܒܪܢܘܬܗ ܗ̣ܘ ܠܢܦܫܗ ܗ̇ܘ ܗܘܐ. ܘܠܡܪܫܘܬܐ ܥܠܝܬܐ
ܘܠܡܦܩܘܬܐ ܐܣܒ. ܘܕܒܝܐܝܬ ܘܐܝܟ ܕܐܕܡ ܗܘܐ. ܠܡܓܒܪܘܬܐ
ܕܐܠܗܐ ܢܦܫܗ ܐܝܬ ܗܘܐ. ܘܒܗ ܡܕܒܪܘܬܐ ܗܘܒܒ. ܘܡܢ ܒܪܘ
ܫܢ. ܘܠܒܝܬ ܐܒܗ̈ܘܗܝ ܐܙܠ ܗܘܐ. ܠܐ ܡܫܟܚ ܗܘܐ ܕܢܣܒܪ ܒܗ
ܗ̇ܢܘܢ ܕܒܢܝܢܫܐ ܗ̇ܘܝܢ ܗܘܘ ܠܗ. ܡܛܠ ܐܘܟ̈ܣܢܝܘܬܗܘܢ ܗ̇ܢܘܢ
ܕܠܝܬ ܠܗ ܕܢܩܘܡ ܗܘܘ. ܥܡ ܠܗ ܡܢ ܠܘܬܗܘܢ ܘܠܐ ܐܬܟܠܠ
ܠܗ ܐܦܠܐ ܥܠ ܢܦܫܬܐ ܕܗܡܢܝ̈ܬܐ ܕܣܝ ܗܘܟܐ ܠܡܥܡܠ. ܡܬܕܒܪ
ܗܘܐ ܕܝܢ ܒܐܟܣܢܝܘܬܗ ܒܕܝܢܘܬܐ. ܘܡܣܟܢܐ ܕܐܠܗܐ ܗ̇ܘ
ܕܠܗ ܠܗܐ ܗܘܐ. ܠܗܕܐ ܡܕܝܢܬܐ ܕܠܝ ܐܬܐ. ܗ̇ܝ ܕܒܗ̇ ܚܠܝܠܐ
ܕܡܕܝܢܬܐ ܡܬܬܕ ܗܘܐ. ܘܒܗ̇ ܕܠܝ ܒܒܝܬܐ ܚܡܪ ܗܘܐ.
ܘܒܘܠܚܢܐ ܐܠܗܝܐ ܢܦܫܗ ܡܥܪܪ ܗܘܐ. ܘܒܬܠܝܐ ܡܕ̈ܝܬܐ ܡܢ
ܦܪܟܠܝܘ ܗܘܕܝܐ ܓܒܝܪܐ ܐܬܪܕ.. ܘܥܘܦܪܐ ܕܕܘܒܪ̈ܐ ܡܫܬܪܐ
ܡܢ ܠܘܬܗ ܚܒܫ ܗܘܐ. ܕܡܛܠ ܗܕܐ ܥܠ ܡܫܠܡܢܘܬܐ ܕܡܕܝܢܬܗ
ܕܐܦܝܣܩ ܐܬܥܒܕܬ ܕܐܡܪ̈ܝܢ ܗܦܟ ܐܝܢܐ ܘܕܐܝܢܐ ܫܘܠܡܐ
ܗܘܐ ܠܗ. ܒܗܠ ܒܢܝ̈ܐ ܕܫܪܒܗ ܬܗܪܘ ܒܗ. ܘܡܢܘ ܕܟܠܦܐ
ܢܥܒܕ ܡܘܡܢܐ. ܘܠܐ ܢܬܕܟܪ ܥܠ ܠܫܒܘܬܗ. ܘܥܠ ܦܪܗܣܝܐ
ܕܠܗ ܘܥܠ ܡܣܟܢܘܬܗ ܘܥܠ ܡܣܒܪܢܘܬܗ ܘܥܠ ܒܪܬ ܩܠܗ
ܕܠܘܬ ܡܬܒܣܝܢܐ ܘܥܠ ܦܘܫ ܦܬܓܡܗ ܕܠܘܬ ܕܝܢܐ. ܘܬܘܒ ܡܢ
ܒܗܠ ܠܡܬܕܡܪܘ ܥܠ ܗ̇ܝ ܒܘܡܝܘܬܗ ܕܓܒܪ ܗܘܐ ܒܗ ܓ̈ܠܝܢܐ
ܕܐܠܗܗ. ܒܕ ܓܒܪ ܐܪܕܘܦܝܐ ܕܥܠܡ ܕܬܪܬܝܢ ܩܢ̈ܘܡ ܐܬܬܟܪܝ ܗܘܐ.
ܒܥܕܢ ܬܠܬ ܕܠܗ ܕܐܪܕܘܦܝܐ ܐܓ̈ܪܬܐ ܕܡܒܣܡܢܘܬܐ ܗ̇ܘܝܢ
ܡܕ̈ܝܢܬܐ ܐܬܝ. ܗܠܝܢ ܕܒܗܝܢ ܦܘܫ ܗܘܐ ܕܥܠ ܐܝܟ ܒܓܠܝܠܘܬܐ
ܘܓܝܐܬܐ ܘܒܥܡܠ ܓ̈ܒܝܐ ܕܡܓ̈ܒܪܢܐ ܕܡܕ̈ܝܢܬܐ ܢܕܒܝܘܢ

ܕܫܘܠܛܢܐ ܕܡܠܟܘܬܗܘܢ ܥܠܝܗ ܗܘܘ. ܘܠܡܘܟܐ ܚܫܝܟܐ ܠܡܫܐ ܗܘܘ. ܘܠܣܢܐܝܗܘܢ ܡܠܟܘܬܐ ܒܙܘ ܗܘܘ. ܒܪܡܫܬܗ ܡܢ ܫܘܒܚܗܘܢ ܕܠܘܬ ܚܕܕܐ ܐܬܦܪܫܘ ܗܘܘ ܘܡܪܕܐ ܕܠܐ ܥܝܕܐ ܠܘܩܒܠ ܚܕܕܐ ܡܚܝܢ ܗܘܘ ܘܐܣܘܬܐ ܠܡܘܪܕܢܐ ܕܒܠܒܕܒܘܬܗܘܢ ܠܐ ܐܬܬܣܝܡܬ ܒܕܡܐ ܕܥܝܕܐ ܕܒܠܝܢ ܒܟܘܠܗ ܡܠܟܘܬܐ ܕܪܗܘܡܝܐ ܐܬܦܪܫ. ܡܢ ܒܬܪܟܢ ܕܝܢ ܕܫܡܥܐ ܒܪܡܫܬ ܢܗܘܪܐ ܕܚܝ. ܘܒܪ ܫܒܬܗ ܒܪܬܐ ܕܐܠܗܐ ܕܟܠ ܒܟܠ ܘܡܘܠܟܢܐ ܐܠܗܐ ܒܟܠܗ ܒܪܝܬܐ ܐܬܡܟܟ.܀..

ܡܕܒܪܢܘܬܐ ܕܐܦܝܣܩܘܦ ܒܫܢܬ ܬܠܬ ܕܕܘܩܝܐ ܕܒܡܫܝܬܐ.
ܒܡܦܪܢܐ ܡܕܒܪܢܘܬܐ.܀.

ܫܘܐ ܡܕܢܚܐ ܘܦܘܪܢܣܐ ܒܝܫܐ ܘܡܫܟܢܐ ܕܒܝܢ ܫܘܠܛܢܐ ܕܪܘܡܝܐ ܠܒܝ ܗܘܐ. ܘܡܢ ܫܘܪܝܗ ܐܝܟ ܕܒܗ ܐܠܗܐ ܢܩܡ ܗܘܐ ܕܢܬܦܠܓ. ܘܦܠܓ ܡܢ ܗܘܢ ܕܗܘܘ ܡܕܒܪܢܘܗܝ ܐܪܕܘܦܝܐ ܦܠܓܐ ܕܒܠܝܢ ܢܓܠܐ ܗܘܐ. ܡܫܬܡܫܢܘܬܐ ܗܘܐ ܕܝܢ ܗܘܝܐ ܘܡܬܓܫܡܐ ܕܠܐ ܪܫܘܬ ܢܦܠ ܠܒܘܠܗܘܢ ܐܝܠܝܢ ܕܡܫܬܢܝܬܐ ܥܒܕܝܢ ܗܘܘ. ܘܦܫܝܩܐ ܠܟܠ ܐܢܫ ܐܬܚܙܝܘ ܗܘܘ. ܘܕܝܢܝܗܘܢ ܡܢ ܡܕܡ ܕܒܢܝ ܗܘܐ ܠܗܘܢ ܐܬܦܪܫܘ. ܐܝܕܐ ܗܘܝܠ ܡܠܬܐ ܐܝܬ ܕܦܩܐ ܕܬܫܡܫܬܐ ܐܝܟ ܕܬܫܪܐ ܟܠ ܫܘܒܚ ܐܠܗܐ ܕܦܘܪܩܢܐ ܐܦܝܣܩ ܗܘ ܕܒܝܘܡܘܗܝ ܐܦܠܐ ܠܡܦܪܩ ܥܡܡ ܡܟܠܐ ܗܘܐ. ܒܝܘܡ ܕܝܢ ܡܢ ܢܕܢܚܐ ܗܘܐ ܕܠܘܩܒܠܐ. ܘܡܢ ܡܕܒܪܢܐ ܗܘ ܕܒܗܘܬܪܗ ܕܒܠܒܐ ܗܘܐ ܡܫܬܡܫܝܢ ܗܘܘ. ܘܒܦܠܝܠܘܬܐ ܕܐܒܗܘܗܝ ܠܡܬܪܕܘ ܒܒܝܪܘ ܡܕܢܚܐ ܐܬܬܪܕܝ ܗܘܐ. ܘܒܗܘܬܪܐ ܕܡܠܟܝܐ ܦܠܓܐ ܒܢܫ ܗܘܐ. ܐܠܐ ܗܠܝܢ ܠܐ ܡܕܡ ܐܝܬ ܒܗܝܢ. ܕܢܦܩ ܠܗܕܐ ܬܫܒܘܚܬܐ ܕܡܢ ܡܬܬܒܥܐ. ܐ̄ ܕܝܢ ܦܠܓܐ ܕܡܠܟ ܗܘܟܢܐ ܬܘܪܬܐ ܕܗ̇ܝ. ܢܦܫܐ ܡܕܝܢܬ ܒܟܠ ܢܦܫܗ ܘܙܕܡ ܦܠܓ ܠܬܘܕܝܬܗ ܕܐܝܟ ܒܡܕܝܢܬܐ ܕܐܝܟ ܗ̇. ܡܢ ܚܝܠܐ ܘܡܢ ܢܦܫܐ

ܒܝܘܡܐ ܕܝܢ ܕܐܡܘܢܬܐ ܢܝܚ ܐܝܠܝܢ ܘܒܝܘܡܐ ܘܒܗ ܕܠܐ ܡܕܒܪܢܐ
ܥܪܪ ܐܝܠܝܢ. ܘܕܢܥܒܕܘܢ ܠܡܠܘܬܐ ܚܕܕ ܐܝܠܝܢ. ܘܡܪܥܝܢܘܬܗ
ܠܡܕܒܪܢܐ ܘܠܟܠܠܗ ܠܟܢܫܐ ܕܒܢܝܗ ܡܛܠ ܗܕܐ ܠܡܩܒܠܘܬܗܘܢ
ܒܬܚܘܡܐ ܐܘܪܚܡܗ، ܘܦܩܕ ܒܠܝܢܘܢ ܡܕܒܪܢܐ ܕܠܒܝܬ
ܣܡܥܝܢܐ ܢܥܬܠܝܢܘܢ ܘܬܗܘܐ ܐܬܦܪܝܫܘ ܡܫܬܡܥܢܘܬܐ ܒܟܠܐܢܐ. ܘܟܕ
ܗܘܝܢ ܒܝܬ ܐܘܪܚܐ ܐܬܝܩܢܘܢ ܗܘܘ. ܐܝܟܡܐ ܕܒܪܐ ܡܢܝܢܐ
ܘܠܟܠ ܐܢܫܘܗ، ܕܢܚ ܡܢ ܩܝܢܐ ܫܦܝܪܐ. ܐܬܐ ܡܢ ܕܒܪܐ ܡܕܒܪܢܐ
ܘܬܒܢܐ ܒܝܬ ܠܒܢܝܬ ܐܘܪܚܐ ܕܢܡܘܣܐ ܠܐܢܫܘܗ، ܐܝܟ ܗܘܐ.
ܘܡܛܠ ܕܡܢ ܩܕܡ ܕܢܦܠ ܠܒܢܝܬ ܐܘܪܚܐ. ܒܐܪܥܢܐ ܫܪܝܪܐ
ܕܡܕܒܪܢܘܬܐ ܐܬܒܛܠ ܠܒܢܝܬ ܣܡܥܝܢܐ ܬܒܠܐܝܬ ܟܠ. ܘܐܦܢ
ܕܒܪܐ ܕܠܡܕܒܪܢܘܬܐ ܡܫܠܡ ܗܘܐ. ܠܡܕܒܪܢܐ ܐܬܒܕܩ. ܘܗܟܢ
ܠܐܘܪܚܐ ܕܢܦܩ ܢܦܩܬܐ ܕܐܪܥܢܐ ܕܬܘܒ ܐܫܬܠܡ ܗܘܐ.
ܘܐܡܬܘܗܝ ܕܗܠܝܢ ܐܦ ܕܢܦܫܗ ܫܡܪ ܘܗܢܐ ܐܝܟܢܐ ܠܒܢܐ ܡܢ
ܠܒܬ ܫܘܪܐ ܕܐܠܗܐ ܐܬܩܢܒ ܠܗ. ܢܠܦ ܐܝܟܢܐ ܕܬܫܡܫܬܐ
ܕܠܬܗܘܢ ܘܐܝܟܢܐ ܕܡܕܒܪܢܘܬܗ ܕܕܢܦܫܗ ܕܠܒܬ ܫܘܪܐ
ܕܐܪܥܐ ܡܕܒܪܢܐ ܡܥܘܬܐ ܦܩܕ ܒܠܝܢܘܢ، ܐܬܬܗܘܦ ܡܛܠ
ܐܦ ܗܢܐ ܒܡ ܗܢܝܢ ܩܕܝܫܐ. ܘܗܘܘ ܒܠܝܢܘܢ ܬܠܡܝܕܐ ܒܡܕܒܪܐ.
ܕܐܬܚܙܝܘܢ ܠܡܥܡܪܘܬܗ ܒܫܘܡܗ ܐܬܬܘܗ، ܗܘܐ ܡܢ ܦܢܝܬܗ.
ܘܕܢܦܫܗ ܐܬܬܘܗ، ܗܘܐ ܡܢ ܠܪܫܘܡܗ ܡܕܒܪܢܐ. ܘܪܘܡܠܗ
ܐܬܬܘܗ، ܗܘܐ ܦܪܘܩܐ ܕܒܕܬܐ ܘܕܕܢܦܩܘܡܗ ܡܕܒܪܢܐ.
ܘܐܝܟܢܐ ܗܕܝܢ ܦܢܝܫ ܘܐܡܬܘܢܕܘܗ. ܘܐܫܬܢܝ ܐܬܪܐ ܬܘܒ
ܐܠܗܘܢܕܪܐ. ܘܬܕܝܢ ܗܢܝܢ ܕܒܬܪ ܒܠܝܢܘܢ ܕܒܫܬܐ ܠܒܢܝܬ
ܐܘܪܚܐ ܐܬܬܠܡܝܕܘܢ ○ ○ ○

ܗܠܝܢ ܒܠܝܢܘܢ ܥܡܐܝܬ ܒܗ ܒܕܒܪܐ ܐܬܬܠܡܝܕܘܢ ܕܪܥܝܢܘܢ
ܢܬܦܠܓܘܢ ܘܒܐܪܒܥܐ ܘܒܗܘܢ ܒܐܕܪ ܗܢܐ ܥܪܒܐ ܗܘܐ. ܘܒܗ
ܒܕܒܪܐ ܥܡܝܠܐ ܣܓܝܐܐ ܕܚܠܬܐ ܗܘܐ. ܕܠܗ ܕܗܘ ܪܥܐ
ܘܚܠܬܐ ܘܕܘܗ ܕܒܬܪܢܘܬܗ ܒܬܪ ܡܢܗ ܗܘܐ. ܘܗܘܢ

ܡܕܝܢܬܐ ܕܐܝܓܦܣ ܘܕܬܡ̈ܢ ܐܠܟܣܢܕܪ̈ܝܐ ܘܕܬܡ̈ܢ ܕܩ̈ܘܢܣܐ
ܘܕܦܠܣܛܐܘܣ ܘܕܦܘܪܡܝܠܘܣ ܘܕܦܠܘܣ. ܒܫܢܬ ܬܪ̈ܬܝܢ ܕܐܪ̈ܘܕܦܐ
ܕܒܢ̈ܩܡܬܐ ܒܩܣܪܝܐ ܡܕܝܢܬܐ.

ܒܐܕܪܐ ܗܘܐ ܕܟܠ ܒܡܕܒܪܝܢ ܒܡܕܝܢ̈ܬܗܘܢ ܒܢܝܫܢ ܗܘܘ. ܐܦ
ܒܗ̇ ܒܩܣܪܝܐ ܗ̣ܘ ܗܢܐ ܒܐܕܪܐ ܗ̣ܘܐ ܗܘܐ. ܒܩܪܘܣ ܓܒܪ ܪܗܛܐ
ܕܝ̈ܕܥܐ ܡܬܝܫܐ ܗܘܐ. ܘܫܡܝܢܬܐ ܒܬܐܓܪ̈ܘ ܡܬܒܕܒܕܐ ܗܘܬ
ܘܗܘܐ ܩܢ̈ܝܢܐ ܘܒܢ̈ܝܢܐ ܒܐܣܛܪܝܢ ܡܕܝܢ ܕܢܗܘܘܢ. ܘܫܒܩܐ
ܘܛܒܐ ܠܗܬ ܟܠ ܐܢܫ ܪܗܛ ܗܘܐ. ܕܐܝܟܢ ܗܘ ܕܢܣܒ ܩܠܝܠ
ܥܒܕܗ ܐܬܕܒܪ ܘܬܠܬܐ ܕܒܡܗ ܒܡ ܥܕܪܐ ܕܦܘ̈ܠܚܢܐ ܐܢ̈ܫܝܢ
ܒܐܣܟܡܐ ܕܣܘ̈ܕܪܐ ܠܬܓܪ̈ܘ ܢܬܦܠܘܢ. ܕܡܢ ܫܘ̈ܬܐ ܢܬܐܟܠܘܢ.
ܗܕܐ ܓܝܪ ܡܣܟܢܘܬܐ ܫܠܛ ܗܘܐ ܐܘܪܚܢܘܗܝ ܕܡܛܠܡܢܐ ܠܚܪ̈ܝܐ.
ܘܟܕ ܕܝܢ ܛܒܐ ܕܗܠܝܢ ܐܬܚܙܝ ܓܒܪܐ ܗܘܝܢ ܘܟܠܗ̈ܝܢ ܐܢ̈ܫܝܢ
ܡܫ̈ܟܚܝܢ ܒܩܘܫܬܗܘܢ ܘܫܠܛܢܐ ܕܦܓܪ̈ܗܘܢ ܒܡܣܟܢܐ ܥܬܐ
ܐܬܚܙܝܘ ܗܘܘ. ܘܟܕ ܗܘܝܢܐ ܠܬܐܓܪ̈ܘ ܐܙܠ ܗܘܐ.
ܘܒܡܦܩܬܗ ܕܡܕܝܢܬܐ ܒܒܪ ܗܘܐ. ܓܒܪܐ ܗܠܝܢ ܛ̈ܒܐ ܠܒܝܬܐ
ܘܡܒܣܡ ܡܢܗ. ܘܐܬ̈ܪܐ ܕܢܦܫܗܘܢ ܗܘܝܘ ܠܥܒܕܬܗܘܢ ܘܦܪܘ
ܘܥܕܡ ܕܢܚܐ ܐܘܪܚܗ ܥܠܡ. ܘܗܘ ܡܕܡ ܕܡܢ ܐܢ̈ܫܝܢ ܒܬܚ
ܗܘܐ ܕܢܗܘܐ ܠܗܘܢ ܒܪ ܠܢܘܡܗܘܢ ܩܕܡܝܢ ܗܘܘ. ܒܒܢܝܐ
ܚܘܝܘ. ܘܡܣܝܒܪܢܘܬܗܘܢ ܡܬܟܪܬܐ ܘܠܐܠܠܬܐ ܕܝܚܝܕܝܗܘܢ
ܕܠܗܬ ܡܣܝܒܪܢܘܬܐ ܫܘܝܘ. ܡܣܩܝܢ ܗܘܘ ܕܝܢ ܒܪ ܦܩܝܢ ܗܘܘ.
ܘܐܦܩܝܢ ܗܘܘ ܕܒܗܘ̈ܠܝܢܐ ܐܢܫܝܢ ܘܕܢܬܒܕܪܘܢ ܒܬܐܓܪ̈ܘ ܗܘܘܒ
ܠܫܘܬܐ ܒܡ ܚܝ̈ܘܗܝ ܐܢܫܝ̈ܗܘܢ ܕܒܢܬ ܐܝܟܢ ܒܡ ܐܘܪܚܘܣ
ܡܣܟܢܘܬܐ ܒܝܫ ܗܘܘ. ܗܕܐ ܓܝܪ ܒܗܠܝܢ ܠܒܝܡܬܐ ܕܢܫܒܩ
ܡܣܝܒ ܕܒܐܬ̈ܠܝܬܐ ܕܠܗ. ܠܟܠ ܐܢܫ ܡܫܬܐ ܗܘܐ. ܘܠܫܘ̈ܩܐ
ܕܦ̈ܘܠܚܢܐ ܒܫܠܝܘܬܐ ܕܐܬ̈ܠܝܗܘܢ ܡܫܒܚܐ ܗܘܐ. ܘܒܠܥܐ ܠܗ
ܘܕܢܫܬܐ ܡܣܢܐ ܗܘܐ. ܕܠܐ ܢܘܪܐ ܘܠܐ ܦܪܙܠܐ ܐܦܠܐ
ܫܘܬܐ ܒܕܪܝܬܐ ܠܦܠܫܘܗܝ ܘܬܢܝܐ ܠܐ ܡܣܟܢ ܠܡܥܒܕܘ.

ܠܐ ܗܘܐ ܕܝܢ ܡܛܠ ܡܕܡ ܕܢܦܩܐ ܠܒܪܝܐ ܐܬܦܩܕ ܗܘܐ ܡܛܠ
ܕܟܠܗܘܢ ܕܕܒ̈ܪܘܗܝ. ܘܟܠܗ ܒܗܡܢܘܬܗ ܕܠܐ ܒܪ ܐܢܫܘܬܗ ܗܘܐ.
ܘܟܕ ܠܢܡܘܣܐ ܕܣܓܕܬܐ ܕܦܬܟܪ̈ܐ ܠܐ ܐܬܛܦܝܣ ܗܘܐ.
ܘܠܐܠܗ̈ܐ ܡܝ̈ܬܐ ܕܠܐ ܢܦܫܐ ܠܐ ܣܓܕ ܗܘܐ. ܡܛܠ ܕܟܕ ܐܢܫܐ
ܗܘܐ ܒܥܢܘܝܐ ܒܟܘܠ ܡܕܡ. ܘܒܢܦܫܗ ܠܐܠܗܐ ܢܩܝܦ ܗܘܐ.
ܘܡܛܠ ܢܟܦܘܬܗ ܘܡܛܠ ܥܘܕܪܐ ܕܕܘܒܪܐ ܕܡܫܝܚܘܬܗ ܫܦܝܐ ܡܟܐ
ܐܦ ܡܢ ܡܕܡ ܕܢܬܠܛ ܠܡܫܡܫܢܐ ܡܢ ܒܚܘܪ̈ܢܗ ܕܡܕܝܢܬܐ ܗܘܕܝ
ܗܘܐ ܘܡܢ ܒܬܪ ܗܟܢܐ ܘܡܫܡܫܢܘܬܐ ܕܒܝܬܐ ܘܟܡܘܟܢܐ ܟܢܫ
ܗܘܐ ܬܡܢ. ܐܬܦܫܛܘ ܗܘܘ ܒܢܝ̈ ܟܢܫ ܒܪܐ ܡܕܝܢܬܐ ܚܙܝܡ
ܒܢܦܘܬܗܘܢ. ܘܟܕ ܠܒܫܬ ܕܢܟܐ ܕܡܫܡܫܢܐ ܐܬܦܪܥܘ ܒܟܠܗ
ܡܫܪܝܬܐ ܕܡܫܡܫܢܘܬܐ ܗܢܐ ܐܬܠܝܛܐ ܕܟܐܢܘܬܐ ܙܟܐ.
ܘܦܫܩܐܝܬ ܗܘ ܕܢܐ ܒܬܫܒܘܚܬܐ ܡܫܪܐ ܠܗܬܘܢ ܐܬܚܙܝ ܘܬܒܪܐ
ܕܚܝ̈ܠܐ ܕܠܐ ܡܚܝܢ ܒܠ ܦܓܪܗ ܐܡܦܪ ܗܘܐ ܘܡܫܪ̈ܝܐ ܕܘܟܐ
ܗܘܘ ܕܠܐ ܡܟܝܠܐ ܕܢܬܒܬܒ ܦܓܪ̈ܗܘܢ. ܐܬܥܢܝ ܘܟܠܗܝܢ
ܟܠܗܝܢ ܗܘ ܫܘܕܪܐ ܚܠܝܬܐ ܕܐܠܗܐ ܐܝܟ ܡܪܒܝܢܐ ܐܬܬܒܥ.
ܘܒܗܘܬܐ ܕܬܬܒܥܗ ܐܚܪܝܐ ܒܡܫܡܫܢܘܬܐ. ܕܡܗܘܬܐ ܕܟܕ
ܢܘܪܐ ܒܝܪܬܐ ܢܗܒ. ܢܘܪܐ ܗܘܬ ܕܝܢ ܪܦܝܬܐ ܘܒܝܪ̈ܬܐ ܗ̇ܝ
ܕܒܗ̇ ܢܗܒ ܗܘܐ. ܐܝܟ ܕܠܐ ܕܠܠܐܝܬ ܬܒܥܐ ܢܦܫܗ ܡܢ ܦܓܪܗ
ܘܬܬܚܝܢ. ܘܬܡܢ ܒܕܡܘܬ ܕܗܒܐ ܦܓܪܐ ܒܒܘܪܐ ܕܢܘܪܐ ܪܒܝܒܬܐ
ܐܬܒܚܪ ܦܓܪ̈ܘܬܐ ܘܕܒܝܘܬܐ ܕܡܫܢܝܘܬܗ ܕܠܘܬ ܐܠܗܗ ܫܘ.
ܘܟܪܝܗܘܬܐ ܕܙܒܢܐ ܥܬܝܩܐ ܕܒܐܝܘܬܐ ܐܬܟܠܠ. ܘܡܛܠ ܕܐܫܒ
ܠܐܠܗܐ ܦܐܪܐ ܕܢܣܡ ܠܪܘܚܗ ܩܕܠ. ܫܘܒ̈ܚܐ ܫܒܩܘܗܝ ܡܫܠܡܢܐ
ܕܠܘܬ ܐܠܗܐ ܡܠܟܐ ܕܟܠ ܝܘܡܐ ܕܢܗܘܐ. ܘܒܟܡܐ ܬܘܒ ܕܗܢܐ
ܡܕܝܢܬܐ ܫܠܝܚܐ ܒܗ ܒܒܕܝܢܐ ܕܡܫܝܚܐ ܕܡܕܝܢܬܗ ܒܗ̇
ܒܡܕܝܢܬܐ ܐܦܝܣܩ ܩܣܪܝܐ ܘܬܠܡܝܕܐ ܕܡܫܝܚܘܬܐ ܗܕܐ ܕܝܢ
ܕܒܘܫ̈ܠܐ ܐܬܚܙܝ ܡܢ ܡܫܡܫܢܐ ܕܗܢܐ ܡܛܘܠ ܒܪܢܫܐ
ܢܡܠܠ ܕܡܢ ܫܘܒܚܐ ܐܬܟܠܠ ܀ ܀ ܀

ܘܟܕ ܗܠܝܢ ܥܒܕ ܗܘܐ. ܙܕܝܩܐܝܬ ܡܕܡ ܟܠܗܘܢ ܒ̈ܢܝ ܐܢܫܐ ܥܠ ܡܠܬܗ ܕܡܫܝܚܐ ܐܘܫܛ ܗܘܐ. ܘܒܥܒܕܐ ܚܠܦ ܕܗ̇ܘ ܕܐܘܕܝ، ܒܗ. ܗܘ ܗܘܐ. ܘܟܕ ܙܒܢܐ ܦܓܥܐ ܗܠܝܢ ܦܓܪ ܬܘܒ ܒܗܕܐ ܐܬܡܟܬܪ. ܘܒܦܘܪܢܐ ܕܡܕܒܪ̈ܢܐ ܘܕܝܢܐ ܡܣܝܒܪܢܘܬܐ ܒܟܠ ܐܘܠܨܢܐ ܐܘܪܚܗ ܒܗ ܘܐܬܚܝܠ. ܘܟܢܫ ܢܦܫܐ ܒܥܡ ܫ̇ܠܘܢ ܥܘܕܪܢܐ ܠܦܬ̈ܝܐ ܕܟܢܫ ܘܟܕ ܒܟܡܕܝܢܬܗ ܐܣܬܟܠ. ܘܗܢܐ ܐܦ ܠܟ ܒܐܢܦܫܐ ܐܬܟܬܒ ܘܐܘܫܛ ܒܝܬ ܕܝܢ ܡܠܠ ܕܡܢ ܦܠܘܦܢܝܐ ܚܘܒܗ ܐܚܝܢܘܗܝ ܗܘܐ. ܒܡ ܒܢܫܐ ܕܗܘ̈ܦܐ ܕܒܗܢܐ ܐܬܪ̈ܐ ܒܦܠܝܬܐ ܐܬܟܬܒ. ܀.܀

ܡܘܕܝܢܘܬܐ ܕܦܠܟܬܐܘܣ ܟܢܝܐ ܡܗܝܡܢܬܐ ܒܥܝܢܬ ܬܪ̈ܬܝܢ ܕܐܪܕܘܦܝܐ ܕܒܢܩܡܬܢ.

ܚܕܬܐ ܗܘܬ ܕܬܪ̈ܬܝܢ ܕܐܪܕܘܦܝܐ ܘܡܪܟܐ ܕܠܡܘܟܠ ܬܝܪ ܡܢ ܡܕܡܟܐ ܒܥܡ ܗܘܐ ܘܟܒܟܒܐ ܕܦܠܘܦܝܢܐ ܐܘܪܒܝܘܣ ܡܫܡܘܢܐ ܐܬܘܗܝ ܗܘܐ. ܗ̇ܘ ܕܒܗ ܒܪܒܢܐ ܠܦܠܝܢܘܣ ܡܫܡܘܢܐ ܡܢ ܥܘܠܐܝܢ ܐܫܒܪ ܗܘܐ. ܐܬܝ ܗܘ ܕܝܢ ܬܘܒ ܐܚܪ̈ܬܐ ܕܫܠܒܐ ܕܬܪ̈ܬܝܢ ܕܟܝܢ ܠܒܪ ܡܢ ܗܠܝܢ ܡܕܡ̈ܝܬܐ ܕܠܡܕܪܫ ܠܟܠܗܘܢ ܒ̈ܢܝ ܐܢܫܐ ܡܬܠܒܝܢ ܗܘܘ. ܒܡܕܡ̈ܝܬܐ ܒܪ ܒܠ ܡܕܒܪ̈ܢܐ ܕܒܕܬܗ ܕܐܠܗܐ ܒܠܝܘܕ ܦܡܕ ܗܘܐ ܕܢܒܝܘܢ. ܒܐܚܪ̈ܬܐ ܕܝܢ ܐܝܬܝܪ̈ܬܐ ܦܘܡܕܢܐ ܗܘܐ ܡܥܝܢܐ ܕܠܟܘܠ ܐܢܫ ܥܘܫܢܝܐ ܐܠܐ ܗܘܐ ܕܠܦܬܟܪ̈ܐ ܕܠܐ ܢܣܓܕ ܒܠܗܘܢ ܒܢܫܐ ܕܟܠ ܡܕܝܢ̈ܬܐ ܘܢܫܐ. ܐܟܝܢܐ ܢܬܒܝܘܢ ܘܐܬܬܘܣܡ ܠܗܘܢ ܢܚܘܬܐ ܕܠܫܐܕ̈ܐ ܢܝܦܘܢ ܐܝܟ ܫ̇ܠܘܢ ܗܘܘ ܒܪ ܦܘܩܕܢܝܗܘܢ ܕܡ̈ܠܘܟܐ ܕܟܡܣܝܩܬܗܘܢ ܠܡܦܪܥ ܒܗ ܐܠܗܐ ܫܠܡܐ ܕܟܠ ܢܨܝܚ ܗܘܘ. ܘܟܕ ܗܠܝܢ ܕܡ ܫܠܡܐ ܦܡܝܢ ܗܘܘ. ܒܥܒܕܐ ܡܬܥܛܠܝܢ ܗܘܘ. ܠܦܬܟܪܐ ܠܡܟܬܐܘܣ ܟܢܝܐ ܡܗܝܡܢܬܐ ܕܦܠܘܦܝܢܐ ܠܐܘܪܒܝܘܣ ܒܪ ܬܘܡ ܐܬܘܗܝ ܗܘܐ ܐܟܬܠܡ ܘܒܟܬܪ̈ܐ ܒܪܡܘܬ ܡܠܠܐ ܒܠܚܘܕܬ ܐܬܠܟܝ ܗܘܐ.

ܠܒܢܝܐ ܩ̈ܕܝܫܐ ܕܐܠܗܐ ܕܥܠ ܟܠ. ܘܟܕ ܡܠܝܟ ܟܡܠܐ ܙܒܢܐ ܠܗܘܢ
ܐܡܝܪ ܗܘܐ. ܘܕܠܐ ܕܣܠܬܐ ܘܕܠܐ ܐܪܡܠܘܬܐ ܬܡܢ ܦܐܫ
ܗܘܐ. ܒܟܘܡܪܢܐ ܕܕܝܢܐ ܗܘ̇ ܕܬܡܢ ܦܐܫ ܠܘܬ ܗܘܐ. ܫܠܦܘܗܝ،
ܡܫܛܘܢ̈ܬܐ ܘܦܩܕ ܟܠܗܘܢ، ܕܒܢܘܪܐ ܢܬܘܩܠ. ܣܢܐ ܗܘܐ ܓܝܪ
ܕܝܢܐ ܢܘܚܡܐ ܕܡܢ ܡ̈ܠܐ ܕܦ̈ܬܓܡܘܗܝ، ܕܗܘܕܐ ܦܓܪ̈ܐ ܡܬܚܝܝܢ
ܗܘܘ ܘܩ̈ܝܡܢܐ ܥܠ ܠܚܘܕ ܡܚܘܝܢ ܗܘܘ. ܘܡܛܠ ܕܐܝܟܢܐ
ܕܐܬܚܡܗܘܢ ܗܘܘ ܩ̈ܠܝܠܐ ܡܠܝܟ ܒܒܝܬܗ ܕܝܫܘܥ ܒܓܒܪ ܗܘܐ.
ܟܪܝܬܗ ܗܘ̇ ܠܗܘܢܐ ܡܪܝܢܬ ܡܕܝܢܬܐ ܐܘܠܦܢܐ ܡܬܩܢܝܢ ܗܘܘ
ܠܗ. ܘܟܕ ܚܙܬܐ ܗܝ، ܕܒܗ̇ ܡܫܡܫ ܒܪܫܐ ܡܫܡܠ ܗܘܐ ܬܟܠ.
ܘܡ̈ܚܘܬܐ ܐܝܠܝܢ ܕܠܒܘܪܐ ܫܥܝܢ ܐܬܛܠܒ ܗܘ̈ܝ. ܘܡܣܬܪܗܒܐܝܬ
ܕܟܘܡܪܢܐ ܢܠܟܘܢ ܡܬܥܣܩܝܢ ܗܘܘ. ܕܕܠܛܝܢܘܣ ܕܝܢ ܩ̈ܠܝܠܐ ܒܙ
ܫܠܒ ܕܗܠܝܢ ܡܟܝܢܐ ܐܣܬܒܪ ܦܩܕ ܘܡܢ ܡܘܬܐ ܕܒܢܘܪܐ ܠܣܘܕܪܐ
ܐܣܟܡܗ، ܡܛܠ ܕܐܡܪ ܕܠܐ ܫܘܝܐ ܡܪܝܡܘܬܗ ܘܫܘܠܛܢܗ ܡܛܘܡ
ܒܪܝܫܐ ܕܒܢܘܪܐ. ܘܐܫܟܚܢܐ ܣܓܝܐܐ ܕܡܫܘܡ ܒܪܝܫܐ ܐܝܟ ܩ̈ܠܝܠܐ
ܡܪܚܡܢܐ ܥܠ ܫܘܕܪܐ ܦܓܪ ܗܘܐ ܕܠܚܝܡ ܢܬܦܣܩ. ܒܪܡ ܕܝܢ ܒܙ
ܗܘ̇ ܡܕܒܪܢܐ ܕܒܗ ܡܬܟܠܠ ܗܘܐ ܐܫܬܒܠ. ܐܠܐ ܫܘܒܗ ܥܒܕܐ
ܡܢ ܐܠܗܐ ܠܐ ܐܬܦܣܩ. ܐܦܠܐ ܠܥܝܢ ܡܠܠܐ ܡܢ ܒܪ̈ܘܝܘܬܐ
ܡܫܠܐ ܗܘܐ. ܘܟܕܝܢ ܠܘܬ ܐܠܗܐ ܩ̈ܠܝܠܐ ܕܥܠ ܫܠܒ
ܬܟܫܦܬܐ ܕܟܐܦܝܣܩܘܦܗ ܦܘܪܢܣܐ ܡܓܠ. ܘܫܠܐ ܦܣܢܬܐ ܠܒ
ܡܢ ܡܕܡܟܢܐ ܐܬܬܟܠ ܗܘܐ ܗܢܝܡ ܠܟܠ ܐܢܫ ܬܘܕܝܐ ܙܟܐ ܐܢܫ.
ܗܘܐ. ܗܘ̇ ܓܝܪ ܕܠܒܝܫ ܐܬܛܠܒ ܗܘܐ ܒܪ ܥܒܕܗ ܒܟܘܡܪܘܬܐ
ܕܐܠܗܗ ܫܠܝܛܐܝܬ ܡܬܟܠܠ ܗܘܐ. ܘܡܗܝܡܢܘܬܐ ܠܒܝܐܝܬ
ܡܫܬܡܪ ܗܘܐ ܘܐܝܟ ܗܘ ܕܥܠ ܟܠܗ ܕܗܘ̇ ܕܐܘܕ، ܒܗ
ܐܝܬܘܗܝ، ܗܘܐ. ܘܒܦܪ̈ܘܣܐ ܢܗܝܪܐ ܘܦܝܫܐ ܒܥܠܡܐ ܕܪ̈ܘܚܢܘܗܝ،
ܫܐܠ ܗܘܐ. ܘܡܠܬܐ ܕܐܠܗܐ ܒܐܕ̈ܢܐ ܕܠܒܗܘܢ ܒܬܪ ܐܢܫܐ
ܙܪܥ. ܘܕܫܦܝܪܢ ܠܐܠܗܐ ܒܠܚܘܕܘܗܝ، ܠܟܠ ܐܢܫ ܡܦܪܢ ܗܘܐ.
ܘܨܠܘܬܐ ܘܬܘܕܝܬܐ ܠܐܠܗܐ ܒܟܕ ܬܡܝܕܐܝܬ ܩܪܒ ܗܘܐ.

ܒܒܝܬܐ ܕܝܗܘ̈ܕܝܐ ܕܒܢܐ ܐܬܬܒܝܘ ܘܐܝܟ ܐܬܩ̈ܠܠܐ ܥ̈ܬܝܩܐ ܘܡܝܩܪܐ ܒܢ̈ܩܛܬܗܘܢ ܒܐܝܟܘܢܗ ܕܐܠܗܐ ܐܬܛܠܠܘ. ܗ̇ܘ ܐܝܟܐ ܕܡܛ̈ܠܠܬܗ ܐܦ ܪ̈ܚܝܡܘܗܝ ܐܬܦܣܩܘ ܗܘܘ. ܘܡܢ ܟܠܗ ܒܡܕܝܢܬܐ ܕܫ̈ܪܝܡܘܗܝ ܥܘܢܝܗܘܢ ܕܠܘܬܗ ܗ̇ܘ ܐܝܟܐ ܕܐܘܕܝܘ ܒܗ ܐܝܟܢܐ ܀

ܡܘܫܐ ܕܝܢ ܕܐܬܢܒܝ ܒܗ ܐܝܬܘܗܝ، ܗܘܐ ܥܒܕܬܐ ܒܬܪ، ܐܡܪ، ܕܡܕܝܢܬܗܘܢ ܕܗ̇ܢܘܢ ܕܐܡܪܝܢ ܟܠܗܘܢ ܐܬܬܓܠܝܬ. ܘܒܗ ܕܝܢ ܒܡܘܫܐ ܗܢܐ ܐܦ ܙܘܗܪ̈ܢܘܗܝ ܒܐܝܠܦܢܐ ܡܕܝܢܬܐ ܐܣܗܕ. ܡܢ ܦܝܠܘܣܘܦܐ ܕܝܢ ܐܝܬܘܗܝ، ܗܘܐ. ܗ̣ܘ ܙܘܗܪ̈ܢܘܗܝ ܘܡܫܡܫܢܐ ܐܝܬܘܗܝ، ܗܘܐ. ܐܦ ܡܗܡܢܢ ܒܚܕܐ ܡܢ ܦܘܪ̈ܐ ܕܦܘܪ̈ܐ. ܐܦ ܗܘ ܗܒܠ ܒܣܕܪܐ ܐܬܡ̣ܢܝ ܘܐܟܡܬܗܘܢ ܕܗܠܝܢ ܕܒܒܠ ܐܠܦܘܗܝ ܗܕܪܐ ܒܦܘܪ̈ܐ ܗܟܢܐ ܐܦ ܙܘܗܪ̈ܢܘܗܝ ܠܦܒܢܐ ܠܗ̇ܢܘܢ ܕܡܢ ܕܫܠܛܗܘܢ ܒܥ̈ܒܕܬܐ ܕܠܦܒܝܢ ܕܪ̈ܘܚܐ ܢܦܠܝܢ ܗܘܘ. ܒܟ̈ܠܗ، ܕܠܡܣܒܐ ܠܗܘܢ ܡܢ ܕܒܢܝ̈ܐ ܟܠܐ ܗܘܐ. ܘܠܟܠܗܘܢ ܕܫ̈ܠܝܬܐ ܕܡܢ ܐܠܗܐ ܡܒܣܪ ܗܘܐ ܘܒܗ ܒܢܝܐ ܗ̇ܘ ܐܝܟܐ ܕܠܦܒܝܘܬܐ ܒܦܠܚܢܐ ܐܬܕܒܪ ܐܡܪܝܢ ܕܒܗܠ ܘܬܡܢ ܒܐܝܠܦܢܐ ܢܦܫܗ ܠܕܝܢܐ ܩܪܒ. ܘܟܕ ܥܒܕ ܕܦܫ ܠܗܘܢ ܕܝܢܐ ܐܝܟ ܕܢܕܟܝܘܢ ܘܗ̣ܢܘܢ ܡܦܪܗܣܐܝܬ ܡܢ ܕܫܠܛܗܘܢ ܕܢܕܟܝܘܢ ܡܢ ܘܒܬܗܘܢ ܐܬܟܒܫܘ. ܗ̇ܘ ܕܝܢ ܗܢܐ ܒܒܪܐ ܠܦܒܢܐ. ܕܫܡܥܢ ܗܕܐ ܣܘܬܐ ܒܥܠܬܐ ܠܐ ܐܫܟܚ. ܘܐܝܟ ܕܟܠ ܗ̇ܢܘܢ ܕܒܢܝܫܘܬܐ ܒܒܝܫܐ ܡܒܝܫܝܢ ܗܘܘ. ܕܡܢ ܥܡܘܦܐ ܢܦܠܘܢ ܙܢܚ ܗܘܐ. ܘܒܕܡܘܬ ܥܒܕܐ ܡܠܦܢܐ ܕܦܓܕܬܐ ܕܐܠܗܐ ܡܕܡܝܢܘܢ ܐܕܝܢ ܗܘܐ ܒܗ. ܦܟܐ ܗܘܐ ܘܐܡܪ. ܕܠܐܝܟܐ ܡܬܕܒܪܝܢ ܐܢܫܝܢ ܐܘ ܬܒ ܐܝܟܢܐ ܘܠܒܡܘܡܐ ܕܬܫܕܘܢ ܢܦܫܗܘܢ ܒܟܠܗܘܢ ܡܬܪܚܝܢ ܐܢܫܝܢ. ܐܪ̈ܝܡܘ ܒܢܝܐ ܕܬܪ̈ܒܝܬܗ ܠܒܪܘܡܐ ܘܟܠ ܡܢ ܒ̈ܠܟܐ ܟܠܗܘܢ ܠܐܠܗܐ ܘܠܦܪܘܩܐ ܕܟܠܗܘܢ ܗܘ̈ܦܩܗ، ܕܒܠܒܐ ܬܕܒܪ. ܘܠܐ ܬܬܠܘܢ ܠܦܒܝܢ. ܦܘܩܕܢܐ ܕܐܬܟܠ ܠܒܢܝ ܘܬܬܚܙܝܐ ܠܗܘܢ ܠܦܒܘܬܐ ܕܠܐ ܐܠܗ. ܕܦܠܚܢܐ ܕܫܐ̈ܕܐ ܘܐܬܕܒܪܘ ܐܦ

ܕܐܠܗܐ ܐܬܝܗܘܗܝ ܗܘܐ. ܘܠܡܥܡܪܘܬܐ ܦܓܪܢܝܬܐ ܠܘܬ ܟܠ ܐܢܫ
ܐܬܝܗܘܗܝ ܗܘܐ. ܘܗܘ ܗܕܐ ܗܘܬ ܠܗ ܥܠܬܐ ܠܓܠܘܬܐ ܠܡܕܝܢܬܗ
ܕܐܪ̈ܙܐ ܘܡܛܠ ܕܫܢܐ ܗܘܐ ܕܒܢܝܢܐ ܗܘ ܥܠ ܟܠ ܐܢܫ ܪ̈ܓܫܘܬܐ
ܘܕܫܠܝܬܐ ܦܓܪܢܝܬܐ ܢܦܠܬ ܗܘܬ ܘܦ̈ܓܪܢܝܐ ܐܝܟ ܕܡܢ ܡܕܡ ܚܐܦܐ
ܕܟ̈ܦܢܐ ܦ̈ܓܪܢܝܐ ܡܬܓܪܦܝܢ ܗܘܘ. ܘܠܦܓܪܝܬܐ ܠܓܢܝܬܐ ܕܦܬܟܪ̈ܐ
ܡܬܕܒܪܝܢ ܗܘܘ. ܘܐܬܚܫܒ ܕܠܘܩܒܠ ܚܐܦܐ ܕܒܝܫܬܐ ܒܫܠܝܢܘܬܗ
ܢܣܘܩ ܠܓܠܠܐ ܕܫܝܢܐ ܒܟ̈ܠܗܘܢ ܫܠܛܢܝܬܐ ܢܬܒܥ. ܘܠܒܢܝ ܒܝܬܗܘܢ
ܕܒ̈ܝܫܐ ܕܐ̈ܠܗܝܐ ܗܘ ܒܪܝܢܘܗܝ ܢܦܫ ܫܕܐ ܗܘܐ. ܘܒܚ̈ܠܐ
ܕܠܘܩܒܠ ܠܗܘܢ ܕܡܢ ܕܫܠܝܗܘܢ ܠܓܘܝ ܡܬܕܒܪܝܢ ܗܘܘ.
ܡܫܘܐ ܗܘܐ. ܘܠܗܘܢ ܡܢ ܦܓܪܬܐ ܕܦܬܟܪ̈ܐ ܦܠܐ ܗܘܐ. ܘܒܬ̈ܠܐ
ܕܐܡܟܝܢ ܠܡܣܝܡ ܥܠ ܡܕܝܢܬܐ ܠܗܘܢ ܡܚܡܕ ܗܘܐ. ܘܒܪ
ܗܠܝܢ ܐܠܦܘܗ ܫܠܝܐ ܘܡܪܕܘܬܐ ܒܦܪܗܣܝܐ ܦܪܫ ܗܘܐ. ܠܒܢܘܗܝ
ܩ̈ܠܝܠܐ ܘܒܪܝܫܝܬܗ ܡܕܡ ܕܢܗܐ ܡܪܚܡܗ. ܗܘ ܕܝܢ ܐܝܟ ܒܪ ܐܢܫܐ
ܕܪܘܚܐ ܕܐܠܗܐ ܩܠܝܠ ܗܘܐ. ܕܒܗܢܐ ܒܝܬ ܩܠܐ ܐܡܪ ܗܘܐ
ܒܫܪܪܘܬܐ ܕܡܠܬܗ. ܘܒܗܕܐ ܬ̈ܠܝܐ ܕܦܓܪܬܐ ܕܐܠܗܐ ܐܝܬ
ܗܘܐ ܒܗܘܢ ܗܢ. ܠܐ ܗܘܐ ܕܝܢܐ ܗܘ ܕܢܐܡܪ ܘܡܛܠ ܗܠܝܢ ܠܒܝܬ
ܐܘܪܚܐ ܐܫܬܪܪ ܗܘܐ. ܘܡܛܠ ܡܫܟܚܬܐ ܬܘܒ ܠܕܝܢܐ ܡܪܚܡܗ.
ܘܒܟܝܢܘܬܐ ܡܫܝܚܐ ܠܟܠܗ ܦܓܪܗ ܕܠܐ ܪ̈ܫܝܡ ܡܬܟܒܫܝܢ ܗܘܘ.
ܒܪ ܒܢܝܢܘܬܐ ܕܪܚܡܘ. ܠܘܩܒܠ ܕܝܢܐ ܙܕܩܐ ܗܘܬ. ܘܒܫܠܛܢܗ
ܠܘܩܒܠ ܥܠܝܗ ܠܓܡܘܬܐ ܦܐܡ ܗܘܐ. ܘܒܩܘܪ̈ܒܐ ܡܩ̈ܝܐ ܒܕ̈ܡܘܬܗ
ܡܬܒܢܝܢ ܗܘܘ. ܘܠܫܪܪܬܐ ܒܪ ܐܠܗܐ، ܠܕܝܢܐ ܐܦ ܠܗܘܢ ܕܒܢܝܢܘ
ܕܕܝܢܐ ܡܫܒܚܝܢ ܒܡ ܐܬܠܝܛܐ ܫܪ ܒܪ ܙܘܓܗ. ܠܫܘܒܚܐ
ܐܫܬܠܡ. ܘܬܡܢ ܒܣܕܪܐ ܕܩܘܫܬܐ ܐܫܬܟܚܬ ܥܠܘܗܝ ܒܝܕ ܠܠܝܐ ܡܬܝܒ
ܗܘܐ. ܘܡܛܠ ܡܫܟܚܬܐ ܬ̈ܠܬܐ ܡܕܡ ܕܢܗܐ ܬܪ̈ܝܗܘܢ ܫܘܐܝܬ
ܐܬܦܪܥܘ ܘܚܘܒ ܠܗܘܢ ܕܢܒܫܘܢ ܠܬܟܠܬܐ. ܘܗܢܘܢ ܒܪ ܡܬܒܕܝܢ
ܗܘܘ ܐܟܪܝܢ ܗܘܘ. ܠܫܪ ܗܘ ܒܠܘܚܕܘܗܝ، ܐܠܗܐ ܬܠܬܐ ܕܥܠ
ܢܒܝܢ ܐܢܫܝܢ ܘܒܪ ܗܠܝܢ ܬܠܬܐ ܡܕܡ ܒܗܠܝܢ ܒܡܬܐ ܐܟܪܝܢ ܗܘܘ.

ܠܗ. ܢܘܟܪܝܐ ܕܝܢ ܐܝܬܘܗܝ ܗܘܐ ܥܒܕܘܬܐ ܒܣܪܢܝ̈ ܢܦܫܐ. ܒܥܠܬܐ ܡܪܕܘܬܐ ܕܐܪܕܘܦܝܐ ܕܒܢܘ̈ܡܪܬܐ. ܗܢܐ ܗܟܝܠ ܡܕܒܪܢܐ ܦܪܘܫܬ ܐܫܬܠܡܬ ܒܡܘܪܝܐ ܡܕܒܪܢܘܬܐ. . . .

ܡܕܒܪܢܘܬܐ ܕܐܠܦܝܘܣ ܘܕܘܟ ܘܕܘܡܢܝܘܣ.

ܒܥܠܬܐ ܡܪܕܘܬܐ ܕܐܪܕܘܦܝܐ ܕܒܢܘ̈ܡܪܬܐ.

ܒܗ ܕܝܢ ܒܙܒܢܐ ܗ̇ܘ. ܟܕ ܗܘܐ ܕܒܐܬܪܐ ܗܘ. ܕܒܥܠܬ ܒܫܘܪܝ ܫ̈ܢܝ ܠܬܠܡܝܕ̈ܐ ܡܬܟܢܫ ܗܘܐ. ܡܕܝܢ ܗܘܐ ܘܡܫܡܫܐ ܕܬܠܡܝܕܘܬܐ ܕܐܘܪܚܐ ܒܒܐܬܪܐ ܗ̇ܘ ܡܬܕܒܪ ܗܘܘ. ܡܕܡ ܕܝܢ ܠܒܐܬܪܐ ܗ̇ܘ ܡ̈ܕܒܪܢܐ ܗ̇ܘ ܕܒܐܬܪܐ ܘܠܐܘܪܚܐ ܕܡܫܒܚܢܐ ܒܟܠ ܗܘܐ ܘܡܫܡܫ ܒܡܕܝܢܢܘܬܐ ܕܬܠܡܝܕܐ ܐܬܒܪܝܘ ܗܘܘ. ܠܗܢܐ ܕܝܢ ܕܐܠܗܐ ܐܝܟ ܕܠܫܡܗ ܕܒܝܬ ܡܢ ܠܦܠܚܐ ܘܦܠܚܘܬܐ ܒܥܕܪܐ ܥܒܕ ܗܘܐ. ܐܦ ܗܟܝܠ ܐܢܫܐ ܕܐܝܬܘܗܝ ܗܘܐ ܡܫܡܫܢܐ ܒܥܕܬܐ ܥܕܪ ܡܕܒܪܢܘܬܐ ܒܕܘܒܪܐ ܐܦܣܩܘܦܐ ܡܫܡܫܢܐ ܡܢ ܟܕܘ ܐܬܥܕܪ ܗܘܐ. ܡܛܠ ܕܐܦ ܗܟܢܐ ܐܝܬܘܗܝ ܗܘܐ ܐܦ ܒܢܦܫܗ. ܐܦ ܕܝܢ ܥܒܕܘܗܝ ܗܘܘ ܢܦ̈ܫܬܗ ܟܕ ܡܫܡܫ ܠܗ. ܘܡܢܗܘܢ ܒܟܘܠܗ ܕܗܘ ܐܦ ܡܪܕܘܬܐ. ܫܪܐ ܡܛܠ ܕܐܪܕܘܬܐ ܕܡܫܡܫܬܗ. ܘܕܒܪܬܢ ܕܒܡܥܪܐ ܐܠܦܝܢ ܡܬܕܒܪ ܗܘܐ. ܘܕܢܚܝܘܗܝ ܠܒܢ̈ܝ ܫܘܢ ܡܢ ܐܦ ܡܫܡܫ ܗܘܐ. ܘܟܕ ܟܠ ܡܕܡ ܕܢܣܒ ܒܡܕܒܪܢܘܬܐ ܕܟܠ ܐܢܫ ܡܥܒܕܐ ܙܪܥ ܗܘܐ. ܘܟܕ ܦܠܚܐ ܕܐܠܗܐ ܡܕܡ ܕܢܣܒ ܐܟܪܙ ܗܘܐ. ܠܟܠ ܥܢ̈ܝܐ ܕܒܗܘܢ ܒܙܒܢܐ ܐܫܬܠܡ ܗܘܐ. ܘܗ̈ܘܦܐ ܡܢܗ ܡܢ ܟܕܘ ܢܚܬܐ ܡܕܒܪܢܐ ܗܘܐ ܗܘܐ. ܘܬܘܒ ܡܢ ܟܕܘ ܗܠܝܢ ܠܟܠܗ ܐܘܪܚܐ ܐܫܬܠܡ ܗܘܐ. ܘܬܘܒ ܟܠܗ ܐܡܬܟܢܐ ܘܟܠܗ ܠܠܝܐ ܒܐܪܥܐ ܫܪ̈ܝܢ ܕܗܘܐ ܬ̈ܟܠܬܗ ܐܬܬܟܝܠ ܗܘ.. ܐܬܬܟܝܠܘ ܕܝܢ ܕܗܠܝܢ ܐܦ̈ܠܝܐ ܐܦ ܐܠܦܝܘܣ ܒܬܪܐ ܕܢܚܬܐ ܗܘܐ ܗܘܐ. ܟܕ ܗܘ ܕܝܢ ܐܝܬܘܗܝ ܗܘܐ ܡܢ ܙܒ̈ܢܐ ܕܐܠܦܘܪܘܣ ܡܕܒܪܢܘܬܐ. ܘܒܬܪܗ ܕܡܪܝܐ ܒܬܘܒܐ ܕܡܪ̈ܐ ܘܡܫܡܫ̈ܢܐ ܡܫܡܫ ܗܘܐ. ܗ̇ܘ ܕܝܢ ܗܢܐ ܡܕܡ ܕܢܣܒ ܗܘܐ ܡܕܒܪܢܐ ܒܙܒܢܐ ܘܡܠܦܢܐ ܕܟܠܬܐ

ܠܐ ܢܠܦ ܗܘܐ. ܟܕ ܕܝܢ ܠܬܪ̈ܝܢ ܫ̈ܢܝܢ ܠܗܘ ܗܘܐ. ܘܟܕܝܢ
ܠܬܠ̈ܬܐ. ܘܩܢܝܬܐ ܦܫܝܛܬܐ ܐܦ ܟܠܗ ܥܒܕܬܐ ܕܠܐ ܦܘܪܫܬܐ
ܡܟܒܪ ܗܘܐ. ܡܢ ܡܪܝܐ ܕܝܢ ܕܡ̈ܠܐ ܐܠܗܝ̈ܬܐ ܠܐ ܠܠܝܐ ܘܠܐ
ܐܝܡܡܐ ܫܠܐ ܗܘܐ. ܟܕ ܥܠ ܐܦܬ̈ܟܗܘܢ، ܘܥܠ ܟܘܡܪ̈ܗ ܢܦܠ
ܟܠܝ̈ܠܬܐ ܐܝܬ ܗܘܬ ܠܗ. ܗܟܢܐ ܕܡܟܝܟܘܬܐ ܘܡܣܟܢܘܬܐ
ܠܟܠܗܘܢ ܒܢ̈ܝ، ܡܢܗܘܢ ܡܠܡܕ ܐܦ ܥܠ ܫ̈ܒܠܐ ܕܐܠܗܘܬܐ.
ܐܡܝܢܘܬܐ ܐܝܬ ܗܘܬ ܠܗ. ܐܦ ܫ̈ܒܠܐ ܟܪܝܬܐ ܕܟܝܢܐ ܠܐ ܗܘܐ
ܒܝܪܐܝܬ ܡܕܒܪ ܗܘܐ. ܟܠܗܘܢ ܕܝܢ ܡܢ ܒܢܝ ܐܒܗ̈ܘܗܝ ܗܘܐ.
ܘܟܠܗܘܢ ܕܒܕܬܐ ܟܬܠܬ ܡܢܗܘܢ ܥܒܕ ܗܘܐ. ܦܘܪܫܢܗ ܡܪܘܢ
ܗܘܐ ܗܘܐ. ܘܟܠܗܘܢ ܐܚܪ̈ܢܐ ܠܥܢܐ ܗܘܢܐ ܠܐܪܥܐ ܡܬܪܟܢ
ܗܘܐ ܘܐܚܪܢܬܐ ܕܡܬܚܙܝܐ ܐܦ ܡܢ ܡܕܡܝܬܐ ܠܗܘܢ ܫܢ̈ܝܬܗ
ܕܒܢܝܐ ܐܒܗܘܗܝ ܗܘܐ. ܘܕܡܘܐ ܡܢ ܡܕܡܘܗܝ، ܘܟܢ ܗܘܘ. ܟܕ ܟܕ
ܡܟܠ ܕܡܢ ܒܢܝܢ ܠܦܘܪܐ ܡܟܝܢܬ ܟܡ ܣܒܪܘܗܝ، ܡܘܬܪܐ ܐܬܥܪ
ܗܘܐ. ܘܟܢ ܒܥܒܕܐ ܡܢ ܬܪ̈ܒܝܢ ܕܡܒܝܢܬܐ ܠܗܬ ܦܟܝܪܘܬܐ
ܐܟܠܗܘܢ، ܘܟܪܥܒܬܗ ܒܟܠܗ ܡܕܡܐ ܐܦܢ ܠܗ ܕܢܬܐ ܗ̇ܘ. ܐܝܢܐ
ܕܟܠܗܘܢ ܡܬܡܪܐ ܗܘܐ. ܕܡ̇ܠܐ ܠܝ ܠܡ ܕܬܒܟܝ ܠܐܠܗܐ ܘܗܘ
ܟܠܗ ܪܒܐ ܐܟܪ ܗܘܐ. ܕܠܝܬ ܐܠܗܐ ܐܠܐ ܐ ܚܕ ܟܠܗܘܢܘܗܝ،
ܟܟܘܕܐ ܘܟܪܘܢܐ ܕܟܠ. ܟܕ ܕܝܢ ܗܘ ܕܢܝܐ ܡܢ ܡܫܘܬܐ ܕܡܠܬܗ
ܕܗܘܕܐ ܟܠܒ ܗܘܐ. ܟܕܝܢܐ ܐܚܪܢܐ ܠܗܘܟܠ ܗܠܟܝܢܐ ܕܥܪܐ
ܐܬܟܬܪ ܗܘܐ. ܘܥܒܕ ܡܠܬܗ ܡܕܡܝܬܐ ܘܥܢ ܠܐܚܪܬܐ ܘܐܡܪ
ܠܗ ܕܠܬ̈ܟܠܐ ܕܐܬܝܗܘܢ ܗܘܐ ܐܪ̈ܟܐ ܒܡܫܝܢܐ ܢܟܒ ܗܘܐ.
ܗܘ ܕܝܢ ܦܗܕܐ ܡܕܥܐ ܕܐܠܗܐ ܐܦ ܥܠ ܗܕܐ ܡܠܬܐ ܡܬܪܐܬ
ܚܣܝ ܘܡܠܬܗ ܕܗ̇ܘ ܪܟܐ ܕܦ̈ܠܐܦܣܘܢ ܕܡ̈ܢܝܐ ܬܢܐ. ܗ̇ܝ، ܕܐܡܪ
ܕܠܐ ܥܦܪܐ ܡܪܘܬܐ ܕܦ̈ܓܪܐ ܐܠܐ ܠܡ ܚܕ ܡܟܪܐ ܢܗܘܐ ܘܚܕ
ܫ̈ܠܟܐ ܘܡܠܠ ܦܘܢ ܦܬܓܡܗ ܕܠܬ̈ܟܠܐ ܢܓܪ ܗܘܐ. ܗ̇ܘ ܚܕ
ܒܕܘܟܪ̈ܘܗܝ، ܠܡܘܬܐ ܐܫܬܠܡ ܗܘܐ. ܘܪܥܡ ܕܦܘܠܝܐ ܒܪܥܬܗ
ܐܫܬܠܡ ܗܘܐ. ܘܡܟܪܙܬܐ ܕܠܠܬܐ ܟܐܘܪܝܐ ܕܥܡܟܐ ܐܬܦܠܓܬ

ܕܡܠܟܘܬܐ ܒܟܘܬܐ ܕܡܕܒܪܢܘܬܐ ܐܬܒܠܠ. ܡܛܠ ܕܐܝܟ ܕܒܐܓܘܢܐ ܡܫܬܪܐ ܗܘܐ ܐܬܬܓܪ ܗܘܐ. ܘܒܗ̇ ܕܒܗܬܐ ܕܝܘܒ ܡܫܝܚܐ ܠܗܘܦܪܐ ܕܟܝܢܐ ܐܬܒܠܠ ܐܦ ܫܡܫܐ ܢܪܐ ܘܡܕܒܪܢܐ ܕܬܠܡܝ̈ܕܘܬܐ ܗܘܒ ܗܘܐ ܐܬܒܠܠ. ܘܒܕܡܘܬܐ ܕܝܫܘܥ ܡܪܢ ܚܕ. ܐܦ ܬ̈ܠܡܝܕܐ ܐܚܪ̈ܢܐ ܒܕܘܟܬܐ ܐܚܪܢܝܬܐ ܫܘܠܡܐ ܕܫ̈ܡܝܢ ܒܡܕܒܪܢܘܬܐ ܗܘܐ. ܘܠܐ ܗܘܐ ܒܠܚܘܕ ܠܡܕ̈ܒܪܐ ܒܗܢܐ ܗܘܬ ܗܕܐ ܦܠܚܘܬܐ ܐܠܐ ܐܦ ܠܕܪܐ ܗܢܐ ܕܝܠܗ ܕܠܐ ܫܘܡ ܐܬܬܚܡܬ ○ ○ ○ ○

ܐܝܟܢܐ ܗܟܝܠ ܕܒܐܬܪ ܐܬܪ ܐܬܝܠܝܕܘ ܘܗܘܐ ܕܢܬܬܟܘܢ ܐܝܠܝܢ ܕܡܫܡܫܝܢ ܒܐܬܪܘܬܗܘܢ ܒܫܡܝܢ ܗܘܘ ܐܝܟܢܐ ܕܐܦ ܡܪܢ ܐܝܟܢܐ ܕܐܘܡܝ ܕܐܡܪ ܒܠ ܫܡܝܢ ܕܢܘܚܬ ܕܒܫܡܝܢ ܗܘܘܬ. ܘܐܦ ܒܫܡܝܢ ܢܣܠܩܘܢ. ܫܡܝܢ ܕܒܗܘܢ ܒܒܢܐ ܒܠܗ ܕܠܘܩܒܠܐ ܡܫܬܒܗܪ. ܡܛܠ ܕܐܦ ܒܟܘܢ. ܕܐܡܪ ܐܝܟ ܡܒܒܢܐ ܡܦܝܓܢܐ ܕܦܫܝܛܘܬܐ. ܗܘ ܦܪܘܩܐ ܕܟܠܢ ܒ̈ܢܝ ܐܢܫܐ ܕܚܝ. ܐܝܟܢܝܫܘܢ ܗܟܝܠ ܕܫܡܝܢ ܐܬܠܒܟܐ ܢܦܫܐ ܠܡܠܟܐ ܘܠܒܝܬܐ ܕܒܗ ܐܬܢܫܡܐ.

ܡܕܒܪܢܘܬܐ ܕܦܪܘܣ. ܒܥܢܝܬܐ
ܡܕܡܝܬܐ ܕܪܘܒܐ ܕܒܢܝ̈ܡܝܢ.

ܡܕܡܝܐ ܕܟܠܢ ܗܦܪܐ ܗܘܢ ܕܒܠܘܦܢܐ ܐܬܝܗܒ. ܦܪܘܣ ܡܬܦܪܐ ܗܘܐ. ܒܥܕܪܐ ܒܪ ܐܢܫܐ ܐܠܗܐ ܐܬܝܗ̇ܒ ܗܘܐ ܡܛܠ ܕܐܦ ܡܢܡ ܡܕܒܪܢܘܬܗ ܠܡܫܡܠܝܘܬܐ ܦܓܪܢܝܬܐ ܫܡܗ ܐܬܒܠܡ ܗܘܐ. ܘܡܢ ܒܪ ܦܠܛ ܗܘܐ ܘܒܗܘܐ ܒܡܫܡܪܐ ܕܒܢܐ ܘܡܕܒܪܐ ܐܝܟܢܐ ܐܬܝܗ̇ܒ ܗܘܐ. ܘܒܫܡܘܬܐ ܕܪܒܝܫܘ ܠܦܓܪܗ ܡܒܝܢ ܗܘܐ. ܐܡܬܝ ܕܐܦ ܡܢ ܡܕܡ ܡܕܘܬܗ ܢܘܬܪ ܕܒܦܓܪܐ ܡܬܘܬܐ ܢܦܫ ܥܒܪܐ ܗܘܬ. ܠܢܦܫܗ ܕܝܢ ܒܡ̈ܠܐ ܐܠܗܝ̈ܬܐ ܡܫܒܠ ܗܘܐ ܐܡܬܝ ܕܐܦ ܦܓܪܗ ܚܫܠܐ ܕܐܠܗܐ ܩܢܐ ܗܘܐ. ܡܟܐ ܐܬܬܠܗ
ܕܝܢ ܠܫܡܝܐ ܗܘܬ ܒܠܝܒܐ. ܘܡܬܘܬܝܗ ܡ̈ܠܐ. ܘܒܗ ܡܠܝ ܗܘܐ ܡܕܡ

ܢܬܒܥܐ ܗܟܝܠ ܕܬܫ̈ܘܬܐ ܟܠܝ̈ܬܐ ܘܬܫ̈ܥܝܬܐ ܥܒܝ̈ܕܬܐ ܕܢܐܠܦܢܐ
ܐܠܗܝܐ ܘܡܗܝܡܢܐ ܗܘ ܕܠܐ ܡܬܦܠܓܐ ܒܥܬܐ ܢܟܕܢܘܗܝ
ܘܠܡܫܪܪܘܬܗܘܢ ܕܡܢܘܬܐ ܐܝܟ ܚܕܬܐ ܐܡܝܢܬܐ ܦܩܕ ܒܢ̈ܝܢ
ܢܟܕܢܘܗܝ. ܡܬܕܡܪ̈ܐ ܐܢܐ ܕܝܢ ܒܠ ܚܠܝܦܘܬܗܘܢ ܕܡܗܝܡܢ̈ܬ ܒܠ.
ܐܦ ܡܕܢܘܬܗܘܢ ܦܠܚܢܐܝܬ ܐܘܟ̈ܡܐ ܘܦܢܝܐ ܚܠܝܡܐ
ܕܢܟܣܘܢ. ܘܫܒܗܪܐ ܕܪ̈ܚܡܝܗܘܢ ܘܦܪܗܣܝܐ ܕܗܝܡܢܘܬܗܘܢ
ܘܚܪ̈ܝܪܘܬܐ ܕܫܘܟܠܗܘܢ ܘܡܣܒܪܢܘܬܐ ܕܢܩܕܗܘܢ ܘܫܪܝܪܘܬܐ
ܕܦܓܪܗܘܢ ܘܠܐ ܐܬܦܠܓܘ ܒܪ̈ܚܡܝܗܘܢ. ܘܕܠܟܠ ܚܝܢ
ܗܘ، ܚܝ̈ܢܝܗܘܢ ܘܠܐ ܕܒܬܐ ܘܐܪܗܒܘܬܐ ܐܬܚܝܗܘܢ ܗܘܘ.
ܘܐܦ ܫܘܒܚܗ ܕܐܠܗܐ ܘܕܡܫܝܚܗ ܚܠܦ ܕܡܬܪ̈ ܡܢ ܒܠ
ܕܠܒ̈ܠܒܒܝܗܘܢ ܢܟܘܢ ܢܗܒ ܗܘܐ ܠܗܘܢ. ܠܐܠܗܐ ܓܝܪ
ܟܠܗܐ ܕܒܗܠ ܐܝܬܘܗܝ. ܘܠܗ ܡܢ ܒܠܗ ܚܠܡܘܢ ܙܝܒܘ. ܘܐܓܪܐ
ܕܝܘܒܠܘܢ ܕܠܗܬܗ ܒܒܕܪܝܗ ܕܠܬܗܘܢ ܦܒ ܠܗܘܢ. ܘܐܬܪܝܚܒ
ܡܢ ܠܗܬܗ ܘܐܬܟܢܫܘ ܒܠ ܗܝܐܢܐ̈ܘܢ ܘܒܒ̈ܝܬܐ ܩܠܐ ܕܗܘ
ܡܕܢܚܐ ܕܡܢ ܩܕܡܝܗܘܢ ܐܘܕܝ ܗܘܐ ܡܬܚܫܒ ܗܘܘ. ܒܕ
ܐܡܪܝܢ ܗܘܘ ܕܡܢܘ ܢܦܪܘܫ ܡܢ ܡܫܝܚܐ ܒܥܬܐ ܐܘ ܐܘܠܨܢܐ
ܐܘ ܐܪܕܘܦܝܐ ܐܘ ܟܦܢܐ ܐܘ ܡܒܘܬܐ ܐܘ ܣܝܦܐ ܐܝܟ ܕܟܬܝܒ
ܕܡܛܠܬܟ ܒܠܝܘܡ ܡܝܬܝܢ ܐܢܚܢ. ܐܬܚܫܒܢ ܐܝܟ ܐܡܪ̈ܐ ܠܢܟܣܬܐ
ܘܒܕ ܡܟܝܪܢ ܬܘܒ ܗܘ ܗܝܢܐ ܣܘܪܐ ܕܐܠܗܐ ܠܡܣܒܪܢܘܬܐ
ܕܡܢ ܒܢܝܐ ܠܐ ܡܪܕܝܢܐ ܐܡܪ ܕܒܗܠܝܢ ܟܠܗܘܢ ܙܟܝܢ ܐܚܢܢ ܚܠܦ
ܡܢ ܕܐܚܒܢ. ܘܕܡܪܕܝܢ ܒܟܠܗܘܢ ܒܢܝ̈ܬܐ ܒܝܘܡܗ ܕܐܠܗܐ ܦܪܩ
ܒܪܩ. ܘܕܡܬܟܬܪܝܢ ܒܠ ܟܠܗܘܢ ܕܩܠܬܐ ܘܐܘ̈ܠܨܢܐ ܐܚܪ̈ܢ ܘܐܡܪܝܢ
ܕܡܟܝܟ ܐܢܐ ܕܠܐ ܡܘܬܐ ܘܠܐ ܚܝ̈ܐ. ܘܠܐ ܥܝܕܢ ܘܠܐ
ܕܒܬܝܕ ܘܠܐ ܚܝ̈ܠܐ ܘܠܐ ܪܘܡܐ ܘܠܐ ܥܘܡܩܐ ܘܠܐ ܒܪܝܬܐ
ܐܚܪܬܐ ܢܫܟܚܘܢ ܕܢܦܪܫܘܢ ܡܢ ܚܘܒܗ ܕܐܠܗܐ ܕܒܡܪܢ ܝܫܘܥ
ܡܫܝܚܐ. ܒܗ ܗܟܝܠ ܒܗܘ ܙܒܢܐ ܦܘܠܘܣ ܗܘ ܕܒܫܠܝܐ ܕܡܪܗ
ܡܬܬܒܪ ܗܘܐ. ܗܘ ܕܝܘܚܢܢ ܒܟܝܢܬܐ ܕܪܗܘܡܝܐ ܡܕܝܢܬܐ

ܕܥܠ ܡܘܬܪ̈ܢܐ ܕܬܐܘܦܢܝܐ ܕܐܡܪ ܠܐܘܣܒܝܘܣ ܩܣܪܝܐ.

ܡܘܬܪ̈ܢܐ ܦܪ̈ܝܫܐ ܕܐܠܗܐ ܗܢܘܢ ܕܠܡܫܝܚ ܘܡܪܢ ܡܛܠ ܡܫܝܚܐ ܘܠܐܠܗܐ ܕܥܠ ܟܠ ܘܡܠܟܐ ܕܟܠ. ܝܬܝܪ ܡܢ ܢܦܫܗܘܢ ܘܚܝ̈ܝܗܘܢ ܐܫܠܡܘ. ܘܠܐܓܘܢܐ ܕܕܚܠܬ ܐܠܗܐ ܐܬܩܪܒܘ. ܘܒܣܗܕܘܬܐ ܕܡܕܝܢܘܬܐ ܐܬܟܠܠܘ. ܘܠܡܘܬܐ ܗܢܝܐܐ ܐܝܟ ܝܬܝܪ ܡܢ ܚܝ̈ܐ ܕܐܢܫܐ ܓܒܘ. ܘܒܥܠܡܝܢ ܕܚܕ̈ܬܐ ܕܡܫܝܚܘܬܐ ܐܬܥܠܠܘ. ܘܬܫܒܘܚܬܐ ܕܡܫܝܚܘܬܗܘܢ ܬܫܡܫܬܐ ܠܐܠܗܐ ܡܩܪܒܝܢܐ ܕܠܟܠ ܡܢ ܟܠ ܐܪܥܐ. ܡܛܠ ܕܡܫܝܚܐ ܫܡܫܐ ܐܬܚܙܝ ܠܗܘܢ ܗܘܐ. ܘܒܟܠܗ ܕܗܝ ܕܕܘܟܬܐ ܠܫܡܫܘܬܗܘܢ ܡܥܕܪ ܗܘܐ. ܘܬܫܒܘܚܬܐ ܘܐܝܩܪܐ ܘܪܒܘܬܐ ܠܐܠܗܐ ܘܠܒܪܗ ܘܠܪܘܚܐ ܕܩܘܕܫܐ ܡܣܩܝܢ. ܘܡܠܘܬܗܘܢ ܕܡܫܝܚܐ ܕܝܠܗ ܠܡܠܟܘܬܐ ܕܫܡܝܐ ܡܢ ܒܢ̈ܝܐ ܕܢܦܫܐ ܘܕܦܓܪܐ ܡܫܪܝܢ ܘܐܚܝܢ ܕܝܢ ܕܗܠܝܢ ܐܚܝܢ ܥܠ ܡܘܬܪܢܐ ܕܬܠܡܝܕܘܗܝ. ܘܐܬܚܙܝ ܐܦ ܡܢ ܥܒܕܐ ܕܫܠܝܚܐ. ܕܢܬܬܘܦ ܒܡܘܬܪܢܐ ܕܩܪ̈ܝܐ. ܢܬܬܘܦ ܒܥܒܕܘܗܝ ܐܦ ܐܢܚܢ. ܘܢܬܪ ܕܢܬܒܥ ܬܫܒܘܚܬܗ ܕܠܗܘܢ ܫܠܡܬܐ. ܗܢܘܢ ܕܒܠܥܕ ܡܬܓܒܝܢ ܡܢ ܥܡܡܐ ܕܥܠܡܐ ܘܢܚܘܢ ܠܡܫܝܚܐ. ܘܠܐ ܗܘܐ ܒܡܝܬܘܬܐ ܕܒܐܝܕܐ ܬܒܥܝܢ ܚܝܢ ܬܬܥܫܢܘܢ ܐܦܠܐ ܒܢܘܪܬܐ ܕܡܚܬܢ ܒܗܝܡܢܘܬܐ ܐܦ ܠܐ ܒܓܘܢܐ ܘܒܕܘܟܬܐ ܐܪܥܢܝܬܐ ܕܠܐ ܢܦܫܐ. ܐܠܐ ܒܥܠܬܐ ܫܪܪܬܐ ܗܝ ܕܡܬܡܠܠܐ ܡܢܗ ܐܠܗܐ. ܘܫܘܪ ܒܒܪܐ ܗܘ ܕܒܢ̈ܝܐ ܡܬܝܢܐ.

° ° ° ° ° °

www.ingramcontent.com/pod-product-compliance
Lightning Source LLC
Chambersburg PA
CBHW030317170426
43202CB00009B/1033

* 9 7 8 3 3 3 7 2 3 6 4 9 6 *